Bilderberg

ULTIMATE CONTROL

A NOVEL

BY

Nolan J. Reynolds

BRIGHTON PUBLISHING LLC
501 W. RAY ROAD.
SUITE 4
CHANDLER, ARIZONA 85225

Bilderberg

ULTIMATE CONTROL

A NOVEL

BY

NOLAN J. REYNOLDS

PUBLISHED BY
BRIGHTON PUBLISHING LLC
501 W. RAY ROAD
SUITE 4
CHANDLER, ARIZONA 85225
WWW.BRIGHTONPUBLISHING.COM

PRINTED IN THE UNITED STATES OF AMERICA

COPYRIGHT © 2025

Second Edition

COVER DESIGN: TOM RODRIGUEZ

❧ Introduction ❧

M any may disagree with the information in this book which isn't surprising given the fact that many of us are driven by the almighty dollar. This book speaks about many injustices happening around us every day. We simply endure them because it's just too exhausting to do otherwise, mostly because our time is taken up supporting our high standard of living. I was intrigued with the research I prepared in writing this book. It was very interesting and alarming at the same time. As I completed an extensive study on this subject, I was saddened. Mostly, because I've found that most people rely on the news for information instead of researching the material for ourselves. As I spoke to individuals, I was amazed at how they accepted and wholeheartedly believed what the news media broadcasts. It was because of that revelation that I felt obligated to explain what we are going through and also what we have tolerated in the last half-century.

In this novel I have incorporated historical events while still focusing on the fictional plot. With constant talk about the end of the world possibilities, I have attempted to bring to light some information while still entertaining my readers. The story revolves around a family as they struggle for survival during a catastrophic situation. They are driven to survive and create for themselves a new world.

Make no mistake about it, this new world is a very real possibility and is being developed at this very moment.

In this book, I spend time reflecting about my childhood, growing up in a small town by the water called Bayville, Long Island. If the reader has lived in this country during the sixties or seventies, they will relate to my stories. I compare many things from back then to the way they are currently. I infer that things were simpler and pleasant back then. We are so complicated nowadays. Our lives are filled with gadgets that we really don't need.

This book discusses many issues and touches on many points that we have only heard about in the past and have argued about in the present, but little is done to change what we experience every day. It's too difficult to explain, in these few paragraphs, what this book is about.

I warn you that this book will challenge your ideas and teachings. It challenges what life has been for most of us and what life could be like if we are willing to change. Sadly though, many will not.

We often dismiss the facts simply because the mangled truth is presented by the corporate controlled media. In fact, it is not truth at all, it is only perceived to be.

False propaganda is an insult to our country and its people. It has prompted this look into our system through the lives of the family portrayed in this book. Their journey takes us through possible solutions for the gross corruption from those in leadership.

This book offers relief to those who have worked hard for the past forty to sixty years and are still struggling to survive because of these criminals who make decisions for us while profiting profusely.

❖ Dedication ❖

This book is dedicated to the honest, hardworking individuals who were part of the industrialization of our country. I would also like to dedicate the book to John F Kennedy, Jr., whose memorable picture of him playing under his father's desk in the oval office and the famous picture of him saluting at his father's funeral shall always be memories that were a major part of my life, and I'm sure for many others. As we look to the future for answers, we also look for a courageous hero to guide us through it.

God help us all.

❧ Chapter One ❦

Way Back When

The mood is certainly grim. Not just my mood. There's a certain funk in the air that I've felt for some time now and it doesn't seem to go away. I wondered if it was like this for my parents back in the 40s, 50s and 60s. Or were times just really bad right now?

Is today's terrorism the same fright that they felt with the Nazi's storming into European countries, Pearl Harbor, the atomic bomb? I don't know, but there is an uneasy feeling mounting and I wonder if this time there will really be an end to our world as we know it.

Albert Einstein was quoted as saying, *"I know not with what weapons World War III will be fought, but World War IV will be fought with sticks and stones."* Upon discovering the splitting of the atom he was quoted as saying, *"It was the worst discovery he had ever made."*

Harry S. Truman, upon the dropping of the atomic bomb on Japan, uttered the words, *"My God, what have we done?"*

I wake up, breathe in and out, and continue my day. All the while I look forward to going back home from work, for this is my solace. Even in my "happy place" there are still thoughts of the news reports and the overwhelming dismay of people losing their homes because the economy is so crippled. No one mentions the "D" word because we're not in a depression...so that's what they tell us. Are we headed toward a depression?

I listen to older people talk and listen to their wise words. I used to sit and listen to my father-in-law talk. What a wise man. The stories of how a soda was a nickel or how they used to wait for the coal train to go by so they could pick up the fallen coal and bring and take it home to burn for heat. He was a US Navy diver in WWII. He was born in the early 1900s and became a plumber later on in life. He was meticulous in his work. I had a lot of respect for the man and people from his era, my elders. Most have all passed on now, but what a generation. I can honestly say that I miss not having them around for guidance. Just knowing they were around for support was calming; after all, they've been around the block a few times.

There were so many stories of how it used to be in days of old. I've heard that some people even looked forward to Christmas because they would get an apple for a gift under the tree. Imagine that. Shoes were a luxury. I had heard incredible stories of poverty while we all enjoyed the comforts of a kitchen table that was always covered in fresh vegetables, potatoes, pasta, meat, chicken and fish.

I'd sit at the table and watch my grandfather's face after a hard day at work. He had a weathered face that he received from many years of hard labor outside in the cold. He was a bricklayer and became a foreman in his industry. He worked on tall buildings and had no fear of heights. He was strong and had Popeye muscles. He was in the war, but on the other side.

My grandmother worked hard around the house washing clothes and making dinner every night like clockwork. They came from a time where she used the clothesline outside. They were immigrants. They only spent money on what they needed and hardly ever went out to eat, in fact, I never could remember them eating at a restaurant. One time I had gotten excited because they ordered a pizza from the local pizza place. Of course, we had to go pick it up to save money. That had only happened twice. Yes, I guess you can say I never experienced really hard times. My family worked hard so I could play as a child without a care in the world.

Gus's Pizza 1979 Bayville, NY
Photo by: Philip Georgious

Economic woes, religious differences, sexual permissiveness, war with no end in sight; all four were indicators that the world was coming to an end. Some even believe there's a date when this will happen— December twenty first, two thousand and twelve. I remember sitting in the high school cafeteria in 1976 when we were told the world was ending. When that day came I waited. I had lunch and looked at the bricks imagining what they would look like in flames. The end of the school day came, I got on the bus for the ride home, but nothing occurred. The plethora of information available today on the Internet leads us to believe that it will happen this time because of the Mayan calendar.

I've also been told that there is a secret organization that includes some of the most powerful and wealthy people in the world, some being government officials including those from the White House.

The Freemasons have been around for quite some time now. It is believed that they control the world's current wealth and its future. They call the shots from the sidelines. It's almost like they are coaching a Super Bowl game from the skybox. The first time I ever heard of this organization was two years ago when a family member told me while we were eating dinner at their house. There's a lot to be said for the information you can receive at the kitchen table.

Our country has always been plagued with the revolution of black and white differences. What were, or are we afraid of? All this prejudice against anything from race, to religion, to politics was sickening. I once wished that we would all be attacked by aliens so it would unify the world as it did in the movie Independence Day. A part of me still feels this way, uttering my wife's words, *"Why can't we all just get along?"*

Well, for one thing, when you have the idea of capitalism, some may take the greed to the extreme. When one man has more money than a European country, something is very wrong. It tips the scales of fairness. If this wasn't so, we would have enough food to feed the world two times over yet, people are starving because of this greed, because of luck, because of who we happen to come from. Yes there are guiding factors of how hard one is willing to fight but even then the odds are stacked so far against some, that it is nearly impossible to break out of that uphill challenge. I don't begrudge anyone that has experienced the American Dream, but at what cost to the world? How much money does one man need? When there are thousands of our own people starving, it is a major problem. A major, selfish, problem of greed.

The problem is not solved by a few men donating their extra pittance at Thanksgiving or Christmas. For God Sakes, there are 365 days in a year that people hunger. We are all humans and if there is a God, he would want us to care for all humans alike. Not because it's stated in the U.S. Constitution, but because it's stated in the constitution of all humanity. We now have a major problem today of huge proportions.

When my parents were working there were also problems which I'm sure they thought were of huge proportions. We have a rich versus poor war that has been mounting for decades and the culmination seems near.

John Fitzgerald Kennedy was assassinated in 1963, Robert Kennedy and Martin Luther King murdered in 1968, and John Lennon was killed in 1980. For each of these horrific events I remember where I was and what I was doing when these incidents occurred. And just like those shocking events, I knew where I was when I saw those huge towers burn in 2001. Yes, the fire is embedded in my heart and I, along with many people, were depressed over that tragic scene for quite some time. For me it was about a six-month period before I was able to come to terms with the horror. I didn't even know anyone in the building except a few clients. I wonder if this is what the country felt like on December 17, 1941. They say history repeats itself. Logically, I knew it had to be a different time back then because they had different weapons, but it must have been a similar feeling. All five of these incidents involved the government and big business in one way or another.

Car payments, utility payments, mortgage payments, credit card bills, food costs, health insurance; times were getting tougher and it seemed as though the words, "the great recession," has titled an era unfamiliar to many of us. A good night sleep has become a commodity. I read somewhere that, "Worry is the interest on debt that we may never have to pay." That's the funny thing about worry, most of the time what we worry about never even happens. Thinking positive helps, but when times are really bad, what else is there to do but worry? I was never one for being a pessimist—but a realist, yes.

Making more money and minimizing debt was the answer for sure. The only problem was that everyone was now ready to spend money for what they needed, not on what they lusted for or what they craved.

Now times are different. It finally dawned on me that we may have to live the life that our parents and grandparents lived just under a century ago. I started having visions of the show Bonanza, and making food from scratch instead of depending on someone else to sell it to me. Money was becoming more and more scarce. Gold was becoming the investment of choice again and prices sky-rocketed.

Deep down I knew that the over-spending years had to come to an end, sort of like an explosion of our own debt. I wish I could say that this was unlike anything our country's short history had ever experienced, but I'd be wrong in saying that because I am sure the depression was a lot worse. For someone who always had the comforts of living the easy life, this was all new to me. Don't get me wrong, I was never rich, but I lived comfortably like most Long Islanders. We were classified as middle-class or upper-middle class.

For various reasons today's economic climate is a lot different than it was in 1929. There is more information at our fingertips now then yesteryear. I guess we could also say that we've had a lot more experience with finances, such as leading and lagging indicators (economic terms which gauge the financial markets), etc.

The Internet age was finally in full swing and with that came the acceleration of both good and bad information. The invention of the Internet was equal to that of the atomic bomb.

Other countries manufactured and exported everything while we sat idle and exported only minimal items such as waste paper. Countries like China exported everything in sight, but we are great consumers for the high standard of living that we love. We adored spending on things that we really didn't need. We were all so oblivious to the fact that we were in the midst of the de-industrialization of our country. We were doomed.

❖ Chapter Two ❖

A Realization

I was only four years old when I saw a coffin draped by an American Flag on television in the latter part of 1963. The kinds of shows we watched portrayed good morals and values. They were shows like, I Love Lucy and Father Knows Best. I could go on and on about the meaning of this writing but the most important explanation would be to research for oneself the factual material that I've brought into the light within these chapters. I really shouldn't say "brought into the light" because the information has always been there. It just needed to be read and acted upon, but no one cares enough to pressure the authorities into prosecuting the guilty parties.

In the words of the late George Carlin, *"Nobody seems to bother and nobody seems to care."* If we did care, though, we could get on with enjoying a wonderful world without manipulations through greed. I believe the guilty parties are above the law. It seems we have nothing but questions about the murders of our leaders while the answers are deflected by the manipulators. We've spent so much time and money pursuing the sex scandal of 1998 while the country flourished. The sex scandal continually pursued for selfish, greedy gains. False propaganda was used like a well-oiled machine (no pun intended) and in this case was used as a diversion.

Oil has dominated and ruined our country, but no one says a word because we are fooled into thinking that we are dependent on this costly resource. It seems the guilty parties involved in the mass destruction of 2001 were pursued less than the sex scandal was. Why? Why was only six hundred thousand dollars spent on the 9-11 investigation and 40 million spent on the sex scandal?

Were those 3000 plus innocent victims less important than ousting a Democratic President for greedy gains?

We have the means to power the earth's energy needs for the next four-thousand years for free, from inventions that have been blocked by big business. They include solar, geo-thermal, wind, and most importantly—hydro-electric power. The truth is we don't need oil at all.

We have all these officials protecting us, state and local police, governors, senators, as well as congress. Who is overseeing what the President is doing? Who is overseeing what their inner circle is doing? Russ Baker investigative journalist interviewed over five hundred witnesses over a five year period and came to the conclusion that there is a shadow government that rules regardless of who is in the White House. Who is monitoring these criminals? It is obvious that there is a force, much more powerful than the president, going uncontrolled and unpunished. If we, as a people, do not bond together to combat this force, our lives will only get worse while the few benefit and reap the rewards of our work. A few—meaning a few hundred to a few thousand—of the wealthiest people on earth. And we know who these people are. The deaths of the Kennedys, Martin Luther King Jr., and John Lennon would all be in vain. Their lives would have meant nothing for what they were trying to accomplish for all of the American people. We may even be too late.

Before I tell you my family's story, it is important that you understand the underlying facts that forced us to change our way of life. Take for instance what has happened in recent years with the tobacco conglomerates. For decades they have been addicting the masses to a drug that is considered dangerous and highly addictive, yet the drug is still legal because the powerful few benefit from it at the cost of killing millions of people.

"A cigarette is a scientifically designed drug delivery device that is intentionally engineered to deliver nicotine to the brain in seconds."

~ Jeffrey Wigand

Mr. Wigand is a scientist who documented and made public this evidence. It sent the tobacco companies into a tailspin as they lost billions of dollars in court trying to defend their ex-employee's damaging statement. After the settlement was all said and done, and after the release of these true facts, were cigarettes made illegal? No. In fact, in some areas such as New York and California, the cost of one pack of cigarettes rose to fourteen dollars.

Even as Mr. Wigand uncovered the blatant distribution of a highly addictive drug that kills people, did big business continue to administer it and did government allow it? Yes, and at over-inflated premium prices.

7

They should be as illegal as the other highly addictive drugs, but our government continues to profit from it.

In 1962 we had peace in the world. The only potential problems were in the Congo. Vietnam was also brewing with the threat of Communism, but it was a civil war between the North and South Vietnamese. With peace in mind and the country's best interest in heart, President Kennedy, after a third attempt, finally made headway with Russian President Khrushchev. After the world listened to the president's speech, Khrushchev noted that it was the best speech ever made by an American President. Soon, the nuclear test ban treaty was signed.

The signing of that treaty made a specific group of plotters very angry about the entire peace progress. Their precious profit yielding war was at stake. They argued that President Kennedy was a weak leader against the threat of Communism. President Kennedy vowed to maintain peace while ruling with an intelligent hand, but big business thought otherwise. The owners of this country wanted war, a war that generates an 80 billion dollar a year business in those days. Their inner circle would prosper from the escalation of our involvement in a small country that we had no business being in, just as we had no business being in Iraq or Afghanistan. If the war business back then generated 80 billion dollars a year imagine what the Iraq war generates in profit today. They use the excuse that its good for the economy, but in fact it's good for their own bottom line. Sounds like a conflict of interest to me. We vote in officials to help the citizens yet policies are made to suit their own family's needs. Why is this not prosecuted? Since it's not illegal, why is not made illegal? Why isn't it demanded by *"the people"* to enact a law against that practice?

In December of 1963, President Kennedy was to issue an order to bring the U.S. advisors out of Vietnam to avoid a war. Additionally, he made a speech that vowed to eliminate secret organizations which existed when he realized these organizations would threaten our countries well-being. Secret organizations such as the CIA and other top secret groups. After the failed Bay of Pigs invasion in Cuba and accepting blame himself for that failure, his staff leaked to News reporters that the failure was anything but the administration's fault. It was then, that President Kennedy realized what he was up against and was quoted as saying he would *"splinter the CIA into a thousand pieces and scatter it into the winds."* Allen Dulles, director of the CIA at the

8

time was fired along with two others. Coincidently, Dulles was a member of the Warren Commission. Again, conflict of interest? The President was also about to start taxing the oil millionaire tycoons to *'even the slate'* among American taxpayers. That would never happen as President Kennedy was gunned down November 22, one month prior to these actions.

The rest is history; the Vietnam War escalated and corporate thieves made billions from the war, while many young soldiers died or were crippled. Who prospered? Who benefited from the killing? Which corporations prospered and why weren't they ever investigated? Who then became president and why wasn't he investigated? It seems that the CEO's were being protected from criminal prosecution. The new president was never questioned by the people. Today, who prospered from the Iraq war, from the Afghanistan war?

What more do we the people, need as proof to start a true investigation into these multiple murders? Thus, the Kennedy Assassination would be the beginning of our country's downfall, while the guilty prospered.

John F. Kennedy was killed, and then subsequently Lee Harvey Oswald and Jack Ruby. Obviously, they would not have been killed unless they had something to say that would incriminate the guilty parties. After the movie JFK was released in 1994, a private non-governmental group was ordered to investigate those murders. Their efforts were diverted at every turn by the Bush/Clinton administrations and were finally shut down four years later. Why?

"History is written by the winners."

~ *Napoleon Bonaparte*

⇒ Chapter Three ⇐

The Call

My name is David Napoli and this is my family's story.

On Tuesday I woke up, went to work, and started with the usual routine of organizing my day with my many lists. Lists are a saving grace when you have so many things to take care of in a day, a week, or even month. I had lists for everything. There were daily lists, to-do lists (usually acquired from my wife), a weekly list, and of course, a list of monthly/yearly debts. In today's times, this particular list was extremely important to me. I had learned the hard way that the monthly/yearly list should have been a priority when times were good as well. We live and we learn. Hopefully we do. For me, the saying is more accurately stated, "Better late than never."

While I was hustling to scratch off as many items on my list as possible, I was interrupted by a call from my longtime friend John Hodges. I hadn't heard from him in ages. John was a man with whom I went to college with back in 1981. In the eighties, we were just getting through with the silly years of disco, which was kind of a dichotomy because in the seventies some of the greatest music was written, as well as, some of the worst. It was all Classic Rock and Disco.

During that time, everyone said they hated Disco, but in the clubs, the scene was "happenin." In the eighties we really weren't too sure about that sound, but the clubs were still jumping though. In the shadows of an influential era, the sound of New Wave had arrived, Reggae was getting more popular and Rap had not yet hit the scene.

This was when I had met John. He was a slender, black man with a nice build. His hair was in dreadlocks and he never carried books unless he was going to the library to study. He came from a poor background, but was the kind of person that had pride regardless of his status. From the clothes he wore and the way he carried himself, John was a proud, black man and was very smart.

Although we hadn't seen each other in a long time, he was the kind of person that I was immediately drawn to because he had a sincere aura surrounding him. When we first met, we became friends instantly. John tried to better himself by doing what no one in his family had ever done, go to college and get a degree.

Unfortunately, he couldn't afford to continue past the second year of school and had to quit so he could get a job and help his mom feed their family of eight. His dad had left a long time ago; his mom was raising the family alone and needed all the help she could get.

In college, John never let on at how bad things were at home and it wasn't my business to ask. I was nineteen years old and at that age there are normally blinders on. I was oblivious to what was going on around me, unless of course I was at a keg party. My sights were usually set on a beer funnel and of course, hot girls.

When he called I was happy to hear from him and I shifted gears from what I had been doing in order to take the call. The connection wasn't too good and it was obvious that he made the call from a cell phone. He sounded far away, like he didn't have a lot of time to talk.

"Hello. Is Dave there?"

I responded, "Yes, this is Dave."

He asked, "Dave Napoli?"

"Yes that's me, how can I help you?"

"Dave, it's John. John Hodges from College."

"John? John Hodges?" I pondered the name.

"Yes," he replied.

I said, "John, how have you been? How are you?"

He responded in a hurried voice, "Well, that's why I'm calling you. I need your help."

I got the feeling he was in trouble from the sound of his voice, but I couldn't pinpoint what was going on with his vague information. It was certainly obvious that something was wrong, but I hadn't heard from him in so long. I was a bit taken back from the situation. Usually, when someone calls that I hadn't heard from in a while, it was a happy call. It was obvious that this would not be.

I said, "What's up?"

"Can you meet me tomorrow, it's important?" He continued, "I'm near Steinway Street in Astoria. Remember the luncheonette we used to go to under the El?"

"Yes" I replied with a concerned voice.

"Please, meet me there at two o'clock."

Without giving a thought to my responsibilities, I said, "Okay. Is everything alright?"

He answered quickly, "I'm sorry I can't talk right now, I'll see you tomorrow." With that, he hung up the phone.

Now, with all that was going on in the world as well as my own little world, this just added to my worries. It didn't matter though, I was getting used to it. The hits just kept on coming. What's one more thing to worry about? That night I didn't sleep a wink. Usually, with the typical worries, I could get five hours sleep even if it wasn't good sleep. This night would be different because I couldn't stop thinking about our troubling conversation. With all the tossing and turning I would manage to get two-and-a-half hours of sleep.

After the call, I continued with my work as best as I could. The day's responsibilities still needed to be taken care of. I am the kind of person that feels bad if my responsibilities aren't taken care of, and feel like such a loser if they are not met. I'm not quite sure if this was a learned habit I got from school, or if I had received that particular trait from my parents. Regardless, I prided myself on making sure I took care of my responsibilities at hand, whatever they may be. In the ever-evolving computer world, there were many responsibilities that came with the job.

Ever since I had seen an old movie about how the company was developed, I had long since wanted to work for my present employer Computech. These guys had been the ones working out computer solutions in their parent's garages and now they were some of the richest, most successful entrepreneurs in the world. The geeks that we had made fun of in high school now had thousands of people working for them. Yes, God has a funny sense of humor. How much more fascinating does it get than that? I was at parties doing keg stands while they were conquering the world's toughest problems.

I remember walking past a room at the college, as a professor uttered the words, "Do you know what's in that room?" He answered his own question, "They are working on the brain!"

When I first heard those words I was freaked out because it sounded like something out of a Twilight Zone episode. It still kind of freaks me out.

Back then, a powerful computer literally filled up a pretty big room. Compared to today, those computers were primitive. We had no idea what was in store for us in the present, with the exception of Sci-Fi writers. It reminded me of Tomorrow World at Epcot Center.

I continued to ask what's in store for people in the year 2029. Surely, the computers we use today will be archaic by then. The computer industry evolves at an exponential rate. I'm not sure that everyone understands what that means. For years now I equated the evolution of computers to a child's video game system. Each new video system that is developed has an increase in memory and graphics. The analogy is comparable with the computers we use, both business and private. Pretty soon we will be unable to tell the difference between a real football game and a video game portrayal of one. I'm sure holograms will be commonplace along with the developmental process. Nowadays, the only thing that is slowing down technological development is the cost of getting this technology into a consumer's home. I once heard Bill Gates express his frustration over this when he said, "It'll take the average consumer twenty years to get this technology into their homes."

One night I awoke to a documentary on computers. It was one of those nights when I couldn't sleep. I awoke and saw 3:41 on the digital time clock. The show blaring away on the TV was correlating the evolution of computers to the fiction movie, The Terminator. I sarcastically use the word fiction because I believe that when it comes to computers, there is no such thing as fiction. A better, more fitting word may be reality. The gist of the show was: *Will computers be able to teach themselves to think without the aid of humans?* The answer, *"Yes!"*

Needless to say, I couldn't go back to sleep. I still got chills thinking about it. All I think about is my family and how I can help them recover from a futuristic catastrophe. Is this what they felt like in the 1950s when they learned about the atomic bomb capabilities or HG

Well's War of the Worlds simulation? All that runs through my mind is watching that rural town, set on dirt roads, on my Zenith television encased in wood, in black and white, and the worry on the actor's faces. I can't help but joke, will Arnold be here when we need him? Will Christopher Reeves bust through the wall right before catastrophe hits? There was a certain comfort in the movie War Games when the computer asks Mathew Broderick in the last line of the movie, "How about a nice game of Chess?"

So, as I stated earlier, I continued to work in my little cubical until the end of the day. When you work with computers, minutes run into hours and the end of the day comes rather quickly. I guess you could say it is a perk in the industry. Most people watch the clock move rather slowly until quitting time. Not me. How easily a person can be watched, listened to, or spied on. Yes, big brother is watching us, all of us. I often wished that I would hit the lottery so I could retire early and live out the rest of my years with my family on the Caribbean Islands or someplace secluded like that, away from all the dangers of today's problems (mostly created by humans).

I finished up the rest of my work and I proceeded to leave. All the while I was thinking about the eerie conversation I had with that voice from the past. All I could think about was how level-headed John was when we went to school. What possible trouble could he be in?

The thought of calling him crossed my mind, but he didn't leave a number. Of course, I tried to retrieve his number using *69 after his abrupt hang up, but he had called from an untraceable number. All I could do was wait until the next day's meeting. I wondered if I should tell my wife about it when I got home.

My wife Laura, to me, is the voice of reason. She's a kind person with a caring heart. I feel a certain comfort being around her. I met her while I was working at a restaurant trying to earn money for college. She had a kind face and a beautiful, slender body with shoulder-length, blonde hair. The kind of face I could immediately trust. When she smiled, she lit up the room…and my heart.

When I got home I was concerned with telling her about the conversation I had with John. I am always worried about frightening her and instinctively I try to protect her from harm's way. But, I reluctantly intended to tell her.

As I entered the house I yelled out, "Laura?" as I usually do when I come home from work.

She answered, "I'm in the kitchen."

I strolled down the hallway toward the kitchen. The house always smelled so delicious because she always has something appetizing on the stove. Something was always brewing and she was a great cook.

I thought I'd wait until after dinner to speak with her. There was no sense in ruining some great quality time. It was only us left at home along with our youngest daughter Pamela. Over the past five years our other two children, Robert and Harry, had moved out of the house to start a family of their own with their wives Simone and Dawn. They had both become Teachers at the local schools and Pamela just had recently graduated from the French Culinary Institute in Manhattan.

Ever since Pamela was a little girl, anytime my wife would cook dinner, there she was by her mother's side, watching, helping, and taking everything in, like a sponge. As the years rolled on, we didn't realize how much our children had learned from us by example. Pamela wasn't always home for dinner so it was just the two of us on most evenings. In fact, sometimes my daughter Pamela would cook for us and leave us alone to eat her great concoctions.

Laura continued, "How was your day?"

I proceeded to tell her some work-related information about problems we were having implementing the new operating system and all the data entry that needed uploading. Speaking to someone who doesn't work with computers is like talking gibberish. She nodded her head in her usual, understanding way. Even though I knew it was tough for her to comprehend the information, she was considerate in actually listening intently to what was being said. She proceeded to talk about the usual stay-at-home Mom subjects such as what the kids did or what the dog got into. Jigzey was his name, a fuzzy, white Pomeranian with a cute face.

To stretch my legs, I proceeded outside through our back door which was where Jigzey was. Upon seeing me, he started jumping around in a happy, snoopy-like craze. I prepared for the thousand little licks I would get upon releasing him from jail. My wife calls Jigzey a wild man. I really hated when Laura locked him up like that, but it was understandable when dealing with a lunatic all day long. I thought to myself that it was too bad we couldn't do this with some of my fellow employees when they were out of control. Employees like Tom Pratt.

Tom Pratt was a prankster, but I'll tell you about Tom at a later time. Right now I wanted to enjoy my family.

As I sat down to enjoy a wonderfully prepared meal by my one and only, I could hear the television in the other room. We have all the latest gadgets hooked up to it: HD, Blue Ray with a million pixels, surround stereo sound with a one-hundred-inch diagonal computer attached, you name it and we had it. It was the curse of technology.

One day we will be able to launch the space shuttle from our living rooms. I mean really, I just want to get off of this ride and stop the exponential acceleration of technology. No sooner is there a new technology one day and a month later, it's obsolete. It's so exhausting.

Whatever happened to enjoying the latest and greatest for say, five years, before something new and improved was available? Let's go back to getting up and changing the TV channel. When we were growing up we enjoyed the outdoors. Kickball with the neighbor's kids was the best. A mound of sand at the end of the block at a new construction site was fun for hours. When we came home from a day of playing outdoors we were exhausted and our parents had to beg us to come inside. The only thing that exhausts kids today is their thumbs from playing video games, indoors.

"This dinner is delicious, thank you!" I exclaimed.

Laura responded with her usual, "Thank you." She never wavered from her politeness and was always courteous and respectful of other people's feelings. That was the way she had been brought up. I always thought to myself that if there were more people like her in this world we would definitely have peace.

I continued, "I had a hard day staring at that screen."

"I can imagine."

"I try to do my work and everyone is always interrupting me to solve *their* problems," I said.

"Well can't you just tell them that you are busy and can't help them right now?"

"I do, but so many of them ask for my help that it's easier just to fix it so they leave me alone," I replied. Then, jokingly I said, "It's so hard having all this knowledge"

After twenty-six years and after all the jokes it's getting harder and harder to get her to laugh. So, a smile was good enough for me. I wanted to tell her of the phone call from John, but wanted to relax a bit longer before I did.

Laura has always been a stay at home Mom, but now that the kids were grown; she considered going back to work full-time. We could actually use the money, since we made a bad investment three years ago in a business that was doomed from the start. Up to that point, Laura was happy-go-lucky and nothing seemed to bother her; in fact, it was rare that we ever got into a fight or that she would even yell. She used to have an easy-going attitude. And why not? Her family gave her a fantastic upbringing. She had everything a child could ever want or need. Up until that point we were very trusting of anyone we came in contact with. Life was good and we were very happy. Now, although she has a strong positive personality, her trust of others has put a damper on her outlook on life.

I guess you could say we needed something good to happen to us after we lost all that money, three-hundred-thousand to be exact. I got into business with a bad partner. You know, the one everyone warns you about? So you could understand why I am reluctant to relinquish any possible bad news. We continued with our dinner and helped clear the table. Afterwards I went inside to enjoy some TV while Laura put on a pot of coffee.

❧ Chapter Four ❦

The Explanation

It was about seven o'clock now as we watched our shows on television when the phone rang. It was Laura's brother from out-of-state calling to see how we were doing. As I enjoyed dessert and coffee, I anticipated my usual nightly ritual of going to the gym. When she got off the phone I had just about finished my dessert and I started to tell her about my peculiar telephone conversation.

"Oh I forgot to tell you," I started.

"Tell me what?"

I got the strangest telephone call from an old college buddy of mine," I said.

"Really? What did he want?" she asked.

Laura's new retort to odd situations now was to wonder what it is people wanted from us rather than just taking in the information. She was no longer the trusting, naïve person she once had been, which is sad because a part of her sort of like, well, died, sorry to say.

"Well…to be straightforward with you Laura, I'm not too sure," I said. I continued with telling her about tomorrow's meeting.

"Sounds kind of fishy to me," she said.

It was hard to convince her that my friends were sincere now after dealing with such a scoundrel partner from our last business deal, but I tried anyway.

"You don't understand Laura, John Hodges was a good soul when I went to school with him." And I continued to tell her about what he was like. "I'm just worried that he is in some kind of trouble," I explained. I tried to convince her by saying, "If I were in trouble and I called upon him, I know he would be there for me because we were rather close back then."

18

"Okay, but please be careful about what you discuss. Think before you act," she said. "In fact before you make any decisions speak with me first," she warned.

When she spoke like this it now gave me a sense of "beware" which was kind of a good thing because it keeps a person in check, so-to-speak.

I got up and started toward the playroom where I kept my gym bag and made sure I had everything I needed to go workout. I usually headed down about 9:00, five days a week. Laura was usually sound asleep by 9:30 anyway, so it really wasn't a big deal that I went so much. It was about 8:15 and I had remembered that my iPod wasn't charged much. So I proceeded to the computer room and turned on my hard drive so that I can charge the iPod. For someone like me, the computer is like a drug—highly addictive. If I turned it on, I would at least surf the net or my desktop for things that would interest me while I waited. I also loved to play card games against people from other states and countries. This time, I wanted to acquire some new songs for my iPod so I purchased some songs to download so I would have some new music for my workout.

I unplugged my iPod after the download and off I went.

I proceeded to tell Laura that I was leaving for the gym. "Do you want me to bring you back anything?" I asked.

She said, "Yes I'd like something sweet." That meant something like chocolate. By now I knew what she meant. What's funny is that we know each other so well, that before she even starts to ask a question I already know what she is asking and I answer before she even asks the question. A great marriage is sometimes funny that way. Well, a great marriage where you marry your soul mate. And that's what Laura and I are to each other more than friends or lovers, but more importantly, soul mates. I always knew how lucky I was to meet her.

I left with a, "Bye Honey," and walked out the door to my car. We own a silver four door Lexus. A ride every day in a luxury car was sweet. Most of our lives are spent on a couch, bed, kitchen or car, so I made sure that those four items were top notch in our lives, and they were. I worked out for about two hours and left.

When I got home the TV was still on and Laura was sound asleep on the couch. I put my bag away, proceeded to drink my drink and sat down to watch some television. I usually watch a bit of the news before I turn on a movie or watch a sitcom. I sat down with drink in hand feeling good about the workout I just turned in and carried on watching the news. CNN is a favorite program to watch, not only does it broadcast news 24/7, but it seems to give the most accurate accounts of world news than other biased channels. But who really knows what their motivation is for broadcasting honestly. For the life of me I don't understand how news channels are allowed to express their bias political views or which candidates they endorse. Who cares what their personal views are? Whatever happened to news agencies being objective?

Now they're all paid off by governments, big conglomerate companies, and special interest groups. Whatever happened to good honest news broadcasting like when Walter Cronkite used to do the news before I Love Lucy came on? Those days are long gone and that era ended a long time ago. I often think to myself, *Wouldn't it be a worthy scandal if one of the honest news agencies reported on the news agencies who don't report objective, unbiased news?* How fitting would that be if they were caught with their hand in the cookie jar and exposed the culprits? It wouldn't matter because governments and big business always have their fall guys, their scapegoats. That's their ace in the hole so to speak. I was so proud of those two anchor people that quit their jobs sighting that they couldn't work for their News company employer any longer because they refused to report false political propaganda. And the beauty of it was that they did it on air.

So, I listened to the newscaster broadcast the stories one after another, world news, story after story when I found one story rather interesting about a poor Harlem resident who had just won a scratch off ticket three months ago. It was one of those scratch offs where you would win a large sum of money each week for the rest of your life. Well the story went on to say that this person was down on his luck and barely making ends meet when he spent five dollars on a scratch off that would pay ten thousand dollars a week for life. The newscaster went on to say that the person had just won all this money and three months later he lost control of his car, slammed into a telephone pole, and died. What a sad story I thought. After such a rough life, finally winning some money and establishing financial freedom, and then that happens. How sad. I continued watching the news until I got utterly depressed again and needed a light comedy to cheer me up. Honestly, why do I do that to myself if I know it will make me depressed? I can only attribute the logic to humans being gluttons for punishment, so what does one do when this happens? Turn on Seinfeld of course. There is nothing like a Seinfeld show to cheer you up. Years ago Lucille Ball did it for me, but today it's Jerry Seinfeld. I remember it was like 1960-something, the night my dad was mugged in Astoria, Queens, while my mother sobbed in grief. I was only eight years old and I needed something to cheer me up while my mother cried over losing his wedding band that they stole. Lucy did it for me. I always remember how she cheered me up when I was so sad.

Television lulls me to sleep and we are the kind of people that need to sleep with the television on. On Sunday's it's golf, bowling, or Bonanza that I automatically fall asleep to, it's therapeutic. After about two hours I was sound asleep. I woke up about 3:30 in the morning to cottonmouth and immediately got up to go upstairs to bed because I had fallen asleep on the couch. I woke up Laura, too, from her sound sleep, and told her to come upstairs so she wouldn't have a crick in her neck from sleeping on such a bad surface. I helped her up, shut the TV and lights off and started upstairs, but first I needed to get something to drink to bring up with me. I got a cold glass of water with ice and drank it down quickly. I refilled the glass and went upstairs as Jigzey followed us up. He too was in a sound sleep until he heard us get up. Jigzey wasn't as wild at this time of night because he needed his sleep as well. He needed to replenish his little body's energy so he could freshly harass us in the morning at wake-up time.

Morning comes very quickly and the alarm clock radio is never set on the channel perfectly enough to avoid the annoying radio static. With all the tossing and turning and only about three hours of sleep, this was par for the course. I immediately headed toward the bathroom. I washed my face and hands, brushed my teeth, and combed my hair. I had the usual uneasy feeling in my gut as to what this day would bring, all the while looking forward to my coffee. Coffee was my only real vice. I never was a smoker and never drank, unless I had little or no responsibilities for the next few days, which needless to say wasn't likely. I always had many responsibilities; my job, my mounting debt, making sure my family was okay, house maintenance and on and on. It never ended it seems and something always popped up. What is the answer? I asked myself daily. What relieves the stress? In my case it was a sense of financial security. Isn't that mostly everyone's stress reliever? Older people have told me not to look at other people's lives because the grass isn't always greener.

Pamela slept at a friend's house last night so I carried out my usual goodbyes to Laura and Jigzey. Out the door I went, waved to the neighbors, got in the car and left for work. It was about 8:30 a.m., and work was close by. I'd usually make it there in thirty-to-forty minutes unless there was some obstruction blocking the roads. With this entire road repair from the new government programs I needed an all-terrain vehicle to deal with all the mangled roadways. I'd get infuriated with all the road work blocking the way, but our new president was doing the right thing promoting jobs while fixing the destruction left by the previous administration.

Still sipping the coffee that Laura had prepared for me, I entered the tall skyscraper where I worked, said, "Hi" to the security personnel at the front desk, and then proceeded toward the elevators to the 41st floor. Raiden was the full-time security guard that sat day-in and day-out at the front desk. He was a Japanese man and proud of his heritage. In Japanese, Raiden was the mythical name for God of Thunder and Lightning. I've had lengthy conversations with him about his home country in Okinawa. In front of where Raiden sat were twelve small monitors that gave a cross-sectional view of the building's perimeter. Some of the screens had views of inside the main hallways and upper floors. Security had been tightened ever since the world changed in 2001. All employees had tags and personalized fingerprint sensors to enter rooms. As a child, I had only read about this kind of technology. Now, I'm living it. Well, lucky me.

As I felt the wave of movement from the elevator's motion, I sensed I was getting closer to my floor. The doors opened and there, directly in front of the elevator, were the glass doors that led to the gigantic room of approximately two-hundred cubicles. It was evident that most workers were just arriving as groups of two and three employees were huddled in conversation, mostly gossiping. Within the next ten minutes most employees settled down to their work—except Tom Pratt. Tom, Tom, Tom. Tom Pratt, as I mentioned earlier, is a prankster. He's the kind of guy you really wanted to strangle at times, but you didn't because he drew a fine line between really funny and irritating. For instance, one day he had lined up all of Karen's stuffed animals which held up a sign that read, "We all hate you!"

Karen was a fellow worker near our desks. I had the wonderful privilege of being situated next to Tom's desk. Another time, he had sent another fellow worker, Joey Diggs, a computer virus that made his computer talk and whistle like a parrot whenever a female walked by his desk. It wasn't anything perverted, but when it whistled or let out a, "Hey Baby" at women, Joey would always get a mean stare. Yes, Tom was a troublemaker but in a good way. He'd give you the shirt off his back. So, in that respect, I really didn't mind being next to him. Plus, he was incredibly smart with computers. He was also a good soul.

I tried concentrating on my work that needed to be accomplished. We always had deadlines—deadlines for this, deadlines for that. It was unnerving at times the stress and pressure of it all. But computer work was gratifying because the more you pushed your mind to solve the problem at hand, the more you learned without realizing it. And that was interesting about computers; it forced you to stretch your mind to the outer limits. This industry keeps surprising me with the endless possibilities of what you can learn and discover. And computers always pay you back with their own surprises of what they can do. Computers are scary, interesting, and fun all at the same time.

I felt myself getting anxious about the mystery meeting but couldn't do anything but wait until it was time to go see him. It felt frustrating but I told myself to be patient and to put it out of my mind. The meeting would happen soon enough. It was about 12:30 now and just then I got a call on the intercom from my boss Richard Harris to come to his office. Good or bad, there is always an alerted sense of interest when the boss calls you into his office. I wasn't really concerned because I was at this job for six years now and I always got the job done regardless of what it was and Richard knew this. Yes, the concern was more as to what he needed me to do, rather than whether I was in trouble or not. I was stretched thin as it is. What could he possibly want of me? When I arrived at his office, he was on the phone in a heated conversation with someone. He motioned to me to sit down. I stared at the items on his desk to take the attention away from listening to his phone conversation. I noticed the back of picture frames that showed pictures of his family, lots of pens and little desk toys. I always had the urge to fumble around with these items but I knew it wouldn't be professional, you know, playing with toys in front of your boss. Richard was a stern man who worked his way up the ladder by hard work and using his brain. He had been there for about twenty-one years. He was an honest man and always cared about the work put out from his department. Upon entering his office, one immediately felt his presence. He had short, black, nicely-groomed hair, about 5' 11', and always wore a suit. He went to Harvard and was set to retire in another five years.

He hung up the phone and immediately asked, "How are you Dave?"

"Good. A little tired, but good," I replied.

He continued, "You know that Antivirus project you've been working on?"

"Yes," I said.

"Well, we've just been informed that it's very effective against the 12SK35 Trojan Virus that's been haunting the new computers," he explained. "I just wanted to thank you for the work you've been doing, but I need to discuss another project with you," he said.

A big sigh of relief came to me when I heard this news, regardless of how I am viewed within the company. Somewhere in the back of my mind there is always a concern when the boss calls for you.

I answered, "Thank you, I appreciate it." And with the next statement, I continued, "What do you need me to do?" All I could think of was the mound of work I already had on my plate, but being eager to help out your boss is always a good thing when it comes time for your raise or a favor. Plus, I have pride in my work which is probably one of the reasons why I am so good at what I do.

The 12SK35 virus was an insidious bugger that attempted to breach security integrities on sophisticated computers often used by big, government-contracted companies.

"One of our client's needs was to make sure that the information placed on their company's computers will be safe from worldwide hackers. There has been a great deal of concern that terrorists had tried to steal information of a valuable nature from our client's computer.

Luckily, the terrorists were apprehended before the information caused havoc," he explained.

Of course, even though I was curious as to what this information was, I immediately responded with a, "Yes sir, I will get right on it!" We weren't allowed to ask who the client was nor what the information was about. We were used to working on top secret projects because in this day and age, computers are how most of us access or store information. I just had a feeling that this client wasn't your average Joe from the careful way Richard explained it to me. There was a heightened sense of urgency that I felt in starting and completing this project as quickly as I could. So, I put my other work aside and began working on extra security measures for this kind of situation.

It was now about one o'clock in the afternoon and I thought to myself that I would leave in fifteen minutes to meet John for lunch. The day seemed to fly by. When I got back to my seat and used my mouse, it activated a song (of sexual nature) on my computer. The speakers were set on high. As I fumbled to turn off the speakers and shut the program off, I thought to myself, *Tom is going to get his one of these days,* because he was the one that booby trapped my computer. He always got his work done in a timely fashion and always had time to fool around. I hated these guys in college. They always had time to play and they always got A's on their reports or tests without studying so hard. In my next life I wanted to come back as one of these guys on easy street. Anyway, I had to concentrate on my work. I turned my voicemail on and left for my meeting.

⇒ Chapter Five ⇐

Power Corrupts, Absolute Power Corrupts Absolutely

I started toward the car lot where my car was parked. My destination was only about fifteen minutes from where I worked. The Luncheonette we were meeting at had been there since about the mid-to-late sixties. Some would refer to this kind of eatery as a greasy spoon. My wife usually comes up with all those old sayings from hanging around her older relatives. She'd always have some saying that was kind of nostalgic, but cute at the same time.

When I arrived, John had not shown up yet, so I asked for a booth and waited. The waitress brought me a cup of coffee and I grabbed a newspaper, all the while I was concerned about getting back to work because I was on a time schedule.

After about five minutes, John came over to the table. It seemed like he appeared out of nowhere. It was kind of an uneasy feeling. I got up and we both gave a manly hug, the type that two guys usually give one another out of respect. We gave each other a back slap and sort of a shoulder bump. It was the cool manly greeting nowadays. It was good to see him but he had on kind of a weird jacket that I never saw anyone wear before. What I didn't realize at the time was that the jacket was lead-lined and there was a reason for this. His hood covered his head and dreadlocks. He had insulated gloves on and thick pants with boots. Every part of his skin was covered for some reason and it wasn't really that cold outside, maybe about 55 degrees. Surely, not cold enough to warrant what he had on.

"Hey bud," I said. "Good to see you."

"Yea, same here brother," he replied.

So, without wasting time I asked, "So, what's up?"

"I don't have much time," he said. "About two years ago I joined a group that was concerned about the country's well-being," he started. "What I've learned was disturbing and goes back to about the early fifties," he continued. "The U.S. has been incurring debt at an exponential rate and top officials have been meeting to control our economy. This plan is so big that it encompasses the world!" he nervously explained. He was shaking, but I wasn't sure if he was shaking from discussing this matter or if someone or something was after him. It was creepy and I grew instantly fearful of the situation. "Ever hear of the Bilderberg Group?"

I quietly answered, "No."

He quickly went on to explain in a rushed fashion. "The Bilderberg Group is a group which conferences once a year at a location that is not disclosed until four weeks prior to the conference. Most are persons of great influence in the areas of politics, banking and business. There are usually thirty-nine core members with a total of about a hundred-and-thirty members that attend the meetings." He rapidly explained what he had learned through the organization he was a part of.

"So," I asked, "What does this have to do with you?"

"Please give me about five minutes to explain." He continued, "The members can only be invited and the media are excluded from covering the story. In fact, if anyone tries to take pictures or even come near the vicinity, they are immediately arrested. The media is invited with the agreement that they are not allowed to report what they see or hear."

"There is high security in and around the meeting place. The original meeting place was the Bilderberg Hotel in 1954, hence the name given to the organization. The exact location was Oosterbeek, Netherlands. In May of 2009, they met in Athens, Greece, but that proved to be a diversion from the actual meeting place. They are very elusive."

I grew more and more anxious as to where this was leading.

He continued, "In 2005 President Bush signed an agreement that abolished the borders of Canada and Mexico to form something called the North American Union. He did this without the authority of Congress or the American People, but his followers never mention this, brainwashed and blinded by the corporate-controlled media."

They have plans to remove cash from our system and introduce a new currency called the, "Amero." This is similar to what transpired in Europe with the "Euro." Soon, Africa will follow suit as well as the Asians—forming four currencies from the four major continents. When the timing is right, they will make their move in combining all four continents into a one-world currency and a new world order. I was shocked to hear such futuristic information and I grew fearful of what the future held and what he was suggesting.

"There's more", he continued. "There will be a single, central bank, one army, and one center of power in a nuclear-free society—the end result would be a one world economy with major corporations at the helm of control. This totalitarian government has been in the planning process for the last sixty years."

I felt scared and happy at the same time because, as I stated earlier, I thought it would be better if the world were unified. What bothered me though, was the people who were planning this were people with monetary and political interests. Whenever you mix together personal money interests with politics, the people who voted in those politicians always get screwed. The heads of media outlets, who had been invited, were not allowed to broadcast the meetings, discussions, or decisions. Who were they to decide the world's fate without input from the public? And, isn't it treason to discuss world affairs in other arenas other than the world stage, in private no less? I immediately thought that the constitution was to be abolished along with our rights and our freedoms. Holy Patriot Act! What I mean, is that if a president can make decisions without congressional approval then it's the beginning of the end for our country. The foundation of what this country was built on is being quickly destroyed and the America we knew growing up was becoming obsolete.

We were about twenty minutes into this meeting when he told me that there was even more. I still didn't know why it was that he contacted me.

"Dave," he said, "right now they are planning on giving everyone in this country identification tags which contain your social security number and all personal information about each of us. Basically, we are all being officially branded with a barcode, sort of like what they did in the Holocaust. What they are trying to do is give everyone in our society that abides by the government's rules, a barcode identification method. The terrorists will not be identified by this method. As a disciplinary measure, if someone gets out of line they would just shut down the card deeming you powerless to identify yourself or buy anything. The last phase, inside the next five years, is to eliminate identification cards, replacing them with an implanted microchip called the R.F.I.D (Radio

Frequency Identification Device.) They will be implanted in humans and it's only a quarter-inch in size. These devices already exist among items that you own and they can transmit far distances to those that want to know information about you. Our privacy is being stripped away from us along with our freedoms. Parents have already had these chips placed in their newborn babies as a tracking method in case their baby gets kidnapped."

Now, I was completely spooked by this information. How did this world get so utterly screwed up? How did we let these greedy political and influential leaders enslave our people? It seemed to me they did it by using the word freedom, but that's just what they took away from us. What's really freaky is that the masses will demand these devices at first for protection. Scare tactics have become common place in this country since the last half century and intensified to present day as we have witnessed in escalating the Iraq war.

He continued, "Dave, just look at the power these individuals have. First, in the year 2000, a president loses the election, but consequently, with the help of his brother, the Florida Governor, and some supreme court judges, he gets the presidency while losing the popular vote. What does it say about our country when the majority votes-in a president by a close margin, but loses anyway due to manipulation and allowed to forge through a Coup De' tat without major objection from the American public? What does it say about our country when the vote can be manipulated simply because of powerful figures that owe someone a favor? When they can sway the votes of Supreme Court justices, you realize that these people can do anything they want."

"Doesn't this sound like a Nazi Regime," I said.

"Sad, but true, yes" he answered. "Look I don't have much time and I don't want to keep you any longer. Two weeks ago I was fired from my job due to this bad recession. I had a few dollars left and played one of those money-for-life-type scratch-off tickets and I hit big—ten thousand a week for life."

"Wow, that's great news!" I exclaimed. "So, why are you so down?" I asked.

"Well, they've got my number" he explained. "They've been monitoring my actions and they know that I am part of this Anti-Bilderberg Group. We call ourselves 'Veracity.' Knowing that their

Lottery money is funding our group goes against what they are trying to accomplish and it doesn't sit well with these animals. Their money is working against them, so the easiest fix would be to extinguish my life, which would eliminate the weekly payout for our cause. They've tried several times already. They shot up my house and killed two members of my family, to make a point. These crooks are worse than the mafia and they wouldn't let anyone get between them and the prospect of making a tremendous amount of money. These individuals knew the future and in knowing the future, they would monopolize the world. They were currently putting all their ducks in a row while waiting for this new world order. It's insider trading at its purest form except for one small detail. There is no one to reprimand, charge, or incarcerate these criminals...they are the law!"

"So," I said quickly, "What do you need me to do?"

"There is an honest man that was part of the Bilderberg Group who is in charge of a powerful newspaper. He was invited. He has abided by their wishes not to broadcast what he saw and heard. He didn't agree with what their plan was. He went into seclusion to combat these bastards; Veracity is who he now works with to bring this information to light. They are in the process of investigating and auditing his paper. The paper called 'The World Gazette' is now weak and on the verge of being bankrupt. They are no longer a credible source for news. His name is Michael Schooner and luckily many of his colleagues still have much respect for him. To some of them his word is still golden."

"You don't understand the kind of people we are dealing with here. There is no one that monitors the Bilderberg's actions; even congress is defenseless against their actions. It's up to us, the people, to stop them and curtail their greedy ways."

"Michael also told me some distressing news that they have plans to kill 5.5 billion people because there are so many people in the world today rapidly depleting the earth's resources. The world is becoming so over-populated because medicine is so advanced today with prospects of finding more cures due to technology's exponential rate. On the one hand, there are more babies being born, on the other hand, our medical technologies are keeping people alive longer. The world cannot handle the increasing population and they are planning mass human extinction. Bilderbergers—or manipulators, as I call them—were concerned with scientist's predictions from scientifically-proven theorems that there would be nine billion people on earth in a few years. As it stands today, the production of food would not be enough to feed all. Earth's resources would be depleted at a faster rate. So, they have decided, in their secret meetings, to annihilate a great portion of our population only discussing the solution in closed circles or in private sessions. Of course, this excludes themselves and their families. They also know that realizing a new world those with this prior information will make them even wealthier and much more powerful. It's the old saying, 'I wish I had a Crystal ball to see the future'. Well, these people are molding the future at our peril and for their benefit. They start wars that others fight. They call all the shots while making the masses believe that they need it for safety."

I found this hard to believe, but I let him continue.

"They will achieve their goal of controlling the population through Swine flu vaccinations, HIV, Drugs, and chemical agents which will be blamed on terrorists. The fear of terrorism cast unto the public, works well with these tyrants. It used to be that our wars controlled the population explosion. The World was multiplying too fast to curtail the human birthrate."

This past decade, fear was used successfully by the administration to get people to believe the actions of politicians we put into office for protection purposes. They knew about 9/11 well in advance, which permitted them to invade Iraq, a war that we should have never been in. Earlier on, four decades ago, some of the same people escalated the war in Vietnam for monetary gains using communism as the excuse. I hate to engross you in this," he said to me, "but you are already involved! We all are," he continued.

"I am going to tell Michael to contact you when the coast is clear. I need you to listen to whatever Michael asks you to do when he contacts you." He continued, "It will be some time this—"

Just then, a barrage of bullets came through the windows killing the soda clerk and one patron sitting at the snack bar. I wasn't hit, but I felt the stream of bullets whiz by my head. I went down to the ground immediately. John was hit, but what I didn't know was he had constructed this odd get up that he had on from a combination of dentist-like, X-ray protective gear and bulletproof lead casing. He was able to get the bulletproof material from a cop friend of his, which I had learned about after future meetings with Veracity members. The outfit he had on protected him from being seen easily by satellite or any technology the government had in place for situations like this. I knew very well of these technologies because I was one of the individuals that developed it for them. I quickly realized that the government was one of my company's secret clients. Dave hit the floor and crawled his way to the back kitchen. The shots stopped and all that I was able to see was the destruction of what the bullets left behind. Sparks flew from electrical fixtures that were hit. Pools of water and blood were everywhere. Ceiling tiles were all over the place. Smoke filled the diner. I was afraid of getting up to use my cell phone, but the cops had already been called by onlookers and patrons that were able to escape. After a few moments, I slowly got up to see if John was alright, but he was gone. I was astonished that this was happening right before my eyes. I thought when the police would get there not to say anything about my discussion with John, for they were clueless as to what was going on in the world. They were just pawns anyway. Government workers are like sad robots just doing what the government tells them to do. They are in a jerk job and most become jerks themselves in the process. I now believed everything John had told me in confidence; he wasn't the kind of person to make this all up. I felt dreadful for him and equally bad for humanity's future.

Before the cops had arrived I made my way through the place and to the back kitchen where I had last seen John, but he was gone. I noticed a back door, but knew that it wasn't a path of option for John. It all seemed to click. This situation I had stumbled unto was huge. John had this joint cased out well in advance of our meeting. I knew he was gone. He just disappeared into thin air. As I told you earlier, John was a smart individual. This was secret agent stuff and from what I remember of him this was right up his alley.

I looked around curiously as to how it was that John escaped and as I slowly made my way to the back, to get out of harms way I spotted a frail floorboard midway between the outside kitchen door and the swinging doors leading to the dining area. I moved the rubber matting that was on the floor semi over it and noticed a wooden plywood flap. I lifted it carefully and observed that it led to a stairway. I poked my head down and saw it was dark. I surmised that it was a storage area for food production, but I was wrong. There was a light switch on the side, I flipped it and proceeded down the stairway. What I saw was an enormous walkway that led to God knows where. I quickly came up as I thought I would investigate it at another time. I knew the cops would be there immediately and didn't want to blow John's cover if this was truly how he fled the scene. My gut feeling quickly conjectured that this was his exit. My guess was that this led to some escape route. I moved quickly before the cops arrived to ask questions so I shut the flap and placed the rubber matting back over it to conceal the opening.

⤞ Chapter Six ⤝

The Interrogation

As I entered the dining area once again, there were slow movements from guests that had been injured. There was moaning and crying heard all around. The area was all disheveled, damaged, and smoke arose from all the gunfire—even flames. It was a dismal, surreal scene as the police arrived. I could hear the sirens in the distance getting closer before they finally pulled in. It all happened so quickly. I thought it had transpired in only a few moments, but apparently it was more like fifteen minutes.

Officers were consoling the people who were hurt badly first. They also checked to see if the people lying motionless were still alive by checking their pulse around the neck region. From a quick overview, it looked as though two people had been killed. All the while I wondered how badly John had been injured from the shot he took to the chest. *Was that personalized vest bulletproof?* I wondered.

I was stunned at what had happened. I asked a police officer if someone could call my employer to tell them that I was not able to come back to work. I was still in distress over what I had just witnessed. Life throws curveballs at you sometimes, but I never anticipated being a part of this. Part of me was grateful that I had found out this information, but another part of me wished I had been oblivious to it. Sometimes not knowing makes for a better existence, because now I had no choice but to help and of course…worry. I came to the realization that the help I was referring to was not only for the Anti–Bilderberg group, but help for my family as well as mankind. What had John gotten me involved in?

As I usually do, I tried to think about the information that he had given me before the shooting, and quickly deduced that we were all in trouble, that is, humanity was in trouble. I mean, if these people could get away with this, it certainly means that they can do whatever they damn well please. It was bad enough with what they've gotten away with in the last sixty years. No one is monitoring their actions or penalizing them for that matter. It seems no one is holding them accountable for their decisions that they are imposing on the world as I previously stated.

I mean, hell, most of them were the ones elected by the people to watch out for us. They weren't elected to fill their own greedy, personal needs.

There were two ambulances outside, a fire truck, and about twelve cop cars surrounding the area. I was sitting at one of the counter stools clearly shaken up as I noticed two of the officers working their way toward me. When they got to me, they asked if I was okay and if I wanted some water. "Yes, water would be great thank you," I said nervously. I told them I felt okay and I didn't notice any broken bones, just some scratches and torn clothes. I had some blood on my shirt from the people who were shot. There was blood everywhere. Officer Mulcahey introduced himself and his partner Officer O'Brien. The paramedics were busy with the more severely injured people. Officer Mulcahey asked where I was when the shooting started as Officer O'Brien brought me some water. I explained to them that I was having lunch with an old friend of mine in a booth. They asked which booth it was. I pointed to it and they, of course, noticed that it was the window where most of the bullets had entered. They asked if he, my friend, was here somewhere and I told them that I didn't see him. They asked my name and then systematically asked for my friend's name. I was brought up with integrity, so I had no intentions of lying regardless of what John had told me. I didn't believe that the cops knew anything about the plan for the New World Order.

I proceeded to answer any of the questions that they had asked along with John's full name and how I knew him. I told them that we were friends and kept the answers very vague. They handed me their card and said that if I needed anything or remembered anything that I should give them a call. They asked if I needed a ride somewhere and I said no. I didn't want to leave my car behind. I was pretty shaken-up, so I waited about fifteen minutes until I knew I was okay to drive.

I didn't want to upset my wife with a phone call so I proceeded to drive home to tell her in person, so she knew I was fine. But, I wasn't fine though. I was worrying about what John had told me, plus the fact that I would get an "I told you so" when I told her that I was in my meeting with John when it happened. It was daunting. Honestly, I really didn't know which was worse, what just happened to me or telling my wife. The wrath of a woman could be intense at times. So, I secretly smiled to myself. That's how I was built. I guess it's all part of being an optimist; find something humorous and optimistic about any situation.

This characteristic also keeps me positive so that I can get any job done no matter how hard. The matter in which we were embarking upon was of catastrophic proportions. What could I find humorous or positive about that?

⇒ Chapter Seven ⇐

What's to come next?

I didn't know what to do and how to react to this. I couldn't get in touch with these guys because they were so covert about the operation. He left no phone number or address. All I could do was wait until someone to get in touch with me again. All that was going through my mind was about that guy John needed me to talk to. *What was his name?* I thought to myself. His name or the information I was supposed to remember escaped me for the moment. I relaxed my mind, Mike, Michael something—Michael Schooner—that was it. I wondered when it was that I was to hear from him. I also wondered how much time we had before the Bilderberg's major plan of taking out 5.5 billion people was to occur. I simultaneously thought about my family, my kids, my job, my future, and building a bomb shelter or protection of some sort. Oh, and I also thought about preparing a survival kit. *Where do I start?* I wondered. If only I knew what it was that my family would need to survive. I thought about getting stockpiles of food, medical supplies, water, and ammunition to combat those who were desperate enough to steal what we had. I thought, *Do we want to survive and deal with the aftermath?* From my computer background I immediately thought to take one step at a time, one problem at a time. So, of course I thought, *Let me tell Laura what just transpired.* After all, she was my guiding light, my voice of reason I spoke about. Then, I immediately thought about her anticipated reaction.

I parked the car and proceeded through the gate and through my front door. I yelled out in a low but firm voice, "Honey?"

I heard her call out from a room she was cleaning, "Daaave?? What are you doing home so early?"

I proceeded to tell her that the meeting with John had gone awry. Then she said loudly, "I told you so!"

You know, there are certain times in your life when you just wish there was a camera pointed at you with an audience watching so you can just commiserate with them with a stare of encouragement. This was one of those times.

I told her to settle down and began telling her the information discussed at the meeting. A pale look quickly engulfed her face and she now looked like I felt. "What do we do?" she asked in a frightened voice.

In a low, calm, firm, voice I said, "We must prepare our family for this! We must do what we have to do!" I exclaimed. "It will be okay," I said with a reluctant pause as I wondered if it really would be okay.

That night was one of the worst nights in a long time. Laura's way of dealing with an intense situation is to sleep away her problems and it's a deep kind of death-like sleep. I kind of wished I had that trait, but the opposite was true for me. There wasn't any sleep for me. I caught a few winks on an upright lounge chair set up in front of my 100-inch HDTV/Computer set, worrying because that's what I do, worry. I perfected it.

Even with what we knew, we got up the next day and went through the motions of the daily routine. Again, I assured my wife when leaving to go to work that everything would be okay. I would be home shortly after work to discuss and plan our escape route. I also told her that we had time, years, as a matter of fact, before anything was to happen. I believed this in my heart. Even though she believed it, she had a blank, dazed look on her face. She too, went through the motions of her daily routine. I left for work.

In secret chambers down below New York City's bustling streets, John made his way back, semi-repairing his damaged chest along the way, where the bullet nearly killed him. The customized vest did protect his body, but was bruised badly from the impact. It could have been a lot worse. There, in that room, were his comrades, people just like him battling the biggest challenge of their lives. Together they were all a team and well-organized. This underground cement shelter was comprised of six compartments. The main room was filled with computer and technological equipment that monitored and calculated all that was needed to carry out their mission-at-hand.

There were sleeping and eating quarters and even an electronic entertainment room for relaxing. One room was set aside as their personal hospital. It contained surgical and medical equipment and tons of pharmaceuticals for practically any emergency. This was the room John headed to immediately upon entering the cement shelter. He was followed into the room by Stephen Howard, a doctor who joined forces about a year ago, once he heard of the movement. Two others joined them a few moments later to discuss what had just happened. They were Leslie Jorgensen and Paul Scott Wayne. Leslie and Paul were the commanders of this particular shelter station. Paul was a tall lumberjack-looking dude. He was very tall about 6' 5". He was a white man with a short goatee, very sure of himself. Leslie on the other hand had a great body. The kind of body that you could tell went to the gym on a weekly basis. She wasn't too built, like a bodybuilder, but her body was fine, real fine. She had a pleasing voice, brunette with blue eyes. Clearly a beautiful woman—and she was very attracted to John. Anyone could easily sense this when you were in the room with them.

There were eight shelters in all, spread throughout NYC city with approximately twenty members to each shelter station, one-hundred and sixty members in all. Each station monitored a section of Manhattan and all stations were linked to each other through computerized technology. Three were on the east side, three on the west and two were centrally located. We were fortunate enough to have members among us, concerned about our future, to finance the construction of these facilities so we could carry out our mission. It was John Lennon himself who had said, "If I lived in Roman Times, I'd have lived in Rome, where else?" Today, America is the Roman Empire and New York is Rome itself. And that it was. After all, it was the financial capital of the world.

Money is the root of all evil and the Bilderbergs were the gladiators of modern times. We had to take down Julius Caesar himself to free humanity from this evil. Caesar represented all those who thought they were above the law, the ones with all the money, stolen, because there was no one to stop them; stolen, because they could. Stolen, because they took advantage of their top positions with no one with higher authority to stop them or police them. This was all about to change. These politicians, bankers, and oil tycoons were all about to be taken down by commoners, people like you and I. People who just wanted to earn the right to live peacefully and acquire a piece of the American Dream for their families. Not to devour the world, in the process, like locusts making their way through open fields and destroying everything in their path for their own greedy, selfish interests. The leaders of these countries made putting personal profits before the people, a selfish quest.

As Dr. Howard aided John's wounds, Paul and Leslie looked on and asked him some questions. First was Paul, "John, What happened?" he started. "Were you able to make the contact with Dave Napoli?"

I wasn't aware of this or it hadn't dawned on me that I was going to be utilized for my vast knowledge of computers. Something so simple, and yet I didn't realize that this was the reason for the contact. You see, this is what happens with the industry of computers. Computers push you to think beyond your own realm of thinking. It pushes you beyond the enormity of the problem at hand, but sometimes the answer is right under your nose. The answer is a simple solution rather than a complicated fix. Most of the time, like 90 percent of the time, the answer is a complicated one because we are always trying to go where no man or machine has ever gone before. Most of the time this is how it is but we forget about the simple solution, the other ten percent.

"Yes Paul, I was able to make contact, but before I could finish, they found me, obviously!" John said in a semi-annoyed sarcastic tone.

"That's too bad, but it's okay," Paul answered without feeding into John's attitude. "You did make the contact; Michael can finish the job and get him started on what we need!" Paul continued.

Leslie was more concerned with how John was feeling. "Are you okay?" she asked intently while looking into his eyes as if to say how bad she felt for him. She reached out her hand and placed it ever so gently on his knee.

"Don't worry, I'll be fine, a little sore but I'll be fine," he said.

"That's good," Leslie answered.

"We have eight weeks before we put our plan into motion to stop these Bastards!" Paul exclaimed. "We must be ready," he said with authority in his voice. Paul had a very deep, stern type of voice that commanders are known for.

John replied, "Don't worry, we will be, you can count on it, brother!"

Back at work it was hard concentrating on anything and in this industry, concentration was key. I worried about how Laura was doing so I gave her a ring to hear her voice. As I dialed the phone I envisioned her picking up the phone and what I could possibly say to make her feel better. I guess I was really calling her to make myself feel better because just hearing her voice gives me a secure feeling and warmth. "Hi Honey," I said.

She said, "Hi."

"Are you okay?" I asked with a reluctant voice.

"Okay, I'm trying to get some work done around here, the floors and bathrooms are a mess so I thought I would work on that today to keep my mind off of what happened yesterday," she said in a soft worried voice.

"I understand," I said. I continued with, "I'm trying to work on this new project Rich gave me. I'll be home around six tonight."

As she was saying, "Okay," she added "can you bring home some Italian bread? I'm making pasta for dinner and we have none."

I answered by saying the usual, "Not a problem, see you later, I love you."

She responded with her usual, "I love you too," and we both hung up.

Just then, Tom tapped me on the shoulder and said, "Hey man, what are you working on?"

He kind of startled me as I was pensive staring at the screen.

"Oh, you know the 12SK thing," I answered.

"Yea, pretty trippy stuff. You wanna hit the bar tonight?" he asked.

"Nah, I can't, got all this on my mind and Laura's by herself. I just told her I'd be home after work," I said. "Plus, it's Tuesday night and I'm feeling kind of beat."

In a consoling voice, he said, "Dude, if you need anything let me know, that was pretty heavy yesterday."

"Yea, tell me about it," I agreed. "We'll hook up on the weekend."

"Cool" he replied. "Let me know if you need any help with that."

"Will do," I replied.

One thing about working in this atmosphere is that there are numerous interruptions that get in the way of concentration. Although I appreciated Tom's concerns, I just wanted to concentrate on the project so that I could get my mind off of what had transpired at the diner. So I delved into the project head first. The hours seemed to fly by and I made some headway into cracking the intense virus by creating a defense so that it couldn't penetrate the sophisticated computers that were protecting our country's most vital secrets. My eyes were starting to see double from staring at a screen for so many hours at a time. Intensely concentrating on this kind of problem while staring at the computer screen can cause the brain to fizzle. I had about an hour left. It was just about 5:00 when the phone rang.

I answered the phone and the voice on the other side asked, "Is this Dave Napoli?"

I answered with a defensive voice, "Who is this please?"

The voice again asked, "Is this Dave?"

"Yes, how can I help you? Who is calling?" I demanded. I didn't want to be rude if it had been a client or something.

"This is Michael," he replied. "I was asked to call you by a mutual friend." He replied again in a cautious tone. I will call you on your cell phone in an hour, please pick it up when it rings," he instructed.

"How do you have my cell number?" I asked in a curious voice.

"Please answer your phone," he quickly responded, ignoring my question. Then there was silence.

Well, that was it. It was now about 5:05 and I couldn't concentrate on what I was doing after the call. I felt like I had put in a good day's work anyway, so I left the office so I could be with Laura.

The office was clearing out by now as quitting time was the standard 5:00 like most jobs unless there was a deadline to meet.

I put on my coat, grabbed my things, some papers, and keys, and then headed down the hallway toward the elevators. I pushed the down button. There were six elevators in all, three on each side. I watched for which one would open first. I heard a ding and went through the first door that opened and joined the others who had been riding down the elevator from their offices above. We all smiled at each other as I got in and we all simultaneously looked up at the descending numbers of floors as the elevator made its way down to the lobby. I had the same anxious feeling of the mood of the people riding down with me, that we all wanted to get somewhere where we could relax from the stressful day. Sometimes, since I was young, I've had intuitions about certain things. I wouldn't say that I was psychic, but I do have the ability to sense what people are thinking and at times, what is about to happen in the future. It's a gift and a curse all in one. I can't really explain it to someone, unless they have themselves, experienced these similar feelings. Let's just say that most of the time I'm aware and alerted to a certain aura surrounding my perimeter. It's uncanny how I could predict what was about to happen.

⇒ Chapter Eight ⇐

Mr. Bond I Presume?

By now I felt like a secret agent. I thought, with all the secret information, phone calls, and meetings. I couldn't help but joke to myself about the Cone of silence from the 1960's show Get Smart. I thought about Control and KAOS and related it to my own situation. But, growing up and watching that show I always knew it was a satire based on fiction. At least, I thought it was, until recent events. I thought about all the different agent movies as well.

As I exited the elevator I watched my phone like I was waiting for a pot of water to boil. I gave my usual wave goodbye to Raiden. Raiden works until about 7:00 p.m. when he is relieved by the night watchmen George Harris. The building has 24 hour surveillance. After 9/11 no one took any chances in the city. George was a black, slender man. He was quiet, but did his job efficiently. He would notice even if a fly flew by. Both guards were armed with weapons. There were silent alarms installed along with the security cameras so that the police could arrive in minutes if there was an emergency, robbery, or unwanted intruders.

I made my way down the street toward where I parked my car. There's a bakery close by that I usually got fresh bread from when we ran out. Small pleasures such as these is what life is all about I guess. They knew me at the bakery because I was in twice a week for various items as well. Okay, sometimes I brought home these delicious cookies they make. I'm a stress eater, when I worry, I get little sleep and I eat. I guess it's something inbred from growing up in an Italian home. My Grandmother always seemed to use love as one of her ingredients in the great food she cooked. I always found comfort in great foods and great cooking. My grandmother was an Angel. I wouldn't say Italian food was my favorite, but it was right up there with Sushi. So, psychologically whenever something bothers me, food helps me to relieve stress. In some odd way it reminded me of the comfort I had living with my grandparents. The mind is interesting that way. I'm guessing that's another reason why I married my wife. Although she's not Italian, her cooking and her warm, special ways, reminded me of my own family.

So, I proceeded to put my order in at the bakery as I made some cheap talk with the counter person about the week's weather. Weather was always a common interest among strangers and was a friendly way to interact while going through the motions of the purchase, all the while trying to take my mind off the more serious issues of the world. I thought to myself, *All of these people have no clue how their lives are molded by bigger forces around them.* I mean, wealthy influential people making decisions about the future of a counter clerk, a night watchman or a school janitor just going about doing their jobs so that they could feed their families. They had no idea. It does boggle the mind. I left the bakery with bag of purchases in hand and headed toward the car at the parking garage. My office was located three blocks away on Fifth Avenue and 57th street. A very influential area, Fifth Avenue is ranked as the richest street in the world. Where else would Computech be located?

I got into my car, put on the music station, and proceeded home. Music was another soothing stress reliever in my life. I love music, all kinds of music. Thank God for music. It has the power to move people in many different ways. It can calm or infuriate a situation. It can motivate and even bring you back to a certain time period, or bring back a special memory with someone you care about, or in the same respect, cared about. I can find something good in all genres of music, even rap and heavy metal. It's difficult though finding something pleasing about that new screaming heavy metal the kids listen to today. But with my open mind, it's probably synonymous with the way my parents viewed our listening to Led Zeppelin or Ozzy Osborne. I play my music loud and I like to feel the bass. I like to feel the music. Okay, so I get some non-approving stares from the old fogies in the cars next to me at the red light. What's interesting is that these old fogies I talk about are about the same age as I, fifty or so. What happened to them? I often wondered. How can they just let their bodies and minds go like that? Here I am, still thinking I feel like I'm seventeen and they can't even go on an amusement park ride because they're just too old. I saw a friend of mine with a shirt on that read, "If it's too loud, you're too old!" I just love that shirt. I'm more of a shirt that reads, "Old guys rule!" I feel good. Fortunately, I really love to exercise. It motivates me, gets the blood circulating, and it combats aging. Anything that can accomplish that, I'm all for.

I don't live too far from work, Flushing Queens to be exact. We moved there when I got this job in the city because it's so close to where I work. We used to live further east on Long Island, but couldn't deal with the four hour commute every day. This cut it down to a little over an hour both ways total. Sometimes it was an hour-and-a-half during holiday rush hour but I could deal with that. Lately though, I've noticed an increase in cars on the road. Well, I felt uneasy about that also. It just seemed like everything was getting so congested. Even a simple ride to the store at non rush-hour times, the streets were packed with cars. I don't ever remember the roads being this populated. I thought maybe I was paranoid from the discussion I had with John at the diner about the over-population problem and how the Masons were trying to regulate the overpopulation problem. Maybe I was just more aware of it now, which lends one to believe that we are just all sheep being manipulated by wealthier powers. Like blind robots just going about our business. It's just so sad that there are fellow humans that would wish other humans ill-will for selfish, monetary reasons. Maybe that's why I wasn't as wealthy as I could have been. It's easier to get rich when you sell your soul. But I vowed a long time ago never to sell my soul for money.

As I arrived home, I pulled the car into the driveway and got my things, as well as the bread Laura asked for. I exited the car and entered my house. Jigzey came rushing up with his frantic body and tail wagging like he normally does when I come home. The house smelled of that tomato sauce aroma I was used to smelling on Sunday mornings when my grandmother cooked our ritual Sunday dinner.

I yelled out the usual Ricky Ricardo wife greeting I was used to watching on TV in the 60s. "Laura," I called and continued, "I'm home."

She replied "I'm in here." I walked in and gave her my usual kiss hello.

She asked, "Would you like a glass of wine?"

"You know what? That's not a bad idea, sure."

So, she said "Can you get the bottle of Pinot Grigio out of the fridge?"

When we were growing up the refrigerator was called fridge for short. I believe Frigidaire was a name brand popular then and referred to by most of us as fridge in that era. I love when Laura uses terms like that because I relate it to those great old times and I immediately think about family that is no longer with us. In that way, I get a feeling of happiness which comes over me, thinking about those great memories. I really missed those people.

So, I got the bottle out, got the corkscrew, and proceeded to open the bottle from my vast experience in the early years of my employment in the restaurant business. I got two wine glasses out of the cupboard and poured a glass of wine for both Laura and I.

As I handed her the glass, I exclaimed, "This virus problem is kicking my ass. It's so tiring."

Her response to that was, "Come on, you know that if you stretch your mind in solving these problems, you're just learning more. You end up banging your head against the wall and when you come out of it, you're that much more educated on the subject.t"

Even though I knew she was right I still thought about how hard it was learning new material or getting your mind thinking to the outer limits. Computers and human brains are very much alike and with that simple realization it helps to solve some of the most complicated of issues. My wife is funny, when her brain is pushed to the limit; she always exclaims that she "needs more meg." Meg is a computer term meaning megabyte, which is a unit of storage capacity for computer hard drives. In other words, her brain is filled with so much ineffectual information that she needs more storage space with all of the everyday problems our challenging life possesses.

As I was speaking, I went to the silverware draw, took out a spoon, and taste tested her sauce. She watched me like I was Alex Ahente' taste-testing the first cup of coffee from the year's crops. I said, "Wow, that's great as usual!" Laura had a sauce recipe handed down from her relatives. They never wrote anything down, it was memorized from the many Sunday's at her aunt's house when she was little. As she finished cooking I went into the TV room to enjoy some television and relax a bit before dinner. I put the thought out of my mind that I would be receiving another call from Michael. Waiting for the call was a terrible feeling. By now, the hour had come and gone and I wondered why the call never came through. I checked whether my cell phone was on and working properly. I checked it and assured myself that it was working just fine. I tried not to turn on the news because that would only set my mind thinking again and I didn't want to do that for obvious reasons. So, I put on Everyone Loves Raymond for some light entertainment as I enjoyed my glass of wine with Jigzey by my side. He was definitely man's best friend and always stayed with me by my side. It's a wonderful thing about pets, especially dogs. They give you unconditional love all of the time, lots of licks and affection. And they appreciate when you love them back. A comedian once said (I believe it was George Carlin), "Dogs have no concept of time. You can leave and come back in three hours and they will jump around like crazy when you get back because they're glad to see you. You can also leave for five minutes and you'll get the same reaction." Yes, he was my friend and he made me feel good to be around him.

After half-an-hour of watching some TV, Laura yelled for me to come in and eat dinner. She had prepared pasta and meat with some mixed vegetables. The table was nicely set for two as Pamela wasn't home again for dinner. We wondered where she was because we knew she was at that dangerous age where she needed amusement constantly. She could be at any one of her many friends' homes, crashing, after a night of bar hopping. That was the scene that Laura and I were very familiar with at that age too. Worrying about this was the least of my concerns. How much worry can one person take? Of course we called her cell phone anyway just to keep in touch with her and her ever changing plans. The waiting for Michael's call continued...

❧ Chapter Nine ❧

The Plot Thickens

The next morning I awoke with the same nervous feeling of, *What will the day bring*? As I went through the usual daily routine of washing up and preparing for work, thoughts of getting my work done and the anticipation of getting that phone call ran through my brain yet again. Thank goodness for coffee, the nectar of the Gods. I always feel a bit of excitement in the morning when I think of drinking that first sip of coffee which only leads me to believe that I am severely addicted to caffeine, but if that is my only vice, then I'm not doing so bad. And it really is my only vice. I've never smoked, I hardly drank, and drugs were just not an option for me. That's all I needed was to have that kind of addiction—shoot me now. Sometimes with so much on my mind I forget to drink coffee in the morning and about midway through the day I'd get these tremendous headaches. Then it dawns on me that it's actually caffeine withdrawals. I find that very interesting.

So I headed to the corner deli for some coffee and a buttered roll, got back in my car and headed to work. As I headed over the bridge I noticed what a beautiful day it was; the sun was shining without a cloud in the sky. It was a beautiful, clear day.

I arrived at the parking garage and gave the usual greeting to the parking attendant. I started with a quick walk toward my building as I was eager to continue working on my project. Everyone has a quick walk in New York it seems. Rushing to do this, rushing to do that. Plus, that's how you can tell the difference between tourists and native New Yorkers. New York has its own language; from taxi cabs to store owners, from street peddlers to hotdog vendors. New York has character and there is always something interesting going on here. You could usually see camera crews, filming some award winning production or amateurs filming the weirdest stuff. New York is a fascinating place.

I made my way into the building and quickly got on the elevator to get to my floor. I arrived a little after nine. I could already tell, from the hustle and bustle of the office, that everyone was in full swing at their cubicles concentrating on their particular project. On the way to my desk

I caught Karen's eyes looking at me and we immediately smiled and said hello simultaneously. She looked at me as if to say, "How are you doing?" I can just imagine the conversations around the water cooler discussing what I had been through. Some people are just naturally mean and will find something rude to say in the worst of situations. I've been around long enough to know this, but I don't bother with any of that garbage or game playing any more. I just stick to my work and mind my own business. I have a firm belief, that with people like that, karma will get them sooner or later. I began working and two hours and fifteen minutes had gone by quickly when I heard the vibration of my cell phone go off. I answered it.

"Hello," I said.

"Hi Dave, I couldn't talk yesterday, something came up." The voice on the other end said.

Before I asked the question I already knew who it was because it was the same voice from yesterday's call. I knew it was Michael Schooner.

"Who is this?" I asked impulsively.

"This is Michael; I had called yesterday as well. Can you talk?" he replied.

I looked around nervously to make sure no one was watching me and I didn't feel secure speaking to him with my co-workers lurking around so I said, "Yes I can talk. But can you call me in exactly five minutes?"

He said, "Not a problem." And with that he hung up.

I told Tom that I would be taking a break if anyone asked where I was. "Tom, I'll be right back, I'm going downstairs to stretch my legs for a sec."

Tom replied, "Okay" without lifting his eyes from the computer monitor. It looked like he was intently working on something that he was almost finished with.

I left the office and went downstairs to the lobby. I gave a look to the security guard with just a smile, no words and headed outside. Just then the phone rang again and I answered it quickly.

I couldn't believe the situation that was unfolding before my very eyes. It's a kind of strange, dreamlike state that you only see in the movies or when you're sleeping and have to wake up to make it stop. I definitely felt as though I was in some James Bond movie with all this secrecy. I had a certain comfort knowing that even with all this mystery, we weren't alone trying to combat this problem. It seemed that the operation was fairly sophisticated with all the outposts and such. Just then I realized, like a light bulb going on in my head, that there might be more stations throughout the world. If this was so, then there were other nation's citizens who felt the same way we did about humanity being strong-armed into doing what these criminals wanted to accomplish. They were the Wall Street Criminals that played a big part in crashing our economy just a few short years ago. Wow, I thought, this was incredible. This operation is a lot bigger than I considered. This awakening has been brought to life as I thought about Michael's seclusion.

Michael was a good man who was tainted by what he had experienced. He was present at three of the yearly Bilderberg meetings and was severely distraught over what he had heard. When Michael threatened to print the story regardless of his oath, they subtly told him that it wouldn't be a wise choice to do so. In the year after this discussion there were two attempts on his life and he finally made the decision to go into seclusion and to go public with what was happening. I didn't know it at the time of this telephone call, but Michael operates all of his business interests from the Fiji Islands, far enough away from civilization so that he would be safe to continue his efforts. No one, except for his closest compadres knew his exact location.

The west had long reaching arms eager to destroy anyone that got in their greedy path. This is what they would do to a country's leaders as well, when they didn't comply with their offers that they couldn't resist. Either they would let them exploit their countries resources for profit, or they would be assassinated by a rogue bribed bandito. These leaders would have some kind of suspicious accident. The next leader appointed would be someone that they could manipulate to carry out their plan to possess the country's riches. Saving humanity was a noble cause and Michael would go to great lengths to be successful. I awaited his request for what he needed me to do.

"Dave, I don't have much time to talk so please just listen." He started, "The operation we are about to have you embark on is the most important thing you will ever do in your life. We need your help. Our Group was formed about ten years ago when we learned about the exclusion of media coverage from these meetings, where these powerful figures discussed humanity's future. Billionaires want to control all of the world's wealth at any cost so they can dominate the world. The Members who have been funding our cause are being killed and it has damaged our efforts to successfully complete the mission at hand. They are aware of our meetings, but haven't figured out where the locations are because of our ingenious camouflage techniques and intelligent use of new technology. We are being watched through the most advanced technological equipment available and yet they have not penetrated our shields. Mainly because we utilize smart individuals like you. You and your family are being watched because of the meeting with John! Do not discuss anything of what I am about to tell you with anyone!"

I answered briefly with a quick, "I won't."

"With my media contacts I was able to learn of information that is detrimental to our cause. The ultra rich and banking elite has a plan of completing one final step that will change life on this planet so that they can reap the rewards for their inner circle. Once the currency is changed to one global currency, those who had prior knowledge of this will have unlimited wealth and power, as well as total control. The wealth that they have had to this point pales in comparison to what they will have. This wealth will be distributed to the Bilderberg representatives of countries from around the world. Each nation is represented by two or three persons who have given an oath not to discuss the meetings with anyone or suffer the consequences. They tried to bribe me as well, saying things like, 'Why are you worried about everyone else, just worry about your own family's interest!' The benefits of these meetings to those who attend are lucrative, not just with riches, but with power. Some that attend these meetings become presidents and also find themselves in the midst of a big monetary deal becoming wealthier beyond belief like the oil tycoons for example. This has happened time and time again in the last six decades," he said. His rapid pace made me very anxious as I wanted for him to get to the point as to what he needed me to do.

"There are posts throughout the world in various nations that are aware of the Masons. We also have stations situated in major cities like Los Angeles, Chicago and Las Vegas. Much research has been done to uncover and to bring to light the atrocities they have committed and are about to commit from their sixty years of planning. Unlike the Kennedy assassination farce cover-up, we have hard clad evidence hidden to prove what they have done. It is the same old story with these people we are dealing with. There is just no one higher than them in the chain to take them down. If they broke the law, it didn't matter because they are the law. They called the shots from the Dallas assassination to the 9/11 catastrophe. The Warren commission, for instance, was filled with people that absolutely hated Mr. Kennedy. These occurrences helped to facilitate three wars that we should have never been in and it made them billions. Some of the same people that were around then, are still around today, and have benefited from all three wars. We are talking about population control, as well as monetary control. Currency and how governments can access personal information about each and every one of us is about to change in the world. They are terrorists themselves and have used the excuse of foreign terrorism to fuel this current war. The mere freedoms that they talk about are the same freedoms that will be given up to the big conglomerates that surround us," he warned.

I answered, getting in a word edge wise with a faint, "I am well aware of what is going on from my briefing with John."

He then, again continued as his time was limited, "We have intel now that the next catastrophic event will be the taking out of an entire U.S. city. Don't get freaked out by this next statement. The blame will be placed on aliens. In the past sixty years, and more so today with 9/11, they saw how well fear works, and thus, the reason for this annihilation of a city. After this occurrence, it will be like taking candy from a baby. The American public will do anything they ask of them for their safety."

"What do you need me to do?" I asked quietly.

Without acknowledging my question he continued, but I could tell that he wasn't being rude, he just wanted to get the information to me while answering my question.

"First, you need to understand how money is made. Today only three percent of the United States currency is backed by gold, so the Federal Reserve just prints money. It's more of an IOU than real gold-backed money. The money printed is then given to banks and that money is lent out to individuals like you and I. If they get five billion dollars from the Federal Reserve that money becomes worth nine times the value. So, that five billion becomes forty-five billion in no time. Our country is rapidly going bankrupt...ON PURPOSE," he warned.

"Big conglomerates and billionaires are blocking all kinds of technology so they monopolize on the wealth of energy consumption due to supply and demand. In simpler terms, they hide the fact that we have enough free energy on this planet to supply every individual power for the next 4000 years. 4000 years! There is so much technology that civilization could live peacefully without the use of money. Everyone would be equal; no one would need to buy anything. For luxury purposes, extra work would come into play. More importantly we wouldn't be controlled by the extremely powerful. Conglomerates are successful for two reasons. They have power and money to control media and to control the fear levels. They use terrorism for their own benefit. And they know that history repeats itself. If we don't learn from our past we are destined to repeat it."

He continued giving credit to the author of that last sentence, "I believe it was philosopher George Santayana that made that statement or a variation of it. Nonetheless it was embedded in my brain during all the school years I've attended. The conglomerates know that most of our wars have been fought over money, race, and mostly religion."

I thought to myself, *I can understand the differences over money and race, but religion?* Most religions speak of love, caring and so on. I thought to myself that God, or any powerful loving force that created religion or founded religion would never want their people to hate or kill one another. Not so, the people in power use religion as their sword saying it is just to kill someone who doesn't believe the same things you believe, how hypocritical. The Catholic Church, for instance, has thirty-four thousand derivatives of the same religion. With these statistics, we are so doomed. It is so depressing.

While I listened to Michael, my mind wandered off on tangents while still using one ear to hear what he was saying. It had gotten so difficult to keep my mind on only one thought. He continued and I concentrated on having all of my attention on what he was saying.

"Our intelligence is rather sophisticated as well, and we know that you are working on the 12SK35 Virus. We need you to continue working on that project without letting on to anyone, especially Richard Harris, of your lack of progress. In other words, you are to make believe you are diligently working on the project without letting on that you aren't. In the meantime, we need to know everything about that virus because it will help us crack the information needed to decipher what their next step will be. Again they are very close to a sixty year culmination of their master plan to control humans of all nations!"

I replied with, "Can I ask a question?

"Yes, of course," he said.

"Do you know if John is okay? He was hit with a bullet?" I asked.

He replied quickly by saying, "John is fine, a bit bruised but he is fine. His vest saved him. Now do you understand what your mission is, Dave?" he asked.

I replied with a military response, "Yes sir."

He continued, "I am telling you this in confidence, so please do not tell anyone or we will need to take you into seclusion."

I again thought to myself that this was inevitable, as well.

Michael continued, "With what we know about our current broken down monetary system and through the use of technology, civilization does not need to use money. We have enough resources for everyone. Big Business does not want anyone to know this, again, for the obvious reason. Jails are filled with people who need money to survive and are backed up against a wall to feed their family. We have the most prisoners of any country populating our jails. Without the need for money, our jails would not be nearly as populated. "It is a known fact that we have enough food to feed the world twice-over; yet due to the greed of some of the wealthiest people there is a tremendous amount of starvation across the globe."

Again, he continued, but I could tell he was getting antsy about getting the information to me and getting off the phone. "Dave, what I am about to tell you will be the way of the world in the future. It's the only way to survive and we are doing this for all mankind. We labeled our mission, The Geneva Project by a great man who thought up the idea. We will tell you the founder's name at a later time. This was the alternative world we thought best for civilization where everything is free for everyone; free of greed, free of religion, and free of totalitarian control from these conglomerates. Help us Dave!" With that he ended by saying, "I will be in touch very soon," and then the voice was gone.

I returned to my cubical, all the while I was trying to soak in the very informative conversation I just had. I knew that if I was caught, the consequences would be severe, but I believed the world was in trouble with the series of events which had occurred in the past two days. I can't actually say that I was worried or nervous or scared because by this point I had become numb to all senses. My mind continually thought of all the questions it had accumulated from all that has happened. Where was Michael hiding? Who else knew about this? Where's the tunnel in that diner leading to? I could have gone on and on. It was enough to make one go insane. Just then Tom poked his head over the partition that separates our cubicles and startled the living day lights out of me because I was in deep thought.

"Hey bro! Wat up? You okay?" he asked. "You look a bit tattered." He always tried to use funny cool little words to get a chortle out of you. I was glad to speak with someone not so concerned with the seriousness of life.

"I'm fine!" I answered. Interestingly enough, whenever I heard someone use the word "fine" it usually meant the opposite. I really did mean the opposite. It killed me not to be able to discuss this with anyone.

"Dude we're all going down to Kelly's pub for happy hour. Looks like you need a few shots!" he quipped.

I said, "Sure." *What the hell, maybe some alcohol could soothe my nerves*, I thought to myself. It was about 4:00 p.m., almost quitting time, so I concentrated on my efforts on the virus project. I felt like Schindler in WWII stuffing the enemy's ammo with anything but gunpowder to sabotage them. I started to see the ways in which we could use this virus to infiltrate information from the advanced computers used by our government and governments from around the world. As advanced as our personal computers are, and as advanced as we think they are, they are nothing compared to the advancement of computers used in governmental agencies. You could multiply what we knew as Q public by ten, and you would then have the capabilities of what the government could accomplish. It was frightening to say the least what big brother could do with technologies that the general public had no knowledge of.

We didn't know that soon surveillance cameras were to emerge on almost every street corner to watch over us. At the very least speeding and running stop signs would be supplemented with a hefty fine in the mail. But the real underlying purpose of these cameras is to watch people. I will repeat this as you need to understand the implications of that last statement. The real underlying purpose of these cameras is to watch people.

By now I had figured out exactly how they were able to get anything they needed from our country these past ten or so years, they used fear and continued to use fear to get any policies they wanted passed, strictly because the people thought they needed to be protected. Thus with a blatant disregard for our constitution, water boarding, the Patriot Act and the National Defense Act were put into effect. Citizens did very little to protest or stop this from happening. In fact, the National Defense Act was signed by the president on New Years Eve while we were preoccupied with the festivities of ringing in the New Year. By enacting these laws the government can pretty much do anything it wants. We have given up our right to privacy whereas wiretaps don't need a judge's approval before their use. But what I find even more disturbing is the fact that we have given up our right to trial. Any military official can come into anyone's home without cause, without trial and incarcerate any of us indefinitely and ship us overseas if that is what they wish. Thus, the fourth and fifth amendments of the constitution have been violated. The second amendment is what they are after next.

I hate to be repetitive but perhaps this is the only way that people will understand the enormity of the situation. If I say it enough times maybe something will get done about it. At least it is my hope, my hope for a better humanity.

"Nobody seems to bother and nobody seems to care."

~ George Carlin

When I was growing up I remember thinking how sad it was that Russia used such horrid propaganda against their people, yet it was happening right here at home. Terrorism only helped our government's hidden cause and the irony was that our own political figures, politicians we elected to protect us, became worse terrorists then the ones we were afraid of. They had perfected the use of propaganda to get what they wanted. It was a technique I remembered using as a kid. I remembered when I was about nine years old and it snowed in our neighborhood. We used to hide behind the mounds of sand they had at the end of our block's construction site. Our opponents would hide behind another mound of sand now covered with snow. The basic tactic was to throw a snowball with enough arc so the enemy would be so concerned with watching that snowball, with their heads looking up; we threw another one with velocity straight to the bodies of our opponents. It worked every time until they caught on.

That's how it was for the first decade of the new millennium. They have weapons of mass destruction; watch out because they are the axis of evil. While we were worrying about them, the evil doers, our own leaders were on a ranch collecting ten percent interest on Iraq oil profits. Profits made from wars they didn't even pay for, borrowing monies from other countries and sending our deficit into the trillions, while wiping or attempting to wipe out our middle class. During this time, I remembered a show that documented the end of the debate on how Kennedy was assassinated. Although I looked at this documentary with doubting eyes and having visited the Dealey Plaza site in person, I knew that the results of the show, again claiming the one bullet theory correct, was preposterous. A few years later I found out that the channel that was airing this documentary was given a license long ago, by the government, to air its shows for free. Propaganda at its best. Nice Job. Power is a dangerous thing.

It was about 5:00 now and I was glad the day was over. I packed up my things and headed to the car so that I wouldn't bring my work to the bar. When I got to the parking garage I asked the attendant to get my car so I could put the items in. The day grew colder and the wind kicked up a bit so that it felt about ten degrees cooler than it had been the prior week. I placed the items in the car and handed the keys back to the parking attendant. He proceeded to tell me that if I got there after seven pm, the place would be closed. So, just in case, I had him park the car where I could see it and he gave me back the keys. I paid a monthly fee for the service so payment was not an issue. I had a code to get into the parking area.

I buttoned up my top button on my coat and started to head to the bar to have a few drinks with my working companions. It was about five-thirty now and I knew happy hour would be in full swing. Kelly's pub was the kind of bar where you could forget about your problems. It mixed young patrons with older ones due to the fact that there was a college nearby. The owner kept the bar in pretty good shape and the bartenders were always nice with great personalities and great physics. Joe Schmidt was the bartender during this time, along with Pam and Kyle. They needed three bartenders because it got pretty nuts there for happy hour. I knew Joe the best because I had come in a few times when the bar was not as crazy and was able to have a conversation with him while having a few drinks. When I walked in, the bar was jumpin'. The jukebox was on and it was loud. The place was packed. It took me a moment to find my friends as I made my way through the crowd. Tom had a Beer waiting for me when I arrived.

"Here you go buddy," he said with a smile on his face.

"Thanks, bud," I replied in a louder-than-usual voice because of the loud music. The beer went down really fast and it tasted so good. I guess due to the fact that I was thirsty and really needed a drink. That's when they taste the best. That first cold beer after you have been overworked and overtired for days, maybe even weeks for that matter, is the best. It felt good to try and relax for a change.

After about ten minutes, I made my way to the bathroom. There was some rock music on and the crowd was moving to the sounds of Mick Jagger's, "Satisfaction." They had a diversity of music on the jukebox to satisfy all tastes of music and all age groups, all genre's from reggae to rap, rock, disco, and even ethnic as well as the traditional Happy Birthday Song. There wasn't really a line at the bathroom like there normally was with the ladies bathroom, so I quickly went in, went, washed my hands and returned back to the spot where I had been drinking. By now, the group had ordered a round of shots. I reciprocated and bought a beer for Tom. Karen was there along with about fifteen other workers that worked in the general vicinity on our floor. There were three floors owned by Computech in our building, from the 39th floor to the 41st.

By now, the place was getting insane. It was about 6:15 and the place was about to erupt with excitement, all good, no fights, just everyone having a real good time. The bartenders were now dancing on the bar and Joe started for the soda gun as he was about to shoot a short spray of liquid into the crowd. With all those people in there it got pretty hot. As it turned out he sprayed some water and everyone laughed as the party continued. The song ended but a new one came on almost immediately as the bartenders continued to serve everyone drinks.

No one was really intoxicated. I had started feeling a buzz when I looked over and saw a man standing near the wall with a drink in his hand. He was staring at me nonchalantly. It wasn't a stare of sexual nature but one of concern because everyone else in the bar was having a great time smiling and laughing except for this dude. It was about 6:45 now and I started feeling as though I should leave before Laura started to worry. I turned my head so as not to keep eye contact or to show that I was being intimidated by the man and continued hanging out with my co-workers. It was obvious that happy hour was coming to an end. Normal pricing was about to recommence and that led many to get their last round of drinks including our group. By now, bartenders were starting to cut people off because they didn't want to get themselves or the bar in trouble. Nowadays, over-pouring is a serious offense.

The atmosphere didn't lend itself to being able to have any serious discussions about work or anything else because the music and patrons were so loud. It was now about seven o'clock as I turned to see if that guy was still looking at me. He wasn't there any longer and I finished my beer so I could leave. I took a few more swigs and finished the last gulp of the ale and placed the empty bottle on the bar. I said my good byes, gave Karen a hug and shook hands with Tom as I exited the pub. I left while saying, "See you guys tomorrow." At the foyer or vestibule I buttoned up my coat to the top and headed out the door.

I walked rather quickly as I was cold and had just left a cozy, warm bar. I felt a bit nervous in my buzzed state as to why that individual was staring at me. I thought I was being paranoid until I turned around just to make sure he wasn't around but there he was, walking about two blocks behind me. I started to walk faster and faster until I got to the garage door where my car had been parked. I quickly entered the code and went inside. I didn't know who to call or what to do and there was no one inside the car garage. I got to my car, locked all the doors and started the engine. Just then my cell phone rang and I nearly jumped out of my skin. It was Laura.

"Are you coming home?" she asked.

I said, "Yes," in a faint voice.

She immediately sensed that something was wrong so she asked, "Is everything okay?"

I answered, "Not really, I thought someone was following me so I ran to my car. I think I'm starting to imagine things."

But I wasn't imaging things; I know he was following me.

She said in a quick voice, "Just come home—where are you now?"

"I'm in my car heading home."

"Okay," she said. "Come home."

I hung up the phone and slowly headed toward the electronic garage door. I hit the remote door opener and the metal door opened slowly. Just then a figure darted out and banged on my window scaring the living hell out of me. My body jolted and it was evident by my physical reaction that I was startled. It was only Tom, fooling around as usual.

I rolled down my window and yelled out to him, "What the hell is wrong with you? I could have run you over! You scared the shit out of me!"

He responded by saying, "Dude I was just messin', why are you so uptight?"

"No reason man, I'm just stressed from work!" He should only know. I was no longer buzzed from all the excitement and tension so the thought of driving while intoxicated was not a concern. We again said goodbye and I headed back home.

❧ Chapter Ten ❧

Living in Extraordinary Times

I made my way home quickly as traffic was light. Although I did some drinking, my nerves were shot. I needed something to relieve the stress and anxiety of all that was happening. I couldn't wait to get to the gym so I thought about a light dinner and exercise. When I got home I went through all the usual entrance rituals with dog, wife, food, and television, except I wasn't too interested at what was on the tube tonight. I tried to clear my mind of any thoughts. I just needed my body to relax and with the enormous strain on my mind that was just not possible. It was Thursday night, one more day and it would be the end of the work week.

Upon sitting down for dinner Laura asked the question, "Do you think we should just move from here?"

Although that thought had occurred to me, I really didn't want to move as I immediately thought of all the pros and cons with that decision. Where would we go? The physical move itself, getting a job in the area we move to, leaving my kids behind etc. It was just too much and then I thought to myself yet again. These people we would be running away from are just too powerful...and resourceful. They would definitely find us unless we went underground and hid in one of the bunkers. If things got too bad like of catastrophic proportions then living in a bunker would be the only choice as these bunkers were fortified with steel, cement and lead casing. The perfect set up after a nuclear or biological incident. So I answered with my concerns but in a very light whisper while I turned up the TV in case we were being listened to.

"No, I don't think that's the solution as of yet. We need to ride this out and see what happens." I went on by saying, "I feel confident that the rebels are well equipped to help us should we need it when the time comes." Even though I said this with confidence, a part of me wasn't convinced that that would be the case, but I wanted to make Laura feel somewhat secure in that thought. We left it at that.

I finished dinner helped her with the dishes and got my bag ready as the TV was on and could be heard in the background. The ride to the gym was maybe seven or eight minutes long. I gave the dog a pet, put my jacket on, and kissed my wife goodbye. I pulled up the strap over my shoulder from my bag and off I went. Just then my cell phone rang and I answered with curiosity as to who it was.

"Hello," I answered.

"Hey, whatcha doin? It's Larry," the voice said on the phone.

I replied "Hey Larry, I'm heading to the gym, why don't you meet me down there?"

Larry was one of my neighbors that I had become good friends with. He was a good guy. He would help me with things around the house and we'd borrow tools back and forth. It was good to have a friend like this as you never know what help you might need in the future. We went bowling a few times which led to being on a league together for a while. We were like Fred and Barney, Ralph and Ed Norton for a while, until it fizzled out. It wasn't one of those serious competitive leagues, but more so a social event every Monday night where you could drink beer with the boys.

"I can't, I gotta help Joan with the painting," he uttered.

Larry was well underway with painting his entire house. A job that had been put off for years until his wife exploded with, "If you don't paint this house I'm leaving you!" So he actually had little choice in the matter.

"Okay," I said. "I really need to pump some iron."

"Some other time then," he said. After a short pause Larry began with why he had called.

"The reason why I'm calling is that I've been noticing some strange cars parked on our block," he warned. "Keep your eyes open for anything suspicious," he said. This was the sign of the times where neighbors were very cautious of anything suspicious. In the 60s and 70s my parents kept their front doors unlocked, and at the age of nine I was allowed to walk to the corner store for milk, bread, and candy. Times had surely changed. I didn't like it. It definitely hadn't changed for the better. You would think that with all this technology things would be great. Wrong.

I stopped off to get something to drink from the corner convenience store as they had all kinds of power drinks. I got out of my car and headed toward the front entrance as there was another patron going inside as well. He cheerfully held the door open as I made my way in at the same time thanking him for holding the door. I can't help it, but this kindness always triggers a thought in my head as to why people can't be this kind or thoughtful to each other in all aspects of their lives. This gesture goes hand-in-hand with the complimentary wave you get cutting into traffic when you leave a parking lot. If only people could be this kind to each other one-hundred percent of the time. We would have peace in the world with no selfishness. It's just a dream or mission statement. Same goes for the hypocrisies I witness when you go to a holy place of worship. One hour of love and kindness, holding hands and singing songs and five minutes upon leaving, an argument ensues due to road rage over someone's driving mistake or waiting too long at a light. I just don't get it. This brings us to yet another quandary. I firmly believe that religion is a necessity since it preaches great love. I also firmly believe differences in religious beliefs have been the cause for many wars as I stated earlier—in the name of God. Now, God is all about love and helping the fellow man. I doubt he would approve of all this hatred and bloodshed, in his name no less. It's so sad and pathetic.

Walking inside my gym gives me a euphoric feeling of escape. All the weight machines, racquetball courts, all the people with their iPods etc., make me feel good and replenished my body's power. I thought to myself, *How is it possible that I can come here, with all that I am going through?* The answer was simple—escape. After all my learning about computers, I knew that there was a logical solution for every problem. I had random thoughts about everything. I even thought about taking Laura out to a night on the town in Lower Manhattan as we loved to go to shows and bars there. Other thoughts spurred as to what was going on in those bunkers all across Manhattan. After about two hours at the club I proceeded home for the nightly ritual of getting ready for the next day of work. I knew it was important to get some sleep as I needed all the strength I could muster to help solve this global crisis.

The next day came rather quickly as I headed downtown and to work. Most mornings are similar except this time when I got to my cubical my boss Richard was standing there. Without having a chance to put down my things, Richard asked how the project was going. Remembering what Michael had told me I responded cautiously, but sure of myself.

"Fine," I responded, "I have to get past a few obstacles but I am on a direct path of breaking this code."

"Do you need any help with this?" he asked. "Because I can put Jonathon on this with you"

Jonathon was another programmer he relied on for intense projects, but he knew the mention of another tech stepping in would mess with my intelligence. I knew the game all too well.

"No, no, no. I got this," I reaffirmed.

"Okay, because the people that need this information are riding me pretty hard," he said with obvious concern. "They need this information yesterday."

Whenever someone put me up against a wall, regardless of whom it was, I was always taught to take control of the conversation.

"Rich," I started, "you know my capabilities, you know my dedication, and my you know the level of my expertise. These things take time, I'll get it done right and efficiently," I reasoned. "Tell these guys they're just going to have to wait and reassure them that you have the best there is working on this."

"Okay," he responded. "I hate to do this but I have no choice. I can only give you two more days to complete this project and then I am going to give you a team of workers to get this done by Wednesday even if we have to work through the weekend to get it done."

I said, "I won't let you down boss!"

Just then he gave me a stern look as he was interrupted by another worker and walked away.

After this conversation I knew I had to somehow get in touch with a member of Veracity so that Michael was aware of the situation. How can I do it? I tried to use logic as to how I could contact them and the only thing that came to mind was to go to the place where I last saw John. I waited until I was done with work and everyone had left. I called Laura to tell her I would be late. What I had planned to do was to go to that diner location and somehow get inside to see if I could possibly find where that tunnel lead to.

❧ Chapter Eleven ❧

The Diner

I rapidly finished the project of uncovering the protection needed against the 12SK35 virus and had no intentions of telling Richard about this progress or lack thereof. By now I had surmised quite a few facts. I believe that the client Richard spoke of is a governmental agency tied in with big business. Billions of dollars could control anything, even our government. And with the two tied in together, government and business, the little people didn't stand a chance. By now, one percent of the population had forty percent of the world's wealth, forty percent. In the '70s it was more like eight percent.

What was happening was the billionaires wanted more and more while they expected the poor and middle class to pay for their greed. The problem was that the working middle class was being destroyed, and obliterated. It all became so clear. I became vindictive, powerful. I went from being a fearful, scared citizen to making it my own personal mission to conquer these selfish greedy individuals and gluttonous corporations. Nothing would stand in my way. I felt like a superhero. I wish Superman were here and of course I immediately reverted back to my youth as I usually do when the mind wanders, sitting again in front of my Zenith black-and-white TV watching the opening to the Superman show, "…able to leap tall buildings with a single bound, etc." I sure wish there really was a superhero today. We could use Batman and Robin, Spiderman or my personal favorite growing up, Wonder Dog. But, that was all make believe. I knew John Hughes and I were the closest things to superheroes. I was ready.

I had arrived at the Diner location, but no one was around. It was dark by now. I fumbled in my car's compartments for a flashlight and found a solar flashlight I had bought a while ago. I got out and made my way toward the boarded up blown out building. There was no way to get inside as I circled looking for an opening. I couldn't find one. I sat there for about ten minutes wondering how I could possibly get inside. I thought maybe if I pried a loose plank it would be enough to squeeze in. I didn't think I had any tools but I went back to the car to search. I looked around and then opened my trunk. There on the side was a tire iron used to pry open hubcaps prior to fixing a flat. I took it out where it was secured with a wing nut. As I walked back to the building I watched to see if anyone was around because I didn't want anyone thinking I was a burglar or something. That's all I needed right now was to call Laura from the police station letting her know I was arrested for B and E. "That's breaking and entering to you." I love that line, stole it from Morgan Freeman in the movie The Shawshank Redemption. Part of what amused me in everyday life was to quote movies. When someone knew what I was talking about, it just tickled my funny bone. In that case I would just utter another movie line to see how good they were at movie lines. It's the little pleasures of life I guess.

I went around to the kitchen side of the diner where I had seen that secret passage down the set of stairs and noticed a loose board. After prying it open, there was still not enough space to pass through. With the first board open it was now easier to pry a few more boards. At about the third board there was enough space to pass through which got me right to the spot where the hidden staircase was. Once inside I took a moment to look around and I remembered what I had thought originally when that assault happened. The place looked like a war zone waiting for some buyer to come along and revamp the establishment. Without dumping some serious money into it now in its present condition, there was no way it could open for business. The health department codes wouldn't allow it, and those things take time. The Sanitarians as they like to be called take their sweet ass time approving a permit. You know the type of Government workers? Anytime I see them I think they are an inspector for the state, a health inspector. So, please let's just call it what it is instead of trying to hide it. I thought if we could just live the world the way religion wants us to live instead of being hypocritical about it, life would be so grand.

After a few moments I lifted the wooden flap up and shined the flashlight down the stairs. It was just so eerie like something out of the movie, "The Blair Witch Project." With all my strength and courage I proceeded down the stairs and poked my head around, but all I saw was the same thing I saw the last time I briefly went down there, some restaurant storage items and a long dark pitch black passage way leading to who knows where.

I started walking down the dark path shining my flashlight all around. It was kind of musty from the wet streets above whenever it rained. I walked about 20 feet and I said to myself that I must be crazy doing this. No one knows I'm down here. I mean there was absolutely nothing around, but about 50 feet forward I noticed a small light shining through. I made my way to that light and looked up, but it was only a streetlight that came piercing through. This was my first thought of turning around and heading back to my car, but something told me to keep going. I was very cautious. I continued with hesitance as I walked further. 'This is nuts, this is nuts, this is nuts' I kept saying to myself. I decided to walk a little further, no more than a hundred feet before I was to turn around and go back.

I continued walking slowly. I got to about seventy-five more feet and stopped for a second to look around—nothing. My heart started beating faster because I now realized I was quite a distance from my car and again no one knew I was down there. I also knew that the farther I went, the longer it would take to get back. I decided to only go another twenty-five feet more before I turned back. So I started once again, my heart pounding with what I was doing. Slowly I walked while pointing the flashlight all around for something. I didn't even know what I was looking for, an opening, a secret compartment? As I slowly walked I started feeling the walls for anything suspicious. I was about to turn around when two silhouettes jumped out at me, my flashlight dropped and spun. With their arms around me, I felt a gag deep in my throat and felt a burlap sack around my head. I was rendered defenseless as I heard a voice yell "Shut up or I'll blow your damn head off!" I didn't utter a sound as they dragged me somewhere. The wall separated and then what seemed like an elevator proceeded to plummet downward. I could only see what I could, considering the circumstances. It felt endless until the doors opened and they dragged me out. I knew I was about to be killed or abducted or something, I really had no idea. I was soo scared. With my heart pumping vigorously now, I thought I was about to die.

My heart beat faster and faster. It sounded like a stick hitting a rotating fan. At least that's what I thought. I was taken to some room as they propped me up on a chair and was told not to move. The sack was left on my head and I heard them leave. No more than thirty seconds went by when I heard two voices coming closer. I could feel the sweat pouring down my back. One of them quickly pulled the sack from my head in one swift motion. As my eyes adjusted to the bright light I was asked a question at point blank. "Who are you?" one of them asked. I didn't say a word as I was disoriented from the entire harrowing experience. He repeated the question, but in a louder firmer voice.

"Who are you?" He asked a second time. I was startled from his tone.

I answered in a soft scared voice, "Dave Napoli."

He immediately asked another question, but now I noticed over to the right that there was a third person who was dressed in the same kind of attire as the man asking the questions. He was holding a semi-automatic weapon. I knew this because I have had experience in my youth with guns. I was in a rifle club and learned about different kinds of weapons. The attire looked familiar, but I couldn't place where I had seen it before. I thought it may have been on a TV show or something.

"What were you doing down here?" He asked.

I didn't know who I was dealing with and why they were down here. Were they working for the government? I didn't know. I answered, thinking as quickly as I could without divulging too much information.

"I lost a friend and was trying to find him" I said.

"Who is this friend?" He asked.

"I last saw him when he was gunned down in the diner up above. It happened about a week ago." I responded.

Then they left leaving the security-type guy watching me with a blank look on his face, gun still in hand. Fifteen minutes went by which felt like an hour, when I heard some footsteps coming my way. The sounds kept getting closer and closer until they entered the room. I was still bound and needed some water. The two men re-entered with a third man. It was John Hughes.

"Dave, what are you doing here?" He blurted out.

"Thank God John; I was down here looking for you. I needed to find you!" I said frantically.

As I continued talking John unbound the rope holding my hands behind my back. "I can't believe what is happening John. I broke the code to the anti-virus program for that virus you guys use, but I haven't divulged any of the information to my boss. He's expecting it in two days. I know what they are trying to do John. My mind hasn't stopped since I met with you and spoke with Michael and so on. We need to work fast. We are on such a downward spiral that this country is about ready to collapse. The government and the huge conglomerates will own not 40 percent of the wealth but ALL of the wealth rendering the public defenseless against their controls. They have the armies and fear tactics to do it. They've been depleting the country's money and raising the deficit in the process. We are close to seventeen trillion. The American monetary system is about to collapse"

All John could utter is "I know."

"You need to come with me," he said.

I immediately rose up out of my chair but stumbled a little because my legs were a bit weak from the struggle. I followed him from room to room trying to observe everything around me. I wondered if this was one of the bunkers they had talked about. But we weren't in Manhattan. That I knew for a fact because we didn't go very far.

I followed John and the men around a corner then another and into this big room overflowing with all kinds of technical equipment, lots of computers and some machines I couldn't ever distinguish. I guess I should be thinking about how worried Laura must be. I didn't even know what time it was. I took a quick moment to look at a computer screen for the time. It was 7:23. Yep, Laura must be concerned by now, but before I could tell them that I needed to use my phone to call home, John introduced me to an elderly man.

He had a weathered looking face similar to my Grandfather's. I got the impression that he's seen quite a bit in his life. I was curious as to why I was being introduced to him. He had a motivating look about him like he's been in a war or has seen it all. I know I keep saying this, but my interests peaked just by being in his attendance. He had a powerful aura surrounding him.

John started to introduce me to him, "Dave, this is Marcus Philippe. He's the originator of The Geneva Project."

"How do you do?" I said. "The Geneva Project? Hmmm, oh yea, that's what Michael talked to me about. I'm very curious to find out more, Mr. Philippe."

"Please call me Marcus," he immediately responded. He went on, "Yes Dave, I heard a lot about you, I understand you are very good with computer programming."

"Yes, well it always intrigued me so I wanted to learn as much as possible about it. I devoted most of my young life in learning about them," I said.

"Well that's good because we could use your help. The national debt clock is ticking every day and every hour. Once it reaches around seventeen trillion it will be the end of our world as we know it and the Bilderbergers could possibly complete their sixty year plan of total domination!"

I called them this as the term applied to those associated with the wealthy powerful group.

"Do you know who they are?" he asked.

"Well, I was told about them through the brief encounter with John when we met at the diner before they opened fire on us," I responded.

He said, "Well Dave, we don't have much time. I understand you are working on an antivirus program that would block the 12SK35 Trojan Virus efforts in getting secret documents from the master data base in Washington. You do know their next 9/11 type tactic is to create another catastrophic diversion, at which time they could have the power to implant r.f.i.d.'s in all people around the world. At that point they will have total dominance over the human race. We must stop them before they get away with their plan or we are all doomed."

"I understand sir! I will help in any way I can," I responded. "Marcus, I don't mean to be rude but I really need to call my wife. She must be so worried right about now."

"Absolutely, I understand—go right ahead. Make the call, take your time, and we will get right down to it. I just need a little more of your time and you can be on your way. You'll need to use one of our phones since your cell phone is useless with these thick cement walls."

I responded by thanking him while I was led to a phone I could use. John stayed with me all the while until I needed some privacy. He trusted me.

"Dude, make your call and come over to me when you're done," John said.

"Okay," I responded.

⚜ Chapter Twelve ⚜

The Master Plan

I proceeded to call Laura because I knew she had been worrying. I really hated delaying the call, but circumstances were such that it was unavoidable. It was about 8:00 by now, so I commenced dialing my home number.

"Daaave?" a concerned voice answered as she guessed at whether it was me or not. It was obvious that she was worried from the way she answered the call, skipping the usual greeting and instead calling out my name first.

"Yes honey, I'm so sorry, but I was detained with some friends and lost track of time," I said being compassionate as to pacify her worries.

"Are you coming home soon? Dinner was ready an hour ago!" she said.

"Yes, I should be home by nine-thirty at the latest. I'll explain when I get home," I told her a quick 'I love you' and she did the same and hung up the phone.

I returned back to the area where Marcus was standing along with about ten other agents. I call them agents for a lack of a better word since I didn't know what to call them. Agents seemed to apply. As I got closer, Marcus began speaking with me in regards to the project.

"Dave, I will be brief. It is very important that you not give your boss the antivirus program. This will harm our efforts in gaining thousands of important documents. We plan the release of these documents to show the world through our media group organizational website called Leakydocs. The founder of that site works with you in your office and we are about to start the first revolution against big business which is in cahoots with our government and corporate-controlled media. The bunker you are standing in is the eastern headquarters for the eight bunkers across the city, for a total of nine bunkers in this area. We strategically placed it here should our whereabouts of the city bunkers be revealed. We have mirrors set up in case the Leakydocs website is sabotaged upon the release of the secret government documents. Do you know what a mirror is?" he asked

"Yes sir, I am very aware of what they are, imaging websites from other servers so that the site remains live from other areas," I responded

"Correct, it's important at this time that you know who is working with you at Computech on this project. His name is Tom Pratt," he said.

"Tom?" I said to my surprise. *Well that makes perfect sense,* I said to myself.

"You see Dave we have an obligation to help the human race from these vicious criminals and our goal is to first save the world so that we bring it to a better level than where it presently is. Secondly, to bring to justice all these corrupt criminals. Their charges are atrocities against humanity. The guys in Texas, although they proclaim to be followers of the Catholic Church, have blood on their hands and they've had blood on their hands since their involvement in the Kennedy assassination. They must be put to justice," he said with a concerned tone.

"I understand very well and I am glad we have people like you taking care of this situation" I said proudly.

"At twelve noon tomorrow we are planning the release of these documents. These documents will show all of the war's injustices, murders, and atrocities against humanity. We have videos, as well as additional documents which will be released. Tom will most likely be taken into custody, but no one knows you are involved. We need you to do something prior to the release of this information as this information will start the ball rolling toward a new world which we have never seen before. Only then can The Geneva Project succeed. My plan will be put into operation within the next year or so, but first we must expose and incarcerate our enemies or it will not succeed. The Geneva project is a new way of living. We have plans to accommodate human life on water, since land is becoming so scarce and humans are multiplying exponentially. We deal with real science not interpreted information, such as with religion. We deal with exact facts in forming our new colony. As you may have heard in the past, religion and scarcity has been the foundation for which wars thrive. You would think that the United States is helping people in countries when in fact they have been exploiting countries for profit for many decades and we have a growing number of enemies set to destroy us because of this. This all because of the immense greed on Wall Street and from politicians tied in with big business tycoons. I fear for our future but am optimistic due to the organization that we have formed to combat these evil forces. As Tom has said in the past, the releasing of these documents will show exactly what is going on through objective media not biased media bought with big business monies. We will elevate the world to a better place through this information. This is our first goal to make people aware of what is going on and secondly to change it from this monetary system to a system of free resources for all," he said proudly.

As he talked, he led me over to an incredible area. This area had hologram models in 3D of these huge water structures. I was in awe over the magnitude of the project. I got chills just viewing them and I imagined how it would feel seeing the actual structures.

"Our water cities will be able to accommodate millions of people and if we have a catastrophic event happen, like they predict we will, we will be ready to save many people. Save them from imminent peril if that is the case. The president and many dominant wealthy people have already built huge underground communities that could sustain life for a five to eight year period in case of nuclear or bio-chemical assault. The fact is, there are many unknowns for the future, but one thing is certain, these criminals plan on ruling the world much as the Nazi's did in the 1940s. The Bilderbergs are concerned with overpopulation and I wouldn't be surprised if some form of mass killings were to occur without revealing the source of biological warfare. In other words, pinning the blame on overseas terrorists when in fact it was our own people planning and carrying out the attack like they've done before," he warned.

"There is a two phase situation that is affecting overpopulation. Due to stem cell research people will be living longer on the one side. On the other end humans are having more babies. So it's a double whammy affecting the over-population problem that the Bilderberg's want to solve so their existence is not affected," he said.

This again was too much for me to grasp. I needed some sleep and wanted to go home.

"Sir, this sounds incredibly interesting and alarming but I must return to my wife as I told her I would be home by nine-thirty. She is very worried," I said.

Upon that note and in closing he said, "Tomorrow when you go into work act as if nothing has changed and give them the antivirus program, a 'mock program' so they think they have a solution regarding the theft of these documents."

"I will do exactly that Marcus," I assured.

He continued by saying, "And go about your day the same as you would any other day."

"I will," I responded. I had no idea how to leave the premises so I asked, "How do I exit here?"

"John will show you how," he responded.

"It was an honor to have met you sir," I said.

Marcus gave me a firm stare and nodded with a slight smile, acknowledging the compliment as he walked away toward a row of computer stations.

"Come on Dave, I'll walk you out," John said. And with that we both left saying very few words as we were both rather pensive about the current state of affairs.

"I was worried about you," I said.

John responded by saying, "Yes I thought you might be worried but I couldn't risk reaching out to you to let you know that I was fine after what we had gone through."

"It's understandable," I said. Up the elevator we went and I was in the tunnel in no time. He walked with me until I got to the staircase leading to the bombed-out diner. I proceeded up the stairs. I was tired and couldn't wait to get home to see Laura and my little friend Jigsey. I held with me the anticipation of the following day. There was no way that I could have gone to the gym tonight.

I squeezed past the boards I had pried open with my tire iron and I proceeded to go to my car that was parked a short distance away. The ride took no time to get home since it was way past rush hour and for the fact that my mind was racing with all that had occurred. It was about 9:22 when I opened the door to my house. Although the house smelled great from what Laura cooked for dinner, my mind was set on going to bed. Instead of a call from the kitchen to me as usual, Laura came and hugged me at the front door as Jigsey jumped like a wild man around me. I kissed Laura hello and apologized for coming home so late. I explained what had happened and even though she was nervous with all of the week's occurrences, a feeling of security came upon us for the first time in a while learning of the plan. We felt we finally had some great forces on our side to combat the evildoers. Without going to the kitchen for a bite to eat, I immediately retired to the family room so I could relax for a change.

As I sat on the couch, Jigsey quickly jumped onto my lap and gave me a thousand kisses to my face while firmly holding it with his little paws. I thought to myself, *No matter how bad things are around us, to a loving animal unconditional love comes first, which happens to be the best affection there is.* He always made me feel so loved.

Laura brought me some dinner and I began devouring the food as I didn't realize how hungry I really was. Abduction and espionage will do that to you I guess. But as soon as I finished eating I laid my head down on the couch and I was out like a light. Tonight I was a sound sleeper. It felt like two minutes later Laura woke me to go upstairs to bed. To my surprise, I had been sleeping for four hours. I set the burglar alarm and went straight to bed. I took my clothes off and put a T-shirt on and got under the covers. Even though I was so excited about what the next day would bring, I still fell asleep with no problem due to the ordeal that I had gone through.

Morning came quickly. I dreaded getting up because I was still so tired from the night before but I forced my way up out of bed and thought about what clothes to wear. I think a shower was in order so I got into the shower and turned the lukewarm water on as the water ran down my head and body. I kept increasing the water's temperature as hot as I could stand and stayed like that for about five minutes before I got the soap and shampoo to clean myself up. I didn't want to get out of the shower but I knew I had to because today was a very important day. Lately, though, every day was an important day.

❧ Chapter Thirteen ❧

Government under Attack

I said my usual goodbyes and left for work. The traffic was the usual traffic I encounter most days, so getting to work was rather quick. In anticipation of what would happen today, the release of the secret documents, all my adrenaline was pumping, so a cup of coffee was out of the question. I didn't even feel like eating anything either. Upon entering the building I saw Raiden standing there with his usual smile.

I said hello to him as he replied, "Hello, Mr. Dave, how are you today?" He called me Mr. Dave as a kind respectful gesture and I had much respect for him as well.

"I'm okay, Mr. Raiden," I said that as a funny gesture back to him. I was always taught to respect others as you would want them to respect you. We talked briefly about the weather and usual conversation when you don't know what else to say. He said he found my office tag that I had misplaced. I probably misplaced it because I had so much on my mind. I thanked him by saying, "Domo Arigato." That's "Thank you very much," in Japanese. He was appreciative of the gesture of trying to speak his language. In fact, I've found that most foreigners appreciate when someone tries to speak their particular language. We both smiled and upstairs I went.

When I got to my floor and to my working station I noticed Tom was out. I asked Joey where Tom was and said he didn't know. I then turned to Karen and asked her and she responded by saying, "I don't know, but someone said he may have called in sick".

I knew otherwise, Tom was ready to make a press conference today at 11:45 announcing the release of the secret documents. The leaders already knew that this day would come. Tom and his people were ready. They had mirrors in place in case the website went down. He anticipated criminal action on himself as well as others within the Leakydocs staff. But he was ready for all of this as I was told by Marcus that he was doing this for one main reason, to elevate the world to a better place. Disclosing these documents would surely damage the integrity of our country's tainted government which was ironic in and of itself. The government had lost sight of what was fair, what was good. They lost sight of all this because there was no one to govern their actions…they were higher than the law. And when you have no one watching or monitoring your actions you think that you can get away with anything even exploiting countries for billion dollar profits. The day of the overwhelming Wall Street greed was over. Our plan was almost ready to start. It was about 9:45 right about now and I thought it best to meet with Richard so that I could give him my work—or lack thereof.

As I walked to Richards's office I could see that he was busy on the phone. He had a big glass window that he had put in so he could watch what everyone else was doing while he was in his office. Then again we could see what he was doing at all times as well, unless of course, he drew the blinds. I walked in as he motioned for me to sit down as he was talking on the phone. He had a very comfortable couch that I sat on while I waited. I noticed some magazines on the cocktail table and I began reading a little as I didn't know how long he would be. I couldn't help overhearing his conversation as he talked about needing five-thousand computer components to upgrade the computers for the company.

I was getting into the article I was reading when he hung up the phone and asked, "What's up?"

"Sorry to bother you, boss," I said. "Here is the program you needed right away."

"It's done?" he asked

"Yes, I worked on it last night at home. I hope you don't mind that I put in for overtime this week," I suggested.

"Not at all, I'm glad you took it upon yourself to finish this right away," he said without a care.

"Well you stressed the urgency of it when we last spoke so I got right on it for you," I replied.

"Thank you, Dave I appreciate it, a job well done," he said.

As I left his office and turned back to take a quick look at him, I noticed he immediately picked up the phone to call someone else. He didn't notice my look as he stared with his head down as he made the call. I conjectured that he was calling the client, but I knew who he was calling.

I got antsy waiting for the ball to drop, for the document release. I tried to stay busy with tons of other work I had going on, but my mind was on only one thing, the new world. The day seemed to drag on until I looked up and noticed that it was about 11:30.

From behind me I noticed a huge pack of suited men, some with earpieces like the kind you see on television when VIP's are escorted in a movie or on the news. It was a stampede of about ten men, all with stern serious looks on their faces like they were mad at something or someone. I knew they didn't work for the company because I never saw them here before. They headed straight for Richard's office and went inside, blinds were drawn, and the door closed behind them. We all talked amongst ourselves wondering what was going on but I knew. It was starting. They were in there for about fifteen minutes when everyone's cell phones started ringing. The news was hitting the airwaves about the release.

I kept my head down and continued working when Joey Digs came over to me and said, "Hey did you hear?"

I said "No, what?"

"Tom Pratt is on television. You know that company he started last year?" he said

I responded by asking, "Leakydocs?"

"Yes that's the one; well apparently he accumulated thousands of pieces of information on the Iraq war and many other governmental secret operations. He uncovered many illegal acts on video footage as well as documents containing information of illegal procedures and the government is up in arms over the release of this information. It seems that political leaders blatantly defied our country's constitution. He proposes to release this in ten minutes," Joey said.

At that moment, the intercom on my phone went off with Richard's voice on it.

"Dave, can you come into my office please?" the voice asked.

"Sure I'll be right there," I responded.

I dropped what I was doing and left for his office which was about a hundred feet away. My heart raced as I anticipated standing with all those government workers that were in his office. As I got to his office, I tried turning the handle and noticed the door was locked so I knocked and they let me in. When I entered I panned the room until I made eye contact with my boss.

"Dave, we tried using this program but it seemed ineffective against the virus. How long will this take to fix?" he asked.

"It should work, let me take a look at it." I moved to his computer as three or four of us stared at the screen together.

"Okay see right there, I see what the problem is, it should take me about an hour to fix," I told him.

"Get on it," he said.

I left his office with disc in hand as they all stared at me. I got the feeling that they were suspicious of me or recognized me or something. If they were who I thought they were, then they must have known that I was the person John Hughes was talking to at the diner.

I immediately felt nervous and realized that they could incarcerate me at any given moment. There were a few flat screen TVs on now because fellow workers wanted to see Tom on television as the news flashed repeats of his telecast. It was about 12:15 when all the news channels started broadcasting the release of the damaging information. People watching didn't comprehend the magnitude of the release. The government had its first real attack since the sixties. The people were finally battling back once again.

Of course they immediately portrayed Tom as a criminal with almost simultaneous reports of allegations of sex crimes and molestation. The mass public "sheep" didn't think anything of these charges as being linked to political tactics to smear the integrity of a person. The public was so easily manipulated by these powerful forces. They believe most anything as long as the news broadcasts it. I knew better. I knew who owned the media. When others turned to their televisions for the news, I turned on the Internet for the truth.

I went to his site and started reading the documents and wasn't a bit surprised at what I read. It documented all that was going on in the war that was being hidden from the public. In one of Tom's speech's he stated, "The Internet still contains freedom of communication untainted by the greedy ones." He went on to say, "It is our right that information is accessed for all to see. This is our country not yours."

Many of us were tired of voting for presidents who were manipulated by the lobbyists of big business, manipulated by the greedy corruption. We had enough and the middle class was almost extinct by the actions of these selfish, wealthy criminals. It was the start of the new world and I felt good that I was a part of that happening.

As I left to take a break outside, reporters were everywhere, pushing microphones in front of my face asking if I knew Tom. I declined any interviews as I didn't want to say something that would land me in the spotlight. I tried to get through the rest of my day as quickly as possible so I could get home as quickly as I could.

I left, making an excuse that I had an emergency to tend to. When I left, Richard asked my fellow employees where I was. I shut my cell phone off so no one could reach me, especially my boss.

The next day the newspapers flashed Tom's face everywhere. Tom's lawyer was being interviewed on the news in regards to his client. He held the stance that all would come out in court about his rights and the rights of every citizen. The government took the stance that Tom's company put soldiers and citizens lives in danger, but we knew this was all false propaganda. *It's amazing,* I thought, *that it's okay for the government to tell lies, but when citizens do it, they target them as criminals.* It's not right, but then again these guys don't play fair. They have to protect their precious oil and war deals so they can pay for their yachts.

In the morning, as I got into my car to go to work, I turned my cell phone back on and noticed three missed calls. They were all from Richard. I called the office at about 8:45 to let them know I was on my way in. I had to make up a story as to why I left in such a rush yesterday so I wouldn't have any problems.

My story was that I had to take my wife to the hospital because she thought she had broken her ankle. When I got up to the main floor I was asked by some workers if she was okay, and I told them that she just sprained her ankle and was fine. My boss wasn't in yet, but I braced for a confrontation.

Just then, cell phones started going off, people whispering, cries could be heard all through the floor. Radio, Internet, and television broadcasts announced and started showing pictures of Raleigh County, West Virginia. The entire county was obliterated. It looked like a scene from Hiroshima. Buildings lie in ruins, blood and body parts were everywhere. The scene looked like something out of a Sci-Fi movie, but it was real.

What I had feared would happen and what I was told would happen was commencing. The president was to make an announcement in thirty minutes to brief the American public, but I knew what was going on. My heart raced worse than it did when I saw those burning towers on 9/11 with people falling out of windows. After all, this devastation was a much bigger event and I feared many more deaths would be reported.

To put this in perspective, the population of Raleigh County is 79, 187. More than twenty-five times the amount of people killed on 9/11. The initial reaction from most people was feeling bad for those poor people and the survivors. My initial thought was, *How is the government going to spin this event to control the world?* It was frightening to know that what I feared would happen was actually happening. Surprisingly, my feelings were to get Laura and my kids to a safe house, to my newly acquired friend's hideaway. I needed to get them and myself to the bunker so we knew exactly what to do next and where we'd be safe.

I intelligently grabbed everything I could as everyone in the office was leaving to be with their loved ones. I copied everything from my computer as quickly as I could onto external drives and memory sticks. Pandemonium abounded, so I was not concerned about being watched. The diversion and concerns of what we were experiencing was enough to do whatever it was that I needed to do.

I tried thinking as quickly as I could about anything else that I could take which might be useful to the members of Veracity. *They were my family now,* I thought. The quicker we could get to them, the safer we would be.

I rushed home. It was 10:00 a.m., but you wouldn't know it. There was bumper-to-bumper traffic as if there was a road blockage from a severe accident. I called all my kids and, of course, Laura. I told them to take all of their belongings and start packing all items that were the most important to them, and necessities, as we were going into hiding.

Thank God I found where the Veracity headquarters was prior to this happening. I got home after three hours and there in the family room were my family gazing into the HDTV. There, clear as day, was the destruction of Raleigh County. They were repeating the president's address to the nation over and over about what had happened, but I had missed it since I was en route home.

Both of my kids and their spouses were quietly watching the set while Pamela was whimpering quietly. Her delusional "party world" had been shattered by this distressing news. Kids are so innocent and oblivious to danger or destruction and the idea that something like this was happening, was unfathomable. It was easier for Laura and me as we have had experience with bad news before. This was cataclysmic though and we didn't know where it would end.

Upon seeing my face, Laura looked at me and said, "Dave, it's worse than we ever imagined. Aliens destroyed Raleigh!"

I looked at her and said, "Calm down honey, I know. I was already briefed about this, but it's not what it seems. I'll explain later, right now, get your things together we need to leave!" I paused for half a second as I noticed the look on her face. She had a look that could only be described as a "deer in headlights look," so I reacted with a stern "NOW!" I yelled this in a panic, only to break her transient stare and get her focused on what had to be done.

❧ Chapter Fourteen ❦

On the Run

We had been stuck in the normalcy bias. What is this you ask? Well, the best way this can be explained, is that in the late 1930s, when Hitler was spewing out all that hatred against Jews, many Jews just ignored it. Only 100,000 of them heeded the warnings and left. However, many affluent Jews stayed behind because they were deeply connected to their communities. They were comfortable in Germany and approximately 450,000 stayed.

They never thought it would actually get that bad. It's the normalcy bias which is going on in our country today. Our country has borrowed so much money that it is impossible to pay back all that debt. They are still spending over four-billion dollars a day. That is staggering, yet common citizens turn a blind eye to that fact complaining only about what they see on the big business controlled media reports and mesmerized over the hyped up TV shows. The hyped up TV shows that proved to be a diversion as to the present life we endure in America.

As we were all getting ready to leave for our safe house, the presidential address came over the TV once again. We were watching CNN, which kept telecasting the presidential address as he instructed what citizens should be doing. We also kept track of the Internet news.

The president started:

"Good morning ladies and gentlemen. Today, we had an unprecedented event never before encountered in American history. At 9:14 this morning the County of Raleigh, West Virginia, was destroyed by alien forces. Military bases all around the country are ready to protect any future attacks from these hostile forces. Needless to say all of our military bases are on high alert, especially at Camp Dawson. We have military capabilities to protect this land from any further attacks and will try to protect the lives of every citizen in the United States. However, our land is just so big that it is difficult to watch everything. Countries worldwide are on standby and are willing to help in any way that they can. Many world leaders have contacted me, as well as

86

leaders from Iraq, Iran and Afghanistan, to express their condolences while putting our differences aside.

"We ask that all citizens remain in their homes with loved ones until further notice. This is all we have at this time and we will brief you all as soon as humanly possible. Any rioting, looting or vandalism will be dealt with swiftly. Today, we are one with the world and there are no more differences between us. This enemy affects all who live on this Earth. Keep broadcast stations open for any new information and may God bless America and the world."

We were all silent as we made our way to the door. There was no question about whether staying would be an option and I was surprised that my kids didn't make a fuss. We were all in shock and in survival mode. There was no way that I would stay at home waiting for thieves to approach. I knew exactly where we were headed and we were extremely lucky to have a place to go to that would protect our family.

As we fled, many thoughts raced through my mind. Would they take out another city before we were safe? What would the future be like? Are we going to survive? These were just a few of the many questions that came to mind.

We drove as far as we could go, but the traffic was bad, bumper-to-bumper. We traveled one block every five minutes. After about an hour of this, a vandal approached our car and punctured the gas tank to steal our gas. Although we were armed with a high powered rifle we opted to go it on foot than to confront the thieves. They fled quickly when they saw the weapon as my gas tanked leaked out all the gas. The kids and Laura almost all simultaneously asked where we should go. The fact of the matter was that I told them we should be there in an hour and that I had a safe place to go. All that lay ahead of us were unknowns. As a protection mechanism I always reminisce to an earlier time when times were easier and times were safer.

As I walked, my mind went back to the days before the Internet, PlayStation, Nintendo, cell phones and voicemail. Times when we spent our summers playing hop scotch and jump rope with our next door neighbor's kids. Those endless summer days and nights sleeping with the windows wide open. Air conditioning was not an option, it seemed. They were filled with simple pleasures like Saturday morning cartoons and finding that neat prize at the bottom of a cereal or Cracker Jack box. Catching lightning bugs in a jar could keep our attention for hours. The summer drink was Kool-Aid or a swig from a hose. Attaching a baseball card to your bicycle spokes was cool and who could forget banana seats. When you got home from school, nearly everyone's mom was home and sandwiches and chocolate milk was a given. Being sent to the principal's office was nothing compared to what your parents would do to you when you got home. Decisions were not made by entering it in your computer's browser, they were made by, you guessed it—eeney, meaney, miney, moe, and that was gospel. Kissing food up to God that dropped on the floor was commonplace. Today that has been replaced by the three-second rule. The worst thing you could catch from the opposite sex was cooties. Scrapes were kissed by Mom to make it better and water balloons were the ultimate weapon. The only mass hysteria back then was when the ice cream man came down the block. Sharing one of those twin ice pops with a friend was always special.

Those were the days. Our parents left the front door wide open and we played all day long until we got tired. Or until it was dusk and you heard your parents calling you to come in for dinner. A foot of snow was a real miracle and when we heard that there would be an eclipse, we'd get ready for a week before it occurred.

Those days were gone and my kids have never experienced them. I felt so sad about that because they didn't even realize how deprived they were. I felt as though they've been cheated from a really wonderful life. That experience has shaped my character and integrity. It has shaped how I respect and treat others…and myself.

We were close to the Veracity headquarters site. When we got to the diner we saw that it was in shambles.

Laura asked, "Dave, what is this place?"

I answered, "You will all see in about five minutes. This was the place where we were attacked and I saw John disappear after the shooting," I answered.

Although it was dark, as we got closer to the building, I noticed that the opening I had made with my tire iron was much larger so we could now all fit through very easily, even with our luggage. We heard some movement inside, but it was only some kids stealing whatever they could get their hands on, but by now any food was spoiled and pretty much everything inside was taken or damaged by the attack. When the kids saw our weapon they immediately scattered. I carefully led my family inside and to the wooden flap in the kitchen, and told my sons to help lift the flap. I still had my solar flashlight with me and I shined the beam down the stairs once it was opened.

Laura looked at me and said, "I'm not going down there!"

I replied, "Yes you are and you need to trust me! Now is not the time for bickering. We don't have much time. The rioting is going to get a hell of a lot worse than what we have seen so far."

She said, "Okay, but you'd better be right because I am very cold and the kids haven't eaten." Not that anyone was even hungry. It's interesting when you are in survival mode. You would think that food is what you would need more than water, but that is not the case. A human needs water every three days to survive, but can go without food for forty-to-sixty days, depending upon their size. After a few days of not eating, you aren't hungry any longer. The problem with water and being on the move is that water is too heavy to carry which creates yet another survival obstacle.

I briefly thought about whom that person was that was stalking me at the bar, but it was a fleeting thought since I had to get my family to safety. So, we lifted the flap and made our way down the stairs carrying our luggage of belongings. No one mentioned that we all thought about whether we'd ever see our homes again. When you are worried about survival all other thoughts become secondary, but nonetheless, they are thoughts that cross our mind.

As we made our way down the stairs, everyone noticed a long, dark tunnel. I was confident as to what we would find, but they looked at me like I was crazy. Even though I couldn't see their faces, I sensed what they were feeling. Close families have that ability to feel without the use of words. Water could be heard dripping as we were well below the city streets. I remembered that from the last time I was down there. We were on our way to the secret passage but, because it was hidden, I didn't know exactly how far to walk.

After a hundred feet I told everyone to start feeling the wall for an opening. I remembered the wall separating on the left before that sack was placed on my head. Finally, I heard a faint voice, "Daddy, where are we going?" It was Pamela. It was clear that she was scared and concerned about our journey.

I replied, "Honey, just bear with me for a little while because I am trying to find some friends of mine."

"Friends?" she asked. "What friends? Down here?"

"I can't explain it right now" I said, to try and offer some comfort in a really bad situation. This tunnel went for miles. What I wasn't aware of was that this tunnel stretched underwater across to Manhattan.

We kept feeling around the wall, but nothing separated and I started to worry if they even knew we were here. I knew they had video surveillance and knew that they'd be watching, but why hadn't they come up for us?

I shined the flashlight down the long tunnel and noticed some silhouettes in the distance. There were three of them and they were walking toward us. Then, they started running toward us.

My family gasped as I reached for my gun and pointed it at the figures. They kept running toward us as if they didn't care. They had weapons of their own. Just then, the wall separated and six arms reached out and grabbed us all. The girls screamed.

Just as they pulled us inside, shots rang out, and one caught me in the leg as the wall closed behind us. We were now in the elevator. As I was bleeding, I looked up and noticed that it was John and two men.

One of the two men looked like Kiefer Sutherland. They looked like some kind of warriors from a Mad Max movie. Their facial expressions were stern and serious like the government officials in Richard's office but more radical like. They weren't wearing suits. John looked at me and smiled and I looked back and said, "Thanks man, it's a good thing you came when you did."

As I lay there exhausted from the worry and bleeding from the scuffle, I introduced John to my family one by one. John looked at them and said, "Don't worry; we have some accommodations where we are going to keep you safe." And accommodations they had, as I have witnessed.

This particular bunker had enough room for 133 guests and could sustain life for two years at a time without needing more supplies.

I was so tired of all this, but what saved me were memories of better times, my childhood, the look of my grandmother's face when all was going bad in my little world when I was growing up. These comforts are what get me through dismal situations whether it was monetary, physical, or ultimately mental. My optimism comes from those feelings that I know few people have ever experienced in their own lives. This is where my mind goes to whenever things are not right in my life. This is where I get my power to continue on. I'm proud to be a glass "half-full" kind of person; and as it turned out, on this particular day, it came in handy.

Once again I looked at John and said, "Am I glad to see you."

He replied reassuringly, "We'll keep you safe."

We felt the elevator plunge downward. After a few moments the doors opened into this sophisticated area of computer screens and surveillance videos monitoring what was going on above us on the city streets. Everyone was working diligently and didn't bother to turn around and look at the new visitors. My family put their bags down and looked at what was going on in amazement. The monitors covered most parts of Manhattan, Downtown, Uptown, and Midtown as well as neighboring and distant towns.

John immediately showed Laura, the kids and their spouses the rooms in which they would sleep. He also showed them the entertainment room to ease their minds and give them some kind of normalcy in this surreal situation.

As they got all situated I remained in the computer monitoring room as my mind is very analytical, as you can imagine by now. My friend told me that I needed to get medical attention for my leg before I got an infection. He knew that if it wasn't tended to, some major complications could result, like infections and such.

My mind was going a million miles a minute trying to absorb all of the information in front of me. It didn't take a brain surgeon to see that these people were working very hard. They seemed obsessed, which led me to believe that they knew a lot more of what was going on in the world than I. I was led away from that area, as much as I wanted to stay, and was brought to the medical room.

This room was so sophisticated that they could have even performed surgeries here. The doctor they had on staff came in as John stood by me. Doctor Howard knew exactly what to do with the bullet wound. He wasn't a young man and it was evident that he knew his way around the O.R. He was in his late fifties and was once a member of the U.S. Presidential staff. And in his experience, tending to White House officials, he overheard quite a few secret conversations in his time. He was like a fly on the wall so to speak. He looked at the affected area and noticed that the bullet was lodged well into the bone. He anesthetized the area with a few shots and worked at getting the bullet out. I couldn't feel any pain just a tremendous type of pressure.

Just then, John's friend Leslie came into the room to see what all the commotion was about. John introduced me to her and I shook her hand as I tried to keep my mind off of what the doctor was doing. We had kept Jigsey in a cage with a handle on it. He wasn't very heavy but Pamela let him out in her room and just then he came running into the medical room, which brought me back to reality for a second. They grabbed him as I was not able to and Leslie brought the little guy back to where my daughter's room was as he licked her face. We could hear Lesley giggle as Jigsey did that to her. That was my dog and that's the effect he had on people.

After the doctor took care of the wound I had a splint and an ace bandage wrapped around my right leg. It really didn't hurt much, mostly because the anesthesia hadn't worn off yet. They gave me some crutches and the doctor gave me some instructions to follow as he handed me a bottle of medicine.

I headed back to the main room with all the technical equipment in it. I continued my study of all the instruments. After I watched everyone work and made a conscious effort not to get in their way or ask questions, one of the workers screamed out, "Chicago!" Everyone took one eye off their screens to see what she was yelling about. Now, four of the thirty six monitors were tuned to a building in Chicago. They showed what was left of the Sears Tower. The collapsed building looked almost identical to the same way the Twin towers had fallen. It was immediately obvious to those in the room that this again was the work of the Bilderbergs.

In the World Trade Tower incident there were many witnesses that heard simultaneous explosions on the lower floors and basements. The members of Veracity know for a fact that these buildings were taken down in demolition fashion. After watching taped reruns it was obvious that the Sears Tower fell in the exact same fashion that those Towers had fallen. I couldn't believe the Sears Tower was gone now as well. It seemed as though things would be happening a lot faster and what we had feared was now taking form. The Bilderbergs were proceeding with the completion of their sixty-year plan right before our eyes.

I once again thought about those poor people in Raleigh. On some of the monitors, news channels were shown discussing the destruction. There were assessments of the damage and it wasn't pretty. The news reporters continued with reports of mass hysteria in Raleigh and surrounding areas. People were out in the streets by the thousands looting and committing other criminal activity which was commonplace during times like these. I wondered about my house, but I cared more that my family was safe. Mass hysteria hadn't hit this area yet, but could erupt at any moment. We were in the best place we could be in given the outrageous state of affairs.

Same as how we felt after 9/11, we knew the world was different now, even more different than it was after the Towers fell. Although most would think that our enemies were aliens, we knew the enemy was ourselves, allowing the powerful people, the ones running things from the sidelines to succeed. I couldn't help, especially at this moment, to think of the words of the great Martin Luther King who said, "He who passively accepts evil is as much involved in it as he who helps to perpetrate it. He who accepts evil without protesting against it is really cooperating with it."

I couldn't fathom how these people could sleep at night with what they were trying to achieve and do to the human population.

I looked around for Marcus but I didn't see him anywhere. I briefly peered over to the area where the holograms of the water city buildings were and I thought about many of the things he had discussed with me. At this time I was not sure whether things would be the same with our plan or what the government's plans were, but I wasn't taking any chances.

I went to have a meeting with my family. I sat my entire family down and discussed with them all that I knew. It was disheartening, but it had to be done so they wouldn't grow restless with their new surroundings.

Wow, I couldn't believe how the things I talked about with John and Michael were now actually playing out. I knew now that it wasn't bullshit. I knew now that my role in all this was very important and that I could not fail. I wouldn't fail; there was so much at stake. I also knew that our happiness was dependent upon going back to a simpler time. My goal was to return back to those times. To those family values and morals of yesteryear. The only question was, would we survive all this? We needed to beat the Bilderbergers before they beat us. I told my family that I needed to go back to the room where everyone was working to see if I could help in anyway.

When I got back there, I was introduced to Commander Paul Wayne Scott.

"Hello commander," I said while shaking his hand.

"Son, we could use your computer skills to decipher some codes we've intercepted from the Chinese government. We have borrowed so much money from them that at any given moment they could devalue our currency and when that happens the riots we are witnessing will be nothing compared to the mass hysteria that will take place. Additionally, many suicides will occur when people will not be able to feed or take care of their families."

He went on to explain the U.S. monetary system. "The United States monetary system is the only currency accepted around the world and has been the strongest currency for decades until recently. It is the world's reserve currency. The luxuries that we have been accustomed to, will be gone. I don't know if you have been traveling lately, but what used to be a widely and eagerly accepted currency around the world, is no longer. Other currencies, like the Japanese Yen, Chinese Yuan and Euro being much more accepted. China is considering eliminating the Dollar and using their currency or combining with Japan's currency as the secure currency for trade. Once that happens, the inflation we will experience here will be of epic proportions. No question about it, we will be in a depression almost immediately. Those families who have not made provisions for what is about to occur, will perish through hunger and disease."

With that he left me alone to monitor the codes and to keep an eye on anything remotely suspicious.

☀ Chapter Fifteen ☀

Attack!

Back at the oval office, the president was meeting with some of his closest advisors. A heated discussion was underway as to what was transpiring in Raleigh and Chicago.

The vice president was there as well and he frantically posed the semi-question, "Mr. President, you *knew* about this? Close to one hundred thousand innocent people were killed! They're people sir, they're just people! How can you do this?"

The president responded with a stern response. The vice president was standing with two other close advisors to the president. They were members of the Bilderberg group which proves convenient as they are always at the heart of what is going on in the world.

The president answered, "Jim, under the circumstances, I'll give you the benefit of the situation and excuse you for using that tone with me. I did what I had to do. The good of the many outweighs the sacrifices of the few and in this case one hundred thousand is a few, compared to the billions of people it will save. This was the only way to get all our citizens on board. Now our plan can be put into effect and the world will be a better place to live in." He gave a slight look to the men standing next to the vice president. One was a senator in line for the presidency and the other a once corporate CEO now head of the Federal Reserve. These are the men who call the shots.

There are thirty-two levels of power in government and the president is only about the seventeenth level. These powerful men of Bilderberg tell the president what needs to be done and the president has no choice, but to do what they say or suffer the consequences. Those consequences are dire if you know what I mean. The president was being manipulated and would have never had done this dirty deed by himself. It seemed he feared for his life and the lives of his family members. The killing of President Kennedy was a message to all future presidents to follow their orders or else. The President really had no choice but to follow their subtle demands.

I thought about why we didn't have a revolution against big business. Why the masses didn't rise up and demand justice. These attacks were crimes against humanity. Wars that commence and result in profit for those who initiate them are crimes against humanity and they should be punished for all the deaths they cause. Many innocent civilians die at the major expense to the profits gained. In the Vietnam War four million Vietnamese died including many innocent civilians. As compared to the United States the total was roughly fifty seven thousand soldiers killed and two hundred thousand injured.

In two thousand and one, after 9/11, we went to war with a country we had no business being in. Upon commencement we immediately gained oil and construction deals exploiting that country's resources for profit. This happened within one month after the start of that war. In normal realities this would have constituted a conflict of interest, but not here, these men are higher than the law. They are the law and they do whatever they want because there is no one that governs them. For the life of me I don't understand why the people don't insist on making it a crime to use your status for personal prosperity. For instance, why aren't officials that we vote in to protect us, criminally prosecuted if they make decisions that benefit their own personal bottom line? The people should demand this law just as they demand drunken driving laws or any other law that protects human life.

The vice president continued with his line of questioning changing the topic to another devastating subject.

"What is the plan sir, if China turns to another currency for their trade dealings? Our dollar is the world's reserve currency and will no longer be if this occurs. I understand the Europeans, China and Japan have had secret meetings without the United States, regarding this subject. The costs of goods will skyrocket and our country will once again be in a depression worse than in 1929 if they switch to another currency and our dollar is devalued."

The president thought for a moment as he lifted his head up to answer. The fact was you could almost see the weight that he was carrying on his shoulders. It had been mounting for the eighteen short months that he'd been in office. The president was a smart man, graduated at top of his class at Harvard, but the problems at hand proved to be too much. There was no quick answer in solving this complex situation that was handed to him by the previous administration.

He looked up and answered the question. "Jim, we go back a long way. You know that the approach I take with everything is to weigh out the facts and figure on what the consequences of our actions will be before we decide to do what we intend to accomplish. The answer is…I don't have an answer at this time. Our country is facing numerous problems that have been cultivating for the past sixty years. We have a war problem, an economic problem, a global over-population problem, a country which is deeply divided and I don't know what else. Is there anything else we can pile onto this mountain of tribulations that I need to solve?"

The vice president looked down as he answered, "I apologize sir." It was evident to many that we faced problems of epic proportions.

Back at headquarters I was doing what I was asked to do. I watched for the codes, but that was boring, so I went on to see if I saw anything else that might be remotely suspicious.

I started investigating the conglomerate websites for any clues or anything that might be useful. I started to see a pattern of patents owned by these corporations and to my surprise I found the evidence linking them to withholding valuable technological information from the public. All kinds of information, the most damaging were the patents for the argument I've had all along. Big business had blocked the development of free energy technology we already had for free energy resources. They did this so they can profusely profit from the sale of oil and lately the profits were record breaking even though the bulk of the population was struggling. They had billion-dollar quarterly record-breaking profits. It was astounding and shameful.

Billions and billions of dollars were made in the last year from oil gouging. The more I found out about these criminals, the more I wanted to put them behind bars and now I had a mission to accomplish. I didn't know how it would happen, but I made it my personal quest to help the human race in this matter.

How come the world doesn't know what's going on here? I knew what had to happen and the leaked documents through Leakydocs surely was an asset to our mission. For years many private citizens knew what was going on, but were too busy to do anything about it because everyone was so busy working two jobs trying to pay for the debt of items they bought on credit. Many items that they really didn't need. Big business knew this fact all too well.

Outside and on the streets above there was civil unrest. The police were out in droves trying to maintain some sanity. There was no way that the people would believe anything else, but what the news channels were broadcasting. Why would they? They thought it was the War of the Worlds all over again. They were brainwashed and it was working. They took the bait hook, line, and sinker...yet again.

We were running out of time. It was only a matter of time before they got whatever they needed to get from the public. Our country turned into a Roman Empire where the elite were filthy rich and the poor had absolutely nothing. There was no middle class. It had been abolished from the manipulations of the rich. Years ago I remembered my dad predicting this. Again, I heard it while we were having dinner at the kitchen table. Big business was on the warpath and they were destroying anyone or anything that got in its gluttonous path.

Now, think for a moment. Imagine knowing that the technology patents these companies possess could change the world for the better. Cleaner, more efficient free energy would be good for all. Except, of course, if the billions of dollars you already have isn't enough. How much money does one family really need? I can't ever understand how these individuals can live with themselves. At what point does a person lose their soul and make a deal with the devil? I just don't get it.

My job was to get this technology out and make it work for the new world Marcus had spoken about. Where was Marcus? I wondered. Just as I thought that, he appeared on one of the many screens monitoring the other eight bunker sites across Manhattan. He was at one of the eastern bunkers closest to our main headquarter site.

He started to speak to all and when I mean "all" I mean that this was a broadcast that reached across international borders. To my surprise I was to learn that there were a hundred-and-fifty bunkers worldwide on the same mission for a new free world. It was the free world that America intended when we first acquired it from the Indians upon settling here. Now there's a dichotomy. Right from the start we started stealing from humans, the Native Indians, in return for our own personal freedom. It was as ridiculous as the propaganda phrase, "The Patriot Act" which directly went against our constitution. What was so patriot about it when every American's freedom was drastically compromised? Again, I just didn't get it. Marcus began his speech.

The sound engulfed the control room with a stereophonic surround sound effect and everyone was captivated while listening diligently. The sound permeated every crevice of the bunker in every room.

He started to talk:

"Ladies and Gentlemen, today marks the first day of our new world. All our efforts make this day as important as the day we knew it was inevitable. We had advanced warnings that this day would become a reality. We shall emerge from this day victorious for all mankind. The new world promises many with luxuries for all not just a select few. There will finally be peace in the world. No one will lack for anything and will share everything. Those of you who work harder shall benefit from the extra work. I stand before you as an equal in the way the old doctrine; the U.S. Constitution proclaimed us to be. I do not stand here as those misguided, self-serving politicians did. We will have a world of truths, not a world of false propaganda. Yes, we will still have our problems, but together we will solve them. No tyrant shall rule our land with the intent of self-profit, causing pain and suffering to others. In this new world, our mission is to develop the already existing technology into realities for humanity. We must hunt the true criminals of the human race. The huge oil conglomerates, for one, are our top priority. We must bring these crooks to justice and charge them all with crimes against humanity. They are no different than the Nazi's that were feared in the early forties. No different than the barbarians that committed genocide for their own wealth and power. Anyone who interferes with the true meaning of living life in peace will be dealt with swiftly."

I looked around at everyone's faces and I saw looks of enlightenment, looks of imagination in a world full of answers. I looked behind me and all the members of my family were watching. They had heard the voice penetrate throughout the bunker as they rushed into the control room to listen on with the rest of us. I caught Laura's eyes for a brief second as she winked at me. I knew from that wink that I did or was doing the right thing. She was always an encouragement to me.

He continued his long speech:

"Our enemy will go to any lengths to protect their insatiable fortunes. That one percent, which owns forty percent of the world's wealth, has met their demise. Their plan to monopolize the world into one currency and one world economy shall not succeed. We must protect mankind. We are their saviors. It will be a difficult road as today's world leaders have an agenda that they feel, they too will not fail. They have reigned over us for many years, far too long. From promoting slavery, to the gold rush, to the fat eighties, all have played a part in what we are experiencing today. We will not stand for another depression and watch millions of innocent people suffer while the 'fat cats' stand by and watch our ruin. We knew the game would change when these 'staged attacks' became a reality."

These guys were masters of propaganda. Above us was pandemonium. People wanted to be safe and wanted the government to protect them as usual.

We listened as the speech continued,

"Be ready for the next phase as it will occur quickly. I predict within the next four months or sooner the people will be led to believe that R.F.I.D.'s are for their own safety and they will demand to have them implanted for their own good. We will not allow them to complete their mission or it will be the end of the world as we know it."

We wondered, or at least I wondered, if other attacks were on the way. This is how I felt when the Twin Towers and the Pentagon were hit. Was it over…or was there more to come?

It was exhausting thinking about all that we were going through, but for the first time I was content as we were heading in a direction that made sense and not in a direction manipulated by greed. As Marcus spoke I grew invincible listening to his words.

He continued with intense dialogue:

"As I speak here today, fourteen water cities are being constructed and will be finished sometime this year; two for every continent, fourteen total. Our cities are being built near Malibu on the Pacific Coast, and off the coasts of Long Island and Cape Cod. They will accommodate millions upon millions of people each, which shall take the pressure off of the land masses which are extremely over-populated today with close to seven billion people. Eventually we will build more cities to accommodate the rising population and to utilize the vast oceans around the world. Today seventy-one percent of the earth's surface is covered by water and the other twenty-nine percent is inhabited by the population. Therefore, our plan must succeed. Work diligently, work steady in an unwavering fashion. In the words of Sir Winston Churchill, 'We shall not fail or falter; we shall not weaken or tire. Give us the tools and we will finish the job.' Well, we are giving you the tools to succeed and succeed we shall."

Upon the ending of his speech, I could hear a stereophonic applause rise throughout the dwelling. We were motivated on an undertaking for success. The Geneva Project will prevail. At that moment I was approached by my two boys who until this point had said very few words mostly in disbelief of what was transpiring. As I worked, staring at the computer screen, I heard a voice behind me say, "Dad, how can we help?"

I turned around to speak with him and I noticed both Robert and Harry were standing there with eyes wide open, eager to help in any way they could. I thought about the question and it took me all of two seconds to answer them about how they could be most helpful.

But before I could answer, Harry looked at me and asked, "Dad, how are you doing? You have been working so hard!"

Harry was always the concerned practical one and Robert was the meticulous one who paid attention to every detail. Robert was a perfectionist. I loved all three of my children very much, but always carried guilt around with me that I wished I took the right path in helping them as much as I could in their lives. I always felt like I short-changed them all with the bad decisions in my life. That is one reason why I was so pumped up about this new project as I would redeem myself, I thought, in their eyes. What I didn't realize or feel was that I was their hero anyway, regardless of the failures.

"I'm okay Harry. I'll be okay, don't you worry," I responded with reassuring demeanor. I looked at Robert and said, "Boys, I don't have to tell you that we are in a new world, but in the long run it will be for the better. This is what I want you to do. The most logical thing for you to do is what you do best. Your teaching ability will come in handy in the *new world*, you must learn as much as you can about the new way of doing things. Learn all that you can about The Geneva Project. I noticed a few computers in your living quarters. Go in there and research as much as you can as you will be teaching thousands of people at a time as to what will be expected of them for the new world to succeed. We must educate people to be more interested in life instead of just going about their business, barbequing in their back yards or watching football games and hyped up television programs thinking all is well. We need to open the eyes of those brainwashed by television ads and news channels. There is a lot more to life than indebting ourselves for conglomerate profit. You see boys, what you do in your lives from this moment on, will be glorious. It will be monumental, to teach others about truly being equal with the concept of those working harder receiving more benefits! As humans this will be the most important task you will ever undertake and you will be remembered as great teachers. No more bigotry, no more wars, no more hatred, no more racial differences, or sexual differences. In this world we incarcerate the powerful who prosper for oneself at the world's peril, instead of good for all mankind. We are in this together as one. No more lies from greedy leaders who benefit from their positions while putting in minimal work effort. We will strive for utopia and with your help we will achieve our goal."

I continued to give them some pearls of wisdom, but I thought for a second at what I could possibly say at this moment to make them understand how important this was. Whenever I think of something intelligent to say I try and quote someone smart. In my mind that someone smart is usually Albert Einstein. If I had to pick someone smart it might as well be someone who was an incredible genius.

I continued with my lecture, "Albert Einstein once said, 'The definition of insanity is doing something over and over again and expecting different results.' So, boys, the reason I am telling you this particular quote is that we, in America, have tried to abide by the system the government has forced on us since practically day one. The American monetary system was doomed from the start and they knew it. They just kept printing and printing money until it became worthless and now they want to rule the world with one monetary system while one percent of the public owns practically everything. Meanwhile, common citizens are practically broke as they work harder and harder to survive. The Geneva Project will change all of that and these criminals will be prosecuted."

They looked at me in amazement but with a diligence in their eyes to start their task.

"We'll get right on it Dad and we'll make you proud of us," they said.

"I've always been proud of you guys," I answered.

I thought of something to say that would bring this whole surreal situation full circle, but I was engulfed with emotion as I peered in their eyes. "We love you Dad," they said in unison.

"Me too, guys, let's get this done," I said, not to distract myself from the work that had to be accomplished.

⇒ Chapter Sixteen ⇐

The Journey

I had been staring at the screen for about an hour-and-fifteen minutes when my mind started to wander, as it usually does. This time I thought about some more games we used to play with neighbors until it was dark out. Games like ringalerio, Simon says, and red-light, green-light, one two three. Just then, walking over to my station was John and command leaders Paul and Leslie.

John started in by saying, "Dave, we made this protection suit for you when you travel outside the safe zones. Remember now you are one of us and need protection because the enemy knows you are with us now. They will not be able to see where you are going as long as you have this suit on."

The suit they were talking about was the suit I noticed on John when I first met with him at the diner. John designed these suits for the organization. They were our particular soldier gear, if you will. But, then it dawned on me that they possibly had intentions of getting me to do something outside the bunker. My instincts are usually spot-on.

I responded by saying, "Thank you, but does this mean I am going somewhere?"

"Well, funny you should mention it," he said "By the way, have you met John and Leslie?"

"Well, yes," I said as I put my hand out to shake their hands. "I met both Paul and Leslie briefly." I could tell Leslie had a thing for John just from her body signals and the way she looked at him when he talked.

John continued by answering my initial question. "We need you to come with us, because Marcus needs your help with software at 'base one' in Manhattan's east side location where he is now. Paul and I will aid in protecting you while we travel there. It's about a good ten miles and since you are hurt we will be traveling in a motorized vehicle that is similar to a golf cart."

I hadn't realized it, but the underground tunnel was like an interconnecting maze that linked all the bunkers together. Like the midtown tunnel, which links New York City to Long Island, this tunnel also ran underwater from about a decade ago when this organization was founded.

I told them I would help them as I noticed John and Leslie quickly look at each other and simultaneously smile.

"I need about ten minutes so I can tell my family," I informed them.

They said, "Okay," and they walked away excluding John.

I looked at John and I said "Hey so what's up with you and Leslie? Are you guys an item?"

He thought for a second, smiled and said, "Yea I kind of care for her. You know man, a girl like that, you make her smile and you've got a lifetime's worth of happiness."

I responded by saying, "I hear ya brother! I got one of those girls. I'll be right back and then we can leave."

I started walking with my crutches toward where my family was staying. As I entered the room I saw Laura lying down, Pamela playing with Jigs, and the boys intensely looking at their computer screens.

"Guys, I have to take a little trip to meet the founder of the project. He wants me to help with some code or something," I said.

"Oh, be careful honey, I'm really worried about this. I just wish it could all be over so we could enjoy our lives once again," Laura said.

"You know I will! I, on the other hand have a good feeling about all this. It may take some time, but in the end we'll come out of this more than okay," I said.

"Okay how long will you be gone for?" she asked.

"Oh, I will be coming back in a few hours or so, in about five or six hours," I assured her.

I then kissed them all and left the room and went back to my station thinking that it has been some time since we all really laughed. You must know what I mean? Laughed so hard that your belly hurt? I hoped it wouldn't be too long before we could relax and feel good again.

I started putting my suit on as John and Paul came over.

"Are you ready to leave?" asked John

"Yes, let's go. I'm ready."

We headed toward the elevators, got in, and felt a jolt upwards until the doors opened into the tunnel area. We all got out and proceeded slowly at first as we looked around. It was dark and we all turned on our flashlights. I noticed from looking at my flashlight that it was solar powered as was much of the equipment that was being used in the bunker station. *Interesting* I thought, *to put this technology to work.* Standing there was a member of the organization. He just finished getting out of our transport vehicle. I didn't realize it at the time but this transport vehicle was fascinating as well. It only went as fast as a golf cart so it would take some time before we reached our destination.

They led the way as I followed. They kept my mind occupied as they made some light conversation. They didn't discuss anything about the mission, where we were headed, or anything like that as they knew someone could be listening. In the way that the riots continued, we never knew who had made their way into the tunnel as curious, anxious minds may guide them to places unknown in hopes of finding some solace. After all, these were bad times and anything was possible. People look in odd places when they aren't thinking straight. And the guys I was traveling with were way too shrewd to get caught up in anything out of the ordinary. They took no chances and I admired that. It made me feel safe having them travel with me. The tunnel seemed never ending.

As we traveled, I tried keeping my mind occupied. I was the only one without a weapon as John and Paul carried concealed semi-automatic rifles under there suit coats. The suits John had designed were big enough to conceal almost anything. If you could imagine the long black coats worn in the movie, "The Matrix," these were similar to those. In a way I kind of liked that I was in a spy-type, real-life movie. It made me feel important, like I was doing something worthwhile and the funny, weird part about it, was that I really was. Again, I felt sort of like James Bond and wondered if I could get John to give me some of those neat toys that super spy's carry around with them. There I went again, thinking about wacky stuff.

We'd gone about two miles and saw much of the same dark, long, and winding tunnel. It seemed endless. We were about eight miles from our destination and I assumed what we were looking for was an opening on a wall like the one we just came from. Why would it be any different than that other opening? I really didn't think we would see any humans down here especially since we were now underwater. Well, we weren't, but the tunnel sure was. I also wondered where they stored this transport unit we were traveling in.

Paul was a hard man to talk to. He had an intense look about him and speaking with someone like that felt odd. He was intently focused. John said few words because of what he has been through outside the bunkers. I was sure that the diner scene wasn't the only time he had been attacked, with winning the lottery and being stalked by high ranking government officials.

We kept to ourselves watching everything around us as we traveled the distance. We were now about halfway there and the ride started to get monotonous. I thought about my family, good times, futuristic better times and anything that would keep my mind occupied while we got to our destination.

In the distance we noticed a light that shouldn't have been there since the tunnel was fully enclosed and we wondered what it might be from. It was about a half-mile away and the only reason we could see it was the tunnel had straightened out at this point. It was at this time that Paul spoke again.

"I think we're coming out of the water. That light is probably from an opening on top," he said.

As we got closer, we kept our focus on that light as it could be a sign of danger. We also kept an eye around us in case there was any movement. We were almost at the light when we realized Paul was correct. It was sunlight from up above. Now we could hear lots of people milling about above probably looting and vandalizing private property. It was probably from people looking for shelter or provisions, supplies, and such. We all kept our focus on our destination point. I had no idea how they would know where the wall opening would be, but I'm sure they had some sort of vantage point.

I was correct. As we got closer, I noticed them looking for something. It was obvious, but they wouldn't say what they were looking for. They talked softly amongst themselves.

"Is it there?" I heard one say.

"No it's a bit beyond. I don't see the marking yet and we haven't gone the distance yet," the other responded.

We kept going on and I thought now would be a good time to explain what kind of world we were building, because by now there was concern that this new world or utopia would be impossible to pull off. It required imagination. I attempted to think like a pacifist and forget all the environmental learning habits instilled while growing up in this culture or environment of extreme hostility. Believe it or not we had been brainwashed in more ways than one.

One may think that this new world we were building was some kind of communist or socialist regime, but they would be wrong in thinking that. There are no rich, there are no poor, and there are no ruling parties, no kings, queens, or dictators. There is only one enforcing entity that governs and prosecutes those who try and profit profusely from others. Greed is the enemy in this world. There are only equals. Everyone works for one common goal and that is to exist in a world where there is no money, no racism, hatred, bigotry, or prejudice. John Lennon once said, *"You may think I am a dreamer, but I'm not the only one."*

We all strive for peace, true peace. Not some politician's words about peace such as the ploys they concocted about peace in the Middle East, where the word peace is used for some profit war manipulation. I detest politicians and leaders who make a mockery of the human race for their own personal greed. These are the people we would incarcerate. The greedy, selfish, hypocritical ones who destroy our lands while trying to convince people that they are not the evil ones. They are the locusts that destroy everything in their path while profiting from it. These are the ones who proclaim other races as evil doers when it is they themselves who are the evil doers.

This was the plan to save our planet from their tyranny over the human race. I'm convinced that when John Lennon was killed, a sigh of relief came over those leaders who worried about their precious, almighty dollar just as they were content with the assassination of JFK to escalate the Vietnam War for profit. It was big business at its worst. That is why John Lennon was feared by the government. That is why he had over three-hundred pages of information in an FBI file. He was feared because of his millions of followers who truly wanted to live for world peace. Music is a very powerful tool and John Lennon was an incredible song writer. He spoke the truth, cared about the human race, and was the government's enemy. J. Edgar Hoover, director of the FBI, the man who had enough power to intimidate sitting presidents, considered John Lennon a radical who was a danger to the National Security of the United States. Now isn't this interesting that they would label John Lennon as a "tax evader" and try to have him deported, yet millionaires and billionaires constantly push for "tax cuts"? It is laughable and such a disgrace.

It's easy to detest what once was. I once heard from a wise person that when you hate, you're only hurting yourself; the person you may hate, doesn't care.

We continued and could sense that it wouldn't be much longer before we were at our destination. I assumed the bunker was similar to the one we had left. I was curious in speaking with Marcus again about what he could possibly need me to do.

My brain was going a mile-a-minute thinking about the endless opportunities that Marcus had talked about. We would be able to bring forth technology that was not blocked by others. We would advance in leaps and bounds like other planets. I thought about how imprisoned we were by not being able to utilize all of our technology because another powerful being stopped us from that advancement. I thought about all those millions and millions of planets in our solar system. The possibility that there is other life out there is definite and the possibility that there isn't any other life on any of those millions of planets is highly, highly doubtful regardless of what the past media would have you believe. It was ironic that today they wanted to use that true information about aliens to their advantage since it now suited them well to purport the feeling of fear into the masses.

I can't be positive that we are the most primitive of all those extra-terrestrial beings, but I can say, with certainty, that there are other beings out there that are far superior to us. Here's a simple fact that stops our world from excelling, the barrier that stops us from developing as a world is to be able to afford all the gadgets that's accessible to humans. As I mentioned earlier, Bill Gates once said that he is frustrated because by the time the human race affords a new technology in their homes it will take twenty years of time to do so. A simple example was the

HDTV's that we read about in magazines five or ten years ago, that only today are being widely used. Now, what if perhaps we didn't have to worry about paying for it and people worked together to get those things for the good of all? Now, wouldn't that be nice.

Just then, John said, "Here it is!" He had located the mark where the elevator was and with a touch on the surface of the wall it split into two sliding doors. As we all slipped inside those walls a member came out to hide our vehicle but I was not able to see where he was to put it. I was glad finally that we found the destination because my ankle was starting to hurt from the distance and the rumbling of the ground below that we were traveling on.

There, on the wall in front of the elevator, was a small monitor. Paul pushed the button and the screen turned on. We could see a lot of movement in the background, but no one seemed to pay attention to the alert as a head figure appeared on the screen. It was Brian McKinley. He was one of the commanders of this particular bunker. When I looked at his face I could see that he'd been through something profound in his life. It would take me about two years to figure out what had happened, but I eventually came to learn that he had a very hard upbringing. He had been homeless most of his young life and lived from shelter-to-shelter.

When I looked at his face, his eyebrows seemed to come together, causing a sad, concerned look most of the time. I guessed I had taken an interest in knowing him right from the start. I was taught at an early age to care about people and living things.

Upon seeing Brian's face I was drawn to him immediately. He spoke briefly letting us know that someone would be down to fetch us.

"Hang tight," he said.

We didn't answer as the monitor shut off quickly. We heard the elevator starting to move and we waited patiently until it opened. The elevator finally opened from its long ascent and we all got in.

Jane Dunn was one of the workers at this bunker. She did as she was told and did it efficiently, sometimes to a fault. She was someone we wanted on our side when we needed to get something done correctly. As the doors shut, we all did what most people do when they get in an elevator, not say a word and look at the rising or descending floor numbers like it was something we had never seen before. But there were no numbers, as this wasn't your usual elevator. So, we all looked up briefly from habit and then looked down as if we didn't intend to look up at all.

When we got to the bottom level, the doors opened into the control room which looked identical to the main headquarters we had left behind. Brian greeted John and Paul with a handshake and shoulder butt. John introduced me to Brian and as we made eye contact, we shook hands. Marcus walked over to us and said hello.

"Please make yourselves comfortable while I get some water. Would anyone like something to drink?" he asked.

John said, "I would—how about you guys?"

Both Paul and I said okay.

We sat down in a lounge area that was semi comfortable. I looked all around taking in what was in that region of the room. I was very impressed by the advanced technical equipment in the area.

❧ Chapter Seventeen ❦

No Mountain High Enough

As we sat there and waited for Marcus to come and talk with us, we were all busily looking around the room at the fascinating images. It was hard not to notice the fifty digital screens that were above the work stations. One person, I noticed, just sat and watched all of the screens as he was on watch for anything peculiar to occur and making sure they were all fully operational. Regardless, it was impressive. One by one, image by image, control room by control room, it was becoming very evident that this new world being created would be a mesmerizing new era.

Marcus came back with some bottled water and asked me to follow him. The other two wandered off to speak with fellow workers they knew. I knew no one except of course John, Paul, and Marcus.

Marcus began speaking, "How was the ride?"

As we talked he led me into another room.

"Ummm, the ride was fine but I am in *some* discomfort with my leg," I said. I continued by saying, "I've never taken a bullet before!"

"Really, you have never been in combat?" he asked in an interested tone.

"No, never, this is all new to me but I'll be fine as I can take pain rather well. After all I go to the gym quite a bit so I'm in pretty good shape," I told him.

I could tell from his mannerisms that he was only listening with half-an-ear. He was preoccupied with all that he wanted to accomplish and we quickly started to discuss what he needed me to do.

We came into a room that had a rather large replica of one of the water cities, those of which were to be built around the world. As I entered the room my eyes lit up as I said, "Wow! This is incredible. I mean I read your articles and saw some of your videos, but to see this right before my eyes is wonderful!"

113

"Yes I see you are impressed," he began. "What you see here is a miniature model of one of our water cities that will soon house millions of people from around the world. This replica is complete with all of the capabilities that we want our real water cities to have. It is equipped with solar and tidal power and we are currently working on geothermal or if it's even possible to have geothermal on water. What I need you to do is to come up with a security program that automates all the mechanics needed to make this city run as easily as possible on free resources. Cooling, heating, lighting, plumbing, electrical outlets all must be run on computer-generated systems with a back up manual system should we go off line. We have the schematics for this system; we just need someone with your expertise to simplify the process for all the cities to utilize. We want to implement a single, programmed system, for all the units. Do you understand?" he asked.

My mind had a hundred questions, but that's only because the answers to those questions would help me build the correct program.

"Yes," I said, "but I will have quite a few questions to be answered before I can complete this task."

"Fire away," he said.

"Well, no, let me get my brain around this first then, believe me, I will have some questions for you and others."

"Okay," he said, "but time is of the essence."

"I understand, but I need some time to think about this all before I begin. I also understand I had to come here to see what it was I had to work on. Can I work from headquarters on this as I need to be with my family?" I asked.

He answered by saying, "I understand completely—and yes, headquarters would be fine!"

I was so engrossed in what Marcus was showing and telling me that I totally ignored what appeared to be a robot standing in the corner of the room. My mind couldn't help but ask why it was there or what they were doing with it. "Marcus," I said, "not to change the subject but why is that robot next to the water city replica?" I could tell he was a bit, I wouldn't say bothered by the question, but sort of upset about something when I mentioned it.

"Well," he started, "interesting you asked that question. We are also working on another endeavor that our scientists brought to our attention but we really don't have time to discuss this at this time. We are missing an important piece that would make for another scientific breakthrough. A breakthrough that would help mankind tremendously!"

I saw that he was a bit disturbed with the situation, not with me asking but more so that it bothered him that he didn't have the venture totally figured out yet. So I just let it go by saying a quick, "I understand sir."

We walked back to the control room as I gazed around in awe. The people working were all focused on what they were doing. I didn't mind as I was paying attention to words that were being spoken. I tried listening to one conversation at a time. After about ten minutes of this Paul and John returned to where I had been standing and one of the men asked, "Ready to go back?"

I responded with a, "Yes." I asked if we could go above ground to see what was going on up there. They said it would be a bit risky, but that we could always go underground again if things got out of hand. As much as they knew the risk, they also were obsessed with adventure. They were well equipped with weaponry anyway. They didn't fear the same things that most of us civilians did. By now, they were used to the unknown and going with the flow.

I was fascinated with the replica Marcus showed me and was eager to get started on this new project. We said our goodbyes and upward we went, but what I didn't know was we actually went up a little farther than the tunnel level.

We got out of the elevator and wondered where the wall partition was, but to my surprise, there wasn't any partition, just a manhole cover. There was a little ladder on the side of the wall that led up to the cover. Paul went up first and slowly moved the cover as he looked around up above. I had lost track of time by now so I didn't know if it was night or day.

It was about 4:00 in the afternoon and it was a bright sunny day outside. We all made our way up to the street level. I used my upper body strength to pull myself up due to the lack of leg strength caused from the abrasion. When I made it to the top the two men gave me a boost by lifting me up the rest of the way and I appreciated the

115

assistance. There was no one around as the opening was in an alley away from the main stream of traffic. As we made our way to the street, what we saw was like something I had only read about or watched on a late night Sci-Fi movie. It looked apocalyptic.

Cars were turned upside down. Store windows were smashed. People were running around with food items and other kinds of items from tires to gas cans to—you name it. People were looting everything. We watched out for the military and kept a low profile. What we really concerned ourselves with was confrontation from anyone or anything. We weren't sure what was going to happen. It is a very uneasy feeling this feeling of survival and not knowing what to expect, so nothing was surprising. We expected the unexpected.

We walked about a mile while watching everything around us; homes had been abandoned, there was no electricity or running water any longer. Most people headed toward industrial buildings. We stayed along the tunnel route that only we were aware of so it was pretty desolate.

From around a corner we saw some guy running toward us. At first we thought he would attack us, but he was crazily yelling something like, "It's all gone man, it's all gone!!" And he just kept running past us. I didn't know where he was going and I wasn't about to ask. He looked nuts, but how sad was that? This guy had probably been a normal guy before all this had occurred, but got caught up in that normalcy bias syndrome never realizing that things could have gotten this bad.

I was so glad that I had a place to stay and that my family was safe. We had traveled about three miles when we noticed a whole bunch of cans lying around. It looked like the military had been here. Those cans were tear gas cans that had been deployed to disperse the crazed crowds. In every store that we had peered into, all the shelves had been cleaned out. From toy stores to gas stations to grocery stores—everything was gone! It was strange because I had never seen anything like this before.

I started to miss the things we had taken for granted, like the sound of new music on the radio, television shows, and being able to go get a cup of coffee at the corner store or taking a ride in your car to the nearest convenience store for some bread. I knew that it would be a long time before we could enjoy simple pleasures again, like riding a bike around town for instance.

After five miles of walking with crutches I started to tire, but I didn't mind because I missed the daily work out at my gym. I thought if I hadn't been in such good shape that this ten mile trip would be impossible. We were halfway back when we saw three figures walking toward us. As they got closer we noticed one of them had a gun. Paul was wearing a satchel around his waist that contained items he may need, like a flashlight, can opener, and some other items like pepper spray for protection. Pepper spray, though, was the least of his arsenal. With all of the artillery he carried in the large coat he wore, he was a small army all by himself.

The guys were about fifteen feet away from us now and John instantly stepped in front of me for fortification.

"What can we do for you boys?" Paul asked with a stern, sort of like Clint Eastwood-style face. The one in the middle was your typical gangster-looking asshole that tries to intimidate with a look, a word, or just a nasty stare.

"What can you do for us?" he asked as he smirked.

He lifted the rifle in his hands a bit so it was in plain view.

"You can hand me that 'man purse' right now," he said forcefully.

Paul looked at him with a mean look and said, "You really don't want to do this man," trying to give them a way out of the altercation.

"We don't?" he asked. "I don't think you understand—I'm not asking, I'm telling you to hand over that purse and whatever else you guys have or I'm going to blow your f...ing—"

Before he could get the words out Paul spun around with his long legs and gave him a round house kick to his face as the aggressor turned away from the impact spewing out blood and...a few of his teeth.

John swiftly ran and kicked the weapon away as the other two fled. The guy laid there practically knocked out as we walked away leaving him there on the ground bleeding profusely. I kept watching as his lifeless body just lay there in the street. He wasn't getting up after that incredible impact Paul had given him.

I looked at Paul with a proud kind of amazement at what I had just witnessed. "Damn dude, you got skillz!" I said kind of feeding his ego.

For the first time I saw Paul look at me with a half, Terminator-type smile appreciating the comment I had just made.

After we walked another two miles we couldn't see that guy lying there any longer. I was so glad I was walking with these two and felt very secure about anything approaching now, but I spoke too soon because a Jeep started riding toward us. Paul and John knew right away that this was a military vehicle as we ran for cover down one of the side streets.

We were now about three miles away from our destination. I grabbed my crutches in one hand and hobbled over as we hid behind a dumpster. The Jeep stopped at the end of the street. They backed up and started heading our way.

We took off again as we heard a voice yell "Stop or we'll shoot!"

In spite of the warning, we didn't stop and shots were fired as promised. But, we really didn't care because we had on our protective suits. At the other end of the block another Jeep had pulled up with someone in it with what looked to be a grenade launcher. When we saw that though, we all stopped immediately. As they got closer I started getting worried as to what would happen. Would they arrest and interrogate us, or worse, hurt us? Who knew?

A commander-type got out of the Jeep and started walking toward us. He had two guys with him, one on each side. As they got closer the one in the middle called out Paul's name. "Paul?"

I looked at Paul's face, and I noticed for the second time that he cracked a smile. It was a full smile this time. All these men were on our side. They were actually looking for me since I had left the job and my home and hadn't returned. I was someone of interest. As it turned out they had been staking out my work's building for something quite interesting. As the news hit the airwaves about Raleigh and Chicago, people had started leaving in droves. There was no one left in the building where I had worked. What was intriguing to me was that these men needed something which they presumed was in that building. But, I didn't know what it was.

Little did I know what was being kept at my work. Little did I know how much involvement there was with the government. I should have figured it out with the way Richard Harris was acting whenever he met with them or when he would give me a special project to do for them. It turned out that the piece they were looking for would be a control mechanism for the next breakthrough in computer history.

It was a microchip that was in its last staging level for the ability of robots to teach themselves how to think. Anyone with this power could rule the world. If robots got the ability to teach themselves to think, whoever they were associated with could tell them to do anything they wanted them to. Marcus was very well aware of this plan, but perturbed that he didn't have this missing piece in his possession. He was about to find out how even more valuable I was to the project. He had no idea. Now it all made sense why the unusual reaction when I asked him about the inanimate robot standing in that room. Marcus and his scientists were working on super robots, or super beings I should say.

The Bilderbergs were also working on this project for their master plan of ruling the world through a one world economy and one world government. They would be at the helm of that rule. All the power and money that they could possibly want would be at their fingertips. This is why they only invited reporters that could be manipulated into recounting their propaganda story when the time deemed fit. Reporters that showed up uninvited had quickly been arrested by the police.

Now, to me, this was sounding more and more like that Terminator movie I had been thinking about earlier. It was pretty freaky stuff. I never dreamed that I would have the task of recovering a robotic microchip that would save the world, or possibly hurt it. It was a race to the finish between the Bilderberg's and the men of the Geneva Project.

After greeting Paul and John, the man in the middle looked at me as he asked, "Is this the guy?"

John answered, "Yes this is Dave Napoli."

The man that was speaking to me in a third person was Peter Harper. Peter had joined the Veracity Alliance about seven years ago. He was recruited by Marcus to help him with his goal of changing the world for the better. Peter was well known in the underground world as a secret-ops-type fighter that had enlisted in the US Army during the first Iraq war. He was also a member of the CIA and had learned of all the greedy monetary dealings and secret devious operations from his involvement in that group. Those operations weren't altogether for the best interest of our country. Marcus knew he was going to need some extraordinary help from extraordinary people. If there was an important mission to carry out, he needed to be surrounded with the right people to get the job done.

Peter and his men had been on a mission above ground for about a week, away from the secret bunkers as not to divulge the locations to the enemy if they were caught. The mission was to gain as much intel as possible before reporting back to Marcus so communication was forbidden until they had returned safely underground. They were not aware that I had already made contact with Marcus. And Marcus was not aware that I could possibly help them recover the hidden piece to the puzzle. I had no idea where this missing link could be. Peter knew that I worked at Computech assisting the government indirectly with their secret project. He also knew that I was an important integral part for the success of the mission on two fronts, assistance with deciphering computer codes, and for helping to locate the missing piece. That is the missing piece that Marcus and his scientists needed to finish building the Super Beings.

Peter looked at me this time and said, "Son we need your help in retrieving a special piece that could alter our world as we know it. The Geneva Project will certainly fail if we don't recover this item; and we don't even know if it is still at the last known location, which is where you worked."

"Do you have access to that building any longer?" he asked.

I thought for a moment about how I could accomplish this. "Well, ummm, I believe so but I left all my information to get in the building at home which is about twenty minutes from here and then another half hour to the worksite," I said.

Peter immediately said, "Not a problem at all. We will immediately escort you to those two destinations."

I thought to myself how it was interesting that I wasn't hungry in the least bit, but I was thirsty. As I mentioned earlier, a person can go without food for forty-to-sixty days depending on their weight. When it came to needing water, though, one can only go without it for three days before perishing.

I was grateful that I had the conveniences of home two-hundred feet under the surface where I could eat, drink, and wash to my heart's content—unlike the many, poor, unsuspecting soles that were now fighting to survive, above ground.

⇒ Chapter Eighteen ⇐

Back to Civilization?

I now thought about going home because that's where I had left my badge for work. I left it there because I didn't think there would be any need for it. It also had my emergency keys in case the fingerprint sensors weren't working for some reason. We always had some sort of manual back up in this high-tech computerized world, but I also realized that there may be generators powering the building in this case. I wasn't taking any chances of getting there and having to make an extra trip if we found that not to be the case. So, I reiterated to Peter and to the others that it was imperative for us to go to my home first before going to my work.

We proceeded to get in the two Jeeps as we headed toward my house. On the way we noticed the war-like, battered roads that had been pummeled by the thousands of people scurrying to get what they needed to survive. We also noticed dead bodies that had been beaten from the struggle. It wasn't clear whether it were soldiers that had done this or other people fighting to keep what belongings they possessed.

Again, it was surreal to see the war zone like images that we had only watched on television about foreign lands. This was our land though. When I was little I remember thinking that I was grateful that what I saw on television didn't happen on our land, in our own backyard, but that has all changed.

It was evident that we needed to step up to the plate to get our country back on its feet away from those that destroyed it. As we sat in the backseat, Peter and the others talked amongst themselves pointing at things in the distance, usually an animal or bombed-out home, or even an overturned tractor trailer with all its supplies gone.

We passed an abandoned trailer park that looked like a small replica of a ghost town. There were few people around which gave it an extra-eerie feeling. I couldn't help but wonder where they had gone. There were long lines of abandoned cars, doors opened, hoods up—and you could see spilt, dried-up oil and gas mixtures staining the roads. I could envision the struggle that had happened here. Basically siphoning gas wasn't an issue as people went around puncturing gas tanks without a concern of vandalism charges. There were so many of them doing this that the military couldn't contain the problem. Imagine thousands upon thousands of people looting and vandalizing all at once. It was unreal to imagine, and to witness the actual aftermath.

I didn't have to tell them where to go as we plugged in my address to the truck's GPS (Global Positioning Service) unit. Thanks to GPS it was one less burden to have to give or take directions from a person whenever you went places. I believe this was one of the great inventions of the Internet/computer age. I loved it when it worked properly, which was most of the time.

Our Jeep was most efficient since it ran on electrical/water (HHO) /solar power invented by one of our staff members. For the past five years at least our organization was not burdened with the hidden agenda of those blocking the great technology available to all. Veracity used every ounce of that knowledge.

We were approaching my neighborhood. This area looked so different. The grass in the front yards of homes all looked about the same because it wasn't summertime and didn't grow much so in that respect it looked the same; but as I looked around, it was certainly different. The entire neighborhood had been ransacked and I could only imagine what I would find when I got to my own home.

As I neared my residence all kinds of useless items were spread around the outside of it like clothes hangers, broken lamps, pieces of wood and metal, etc. It was a mess. I could hardly recognize that those were items from our house. We pulled up in front of the house and I jumped out as they watched my back walking ever-so-cautiously behind me as I walked toward the front door. Both Peter and Paul were forces to be reckoned with. I felt much protected as I wondered if I would find the items I needed to enter the building where I had worked.

I slowly walked up the steps as I experienced a mental flashback of the many times I got to this point after coming home from work. I pictured Laura cooking in the kitchen and my dog jumping around as I entered, but that wasn't happening. I thought about Pamela showing up after her usual three-day stint of partying with all of her friends. After I came to the realization that these were memories of our previous life, I instantly snapped back to reality and focused on my mission.

I couldn't help inspecting the premises before I went into my bedroom to search for the required objects. As I walked down the hallway to the kitchen area it looked drab. *This isn't my house,* I thought—but it was. As I peered into the kitchen, cabinets were opened and drawers were upside down on the floor. The microwave door was also opened as if someone was desperately looking for anything that could be used for survival.

I had a sick feeling as I looked around. It was like looking into a room and seeing in the mind's eye, our personal items all around were gone. The area was totally disheveled. It may be hard for someone else to envision this happening to them. The reality is that this could happen to anyone when one is dealing with desperate human beings. It has happened in history many times and is happening this very moment, somewhere in the world, as I express this story to you.

The fact of the matter is that we would rather ignore it, than deal with it as a global entity. I knew I was doing the right thing helping my organization do what it had to do to get a better world for all. There was no question about it. I wish I could say that everything would be okay. I wish that we would all join together: Chinese, Black, Jewish, Muslims, Italians, Greeks, Spanish, Whites; all working together toward an unselfish goal of free commerce. If only we could break down those barriers that have been put up by the one percent greedy, ruling class of the world. If we could only put our differences aside so that we could live together, work together, play together and break down those fences.

This brings me to a famous person and writer, Henry David Thoreau who said, "I am amused to see from my window here how busily man has divided and staked off his domain. God must smile at his puny fences running hither and thither everywhere over the land."

I worked my way to the bedroom and where the furniture used to be. They had been moved as looters looked behind the furniture for anything they could find. I straightened out the dresser and night tables and started looking in drawers that were opened, but didn't find anything. I was attempting to leave no stone unturned, so to speak. I looked into every crevice of the room, but nothing turned up. The looters even found some emergency money I had hidden away that I had forgotten about. It was only about a thousand dollars in ten one-hundred-dollar-bill increments. These were also left spewed all over the hallway floor, as money during these times was worthless.

As I went into the master bathroom I noticed that items had been dumped from the medicine cabinet: cue tips, cotton balls, and empty Band Aid boxes were all over the floor. As I looked behind the toilet on the floor, I noticed a key and as I got closer there they were connected to each other as I had left them. The badge was gone, but it didn't matter as I doubt anyone was left at work to check ID's.

I grabbed it at once and said to the guys excitingly "I found them! Here they are!"

We quickly left toward the front door. This time they were walking in front. I stopped for a moment to look at the place where I used to live. I was so sad to leave it, but was interrupted in my thoughts, as the guys yelled out, "Come on!" It was actually what I needed to break me from that disturbing thought process. I looked one last time to see if there was anything I wanted to take with me but there was nothing of interest. We jumped in the truck and off we went to my old place of work.

The new destination was set on the GPS as we heard the robotic sounding voice of the unit tell us which route to take and where to turn. We also took a notice of how long it would take to reach our destination, which wasn't very long. We would be there in about a half-an-hour. The reason they had set their GPS was merely to see how long it would take from where we were to where we were going.

I wondered if the electricity would run out, but this truck was built so efficiently that the solar power, together with the energy generated from the fan belts themselves replenished the electricity. This was much like what an alternator did in a regular gas-powered car. The solar cells were much more advanced than the ones released to the public or allowed by the big business industry. Any kind of water would power this vehicle's water (HH0) engine. Four ounces would allow for one-hundred miles of travel. It was repeatedly evident to me that our new world would contain many of these hidden secrets which would make our new existence that much better.

As we traveled, what I didn't know was that this ride would be a lot more dangerous having to cross a bridge or tunnel to reach the island of Manhattan. They were opting for a bridge to go over since a tunnel may be more risky and would entrap us if the military had a blockade set up. The fact was that there would be a switch way before we got to the bridge for the crossing. All three men, John, Peter and Paul, were high-profile figures sought by the government.

We were heading toward the site of the World's Fair in Flushing, New York which was very close to my house. This was also the site that was used in the famous movie, "Men in Black," as they proclaimed the World's Fair tower to be a spaceship. Well, that was the vision we saw as we got closer and as we pulled into Flushing Meadow Park's parking area near one of the concession stands.

We parked and walked down the stairs and noticed an indoor kiddy park at the base of the stairs directly to our left. And off to the not-so-far distance was the gigantic and famous World Globe. Inside the desolate concession area was a carousel. *How interesting*, I thought, *that such an attraction can fit in such a small area*. There, standing at the entrance to the closed concession were three men I observed, as my entourage escorted me to them.

As we got closer I recognized one of the men as Brian McKinley, commander of the Eastern Bunker we were in. John briefed me as we walked closer to them.

"Dude, this is where we separate, Brian will see you the rest of the way and we'll meet you back here in an hour or so to escort you back," he said. "You'll be okay, don't worry. Brian's good people,"

With that I nodded my head not uttering a word as we made the switch. John and the others turned around and headed back to their vehicles.

I said a hurried hello to Brian and we were off. Like Paul, Brian was also a man of few words. I didn't know this fact, but the reason Brian was less of governmental concern was because the government still saw Brian as one of their own. He was a double agent. He reported to his superiors inside a little organization known as the CIA, the organization that with the help of the FBI facilitated the killing of our beloved president, John F. Kennedy.

Brian had joined Veracity for many of the same reasons I had outlined numerous times before. Men like him were an enormous asset to the organization merely because he could get in and around government controlled areas quickly and efficiently. We didn't know how long this would last, as his cover could be blown at any second, but I didn't want to be around him when it did. Hopefully, I thought, it would never happen until we made the transition into our new world.

Brian, along with the others and I, started walking in the opposite direction from where we'd parked. We strolled through the park as if we were invited to a company picnic or attending a family BBQ. I had never been so close to the famous World Globe situated in the center of the park. I gazed at this gargantuan structure while flashing back to the back seat of my father's Chevy Impala around 1964. I could remember my parents talking about how this would be the only time the worlds' fair would be hosted at this location.

We passed this object to our left as I noticed a huge grass area that went for thousands of yards. We also noticed other buildings around that were also probably used as concessions or lavatory areas. I was guessing that we were heading toward another parking area and I was right.

After crossing an overpass, we came upon a parking lot where there sat a similar Jeep to the one that I was just in, but this one looked more military. It was camouflaged, but used the same solar/water (HHO) electric principals as the other.

I was a bit tired from the walk and couldn't wait to sit down in it to relax awhile. This vehicle too was equipped with a GPS as I told Brian the address of the work location. He punched it in and off we went.

As we left the park we headed toward the Long Island Expressway westbound, toward the midtown tunnel. For small talk, I asked Brian which route we were taking.

"Brian, is the GPS making us take the midtown tunnel?" I asked.

He looked at me briefly and looked back to the road as he was the one driving and said, "No, I think given the coordinates, the Fifty-Ninth Street Bridge makes much more sense."

Usually what went through my head getting to the city is avoiding tolls associated with crossing and using the 59th street Bridge doesn't cost anything, but in this case it didn't matter. There were no workers at the toll booths; it just made more sense since my building was on 57th Street.

As we got closer to the city I could see the skyline very clearly. The usual billboards were left as they were from old advertisements of movies and products. The mechanical billboards were obviously not functioning. There wasn't a cloud in the sky much the same as it was on 9/11 viewing that creepy site on that ill-fated day. I couldn't help but notice the hole that was left on the left side of Manhattan as we approached the city. I doubt there is anyone that doesn't think of that as they approach Manhattan's skyline in today's world.

We veered off the exit just before the tunnel and headed toward the bridge. There was no stadium traffic, rush hour traffic, or traffic in general that we would have normally experienced in this congested area, as everyone had already evacuated. It was odd not to see any traffic, the place that was always saturated with people in cars rushing to get somewhere for money, either making it or spending it. The only thing that could be seen were broken down and vandalized vehicles left on the side of the road that had run out of gas or that had been deserted from the mad rush out of the vicinity. From time to time we'd see military soldiers equipped with rifles standing there as they watched us go by. I guessed that more than likely there would be a checkpoint on the other side of the bridge as we entered Manhattan.

We were now at the entry way to the bridge and as we crossed I again found it odd not seeing very many vehicles around, in front, or beside us. The two men next to, and seated in front of me, were motionless as they stared straight ahead without uttering a sound the entire time. It was weird.

As we crossed midway and headed down toward the city, we noticed the checkpoint. My stomach knotted up as I worried about what may occur here. The road was blocked with military soldiers well-armed in case of confrontation.

Brian looked at me and ordered, "Don't say a word."

I nodded in agreement to his wishes. I wasn't going to argue. Brian slowed down the vehicle and even before stopping had his badge ready to show the officers.

Two MP Officers approached the vehicle and asked, "Where are you boys heading?"

Brian responded something like, "On official business!" as he flashed his badge. They looked at us, looked back at Brian, and waved us in without a fuss. I exhaled a sigh of relief.

❖ Chapter Nineteen ❖

The Future

We were now minutes from where I used to work. I noticed that stores had been closed, windows smashed, street lights were out, and the usual hustle and bustle of this legendary place was non-existent. It was one more odd reality to the ever-changing place we called earth. New York City was desolate. I'm sure they were also experiencing this around the country and around the world.

We pulled up right in front of my building which was strange in itself. We actually found a spot directly in front of the doors to a major skyscraper without some doorman chasing us away. We parked and got out.

As we entered through the manually operated revolving front doors, we realized that our suspicions were correct, there was no electricity. Thankfully, we had a solar powered flashlight in the truck. The Jeep was equipped with many survival gear type equipment for just this reason.

As we entered, it was dark and I dreaded the climb up forty-one flights to my floor hobbling with crutches in hand. I knew where the emergency stairs were because I always made sure I knew where stairs were in case of fire or evacuation. Again, this was a safety mechanism I used just in case of an emergency. Did you ever check out someone's license plate and memorize it just in case they did something illegal? Well, that was my screwed-up mindset after 9/11. We were programmed to be observant of our environment. (Part of the fear strategy on the government's part.) That's what they wanted us so-called "sheep" to do.

We listened and we watched, ever-so-carefully to the color-coded propaganda threat alert. Could these officials be so obviously blatant as to guide the masses in any way they chose? It was sad. They saw how easily we were fooled after we were fed the Oswald story. How easily we could be fooled even as recent as a few years ago, when they had a major network news channel replay the same story they spewed in 1963 on a station that the government owned. It just proved one thing—the same family of killers was still present.

The media was an incredible tool for these guys. If you want the public to believe the lie, "Use the media," was a known saying among the secret societies. But, they couldn't control the Internet yet. This is why we had to work fast. Where was that robotic microchip kept?

I was standing in the lobby when I looked over at the big welcome desk where security stood and where Raiden and I would have numerous daily conversations. I knew that I liked Raiden very much because as I stood there, it made me want to talk with him again. I guess I just missed my friend.

Well, we got to the stairs and started our long ascent up the flights of stairs. I thought, *Thank my lucky stars I'm physically fit and so are the guys I'm with.* It then made me realize how much I missed going to the gym. When I got back to headquarters I thought I'd make use of the fitness equipment. It was harder trucking up those flights of stairs with limited vision and using crutches—but we were troopers. Each of the guys held one crutch as I held onto the railing and hopped up each step.

We were about halfway up when we all stopped to take a breather. Brian and I looked at each other at the same time and smiled.

"Are you okay?" he asked.

"Yes, yes I'm fine. It's not every day that you get to walk up forty-one flights of stairs with only one healthy leg," I answered.

I guessed that running on a tread mill was sort of the same, but not really. We finally made it up to my floor panting for air. Again, we waited a moment before we opened the door to my floor. After we caught our breath, we opened the door, and made our way into the hallway past the locked bathrooms. We could only access these bathrooms through combination two, eight, three, zero. Without electric, though, we needed the key—which I didn't have. I didn't need to go to the bathroom, but my mind works in that way—know all the options available. It's an analytical response learned from being a computer programmer and technician. Computers mimic life in many ways and it's the first thing you realize as you are taught how to use them.

When I got to the door to my office of course it was locked and, of course, I couldn't use fingertip sensors to open it. So, I reached into my pocket and pulled out the key I had gotten from my house. I put it in the keyhole and it opened promptly. We flashed the light from the flashlight inside to see all of the vacant cubical areas. Surprisingly most of the computers were still all there but that's not why we came. *Where is that microchip kept?* I wondered. The first place I thought to look in was Richard's office. I was also surprised that no one was there to protect the chip. It was probably because very few people knew about it. Our group was comprised of those few people.

The door to his office was locked so we just broke the glass to the door to let ourselves in. We shined the light all around, careful not to shine it toward the windows facing the street, but it was pointless because any light could be seen from the street below especially if you were looking for something odd or out of the ordinary.

As we looked around we tried to see if there was a safe or anything that would hold this tiny computer chip. I tried to think as a programmer would, where I would hide such a small device if it were me. It was like finding a needle in a haystack. We couldn't leave unless we found it. We looked in desk drawers, file cabinets, as we turned the place upside down moving things all around. The two guys we were with were at the doors keeping watch as Brian and I looked around for this item. I described what I believed it would look like to him so he could be of assistance. I was just guessing, but tried to make the most intelligent guess possible so we would know that we found it when we saw it. We looked everywhere in his office but nothing turned up. We then went to supply rooms on the floor, and even a lab that we used to diagnose different formulas and special projects, but there was nothing. I started to think out-of-the-box, maybe this item was not on microchip format. Maybe the information was kept on a flash drive due to its complexity.

Brian then looked at me and sternly ordered, "Come on, we have to hurry. We can't stay in one place for too long!"

I responded by saying, "Okay, I've got to think, hang on!"

We then went back to Richard's office and took a closer look at the files for any type of clue that would lead us in the right direction. We found some interesting stuff, even information on all employees; social security numbers, names, addresses etc., but no information on the robotic project. I then stumbled onto a file that was entitled, "Agent Thirteen," which caught my attention. The file was marked, "Top Secret."

I thought, *Now we we're getting somewhere!*

The document didn't reveal anything about a chip or flash drive. Instead, it contained information about some vault that was kept on the 39th floor. We quickly left to investigate this finding. We exited the same way we came in and proceeded down two flights of stairs.

When we got to the entrance of Computech's office area, there was glass on the right side of the doorway, and since our key didn't open this door, we had to get in the same way we did with Richard's office.

We carefully smashed the thick glass and were able to unlock the door from the inside. We weren't worried about alarms going off for obvious reasons. We entered the room and started to look for the vault that was mentioned in the file. We looked everywhere but couldn't find anything resembling a vault.

We then found a room that looked like a kitchen area. It had several refrigerators and microwaves and a small table with three chairs around it. The door was locked, but once again we broke the glass to get inside. We looked around, but no vault. We then looked in one of the refrigerators and saw that the food that was refrigerated at one time had gone bad. There wasn't much. It looked like some sort of discolored potato salad, a few sticks of butter, moldy cream cheese, and so on.

The second refrigerator was a more modern type with a steel-framed door which piqued our interest. *Could it be that this refrigerator held the device we were looking for?* I wondered.

Its door was locked. We looked around for anything that we could find that could pry the door open. We spread out throughout the floor, looking behind desks for any tools until we came to this one cubical that contained all kinds of tools. This must have been a computer tech's desk because it had a wide variety of tools that could open any hard drive and fix any of its components. He even had a crow bar which would be perfect for what we needed. We weren't worried about causing damage to the refrigerator since it may contain the salvation of our world. Plus, there was no electricity so the contents weren't protected by refrigeration.

We ran back to the room containing the refrigerator as the guys stood watch for any intruders. We pried the door open after a few hefty pushes and the top half opened enough for us to see what was inside. The refrigerator was set at a temperature just above freezing and it was still cold inside. We couldn't understand how this refrigerator was still cold inside without any electricity. Inside of it were two shelves. The top shelf was the only shelf we could get to so we reached in and pulled out a box with a top on it. We took it out and placed it on the table.

We opened the top and looked in the interior. As we did, smoke was released. It looked like smoke, but it was actually cold air that hit room temperature like dry ice. Once I again thought, *How could this refrigerator still be cold?* It certainly raised our awareness, but we concentrated more on what was inside the box. It was a test tube which contained something mechanical in it. I thought to myself, *This must be it. We need to get it back to headquarters to have it analyzed.*

Our time there had been exhausted, as we had been there well over our allotted time. Every minute made it much more dangerous for us to stay and avoid getting caught by those who knew about this device.

Being an expert in my field, I knew there was a reason why this was refrigerated and kept at this temperature. Before we left I wanted to see what was on the second shelf so we again took the crow bar and pried the other half of the door to get out what was on the shelf. We quickly did that and noticed another box with a handle on top. We pulled it out and placed it on the table next to the box we had already pulled out prior.

This box looked like some type of carrying case for the same device. There was a vacant spot for a test tube as well and it looked as though this carrying case maintained the temperature needed for transport. The technology used to keep the temperature steady was advanced technology, the same technology that powered our bunkers, our cars and almost every piece of mechanical device we used for our organization's everyday operations, technology that was hidden from the public. Given the lack of time we had I wasn't about to stay there and analyze how the transport unit was being kept cold. We could always do that back at headquarters where we would be safe.

I swiftly made the switch placing the test tube carefully in the slot provided and headed to the door to leave. "Let's go," I said as the guys watching the door headed out in front of Brian and me.

As we got to the door we were encountered by two men waiting at the front entrance to the office we were in. They had noticed the lights in Richards's office from the street below as well as the parked camouflaged Jeep parked out in front of the building. And although

Richard's office was two floors higher than where we were, these guys went searching all floors associated with Computech.

"What are you guys doing up here?" they asked. These guys looked like Marines as they pointed their weapons at us, but they were special ops. These were guys we didn't want to mess with. I wondered who had the upper hand—us or them.

Before we answered, they noticed that two of our guys had weapons.

"Drop your weapons!" one of them shouted.

They started to slowly put down their weapons as Brian pushed me out of the way. He spun around in the air as his foot slammed both guys in their heads with a roundhouse-style kick.

"Whoa!" I said to no one in particular. Watching this, one could almost feel the impact of the force from the air bound rotation. Even though both guys fell backwards onto the ground, they bounced back up almost instantaneously and a fight ensued.

All five guys were going at it full force as I placed the box down and grabbed one of the weapons. I fired two shots in the air as I yelled, "Freeze!"

Everyone stopped as they caught their breath. Brian came over to me as we now had all the weapons.

He looked at me and said, "Good work."

We clearly had the upper hand now as these guys were defenseless without their weapons. We didn't know how many more of them were close by, so Brian quickly made them take their handcuffs out.

He made each of them put one on their wrist and one on a secure fixture. This was done efficiently, and then we immediately left the area. *They must have been on some detail watching this place,* I thought. We weren't going to stick around to find out, so we went down the stairs as quickly as we possibly could and headed toward the front revolving doors of the building's main floor.

As we left the building, six more soldiers started toward us, but this time Brian and the other two weren't as patient.

Brian screamed out to us all to get down. We all hit the deck as a barrage of bullets exchanged back and forth. One of our guys was hit in the chest, but was protected by our heavy-duty vests. Our aggressors weren't as lucky with all of them being struck by multiple shots. They all perished almost at once as we got up, helped our guy up that was hit, and headed toward our escape vehicle. We got in and sped off toward headquarters.

I thought for sure Brian's cover had been blown if it wasn't for one saving grace—and that was that all those soldiers were killed and couldn't tell anyone. Just then I remembered the two we spared back at my office who were cuffed to the desks. It was only a matter of time before they were rescued or before they figured out a way to free themselves of the cuffs. After all, this is what they've been trained to do. Although they had no radios and the telephones were inoperative, at some point other soldiers were bound to check on what we recovered from that refrigerator. That brought my mind to what was in that test tube. It had to be what we were looking for. I was ninety-nine percent sure of it. Who would have gone to the trouble of placing them in a refrigerator that had an alternate emergency power supply? I was thinking that that refrigerator was probably powered by the two most effective alternate resources that we knew so well: Solar and water (HHO) power.

I was concerned about the checkpoint over the bridge, but I had forgotten that we didn't need to go back over the bridge because we had underground bunkers all over Manhattan which were connected by those tunnels. The most logical bunker to go to was the one I met Marcus at and where work was being done with robotic networking, that is, robots that can teach each other how to think. It could be possible that these robots would be our saving grace, the world's saving grace in the future.

The eastern bunkers were strategically placed as were the central and western ones, equally apart for the most protection for its members. Brian then spoke and reassured me that we would be safe in about ten minutes as we headed toward the bunker. We needed to get this device to a secure location and fast.

"We're taking you to Bunker 1 East where you were before," he said.

"The one we walked to, the one where you operate?" I asked.

"Yes, that's the one. You'll be safe there. We'll be there in about eight minutes," he reassured.

I felt a sigh of relief as we headed down what looked to be Second Avenue. I looked around, but didn't know where the entrance was and was trying to figure it out. We slowed down along the street and noticed a Jamaican Reggae style place on Second Avenue with a parking garage next to it. We rode down the parking garage driveway as I noticed those arrows directing the travel path for parking. When we got below, there was no one there.

Brian parked the Jeep near a cement stairwell that led to an elevator which looked immobile. We got out looking all around us and we headed down the cement stairwell. It was cold as we walked down to the decrepit elevator entrance to our bunker. He pushed a button and a monitor turned on. Again I noticed people working in the background scurrying about and knew it was the bunker I had been to.

One of the members looked into the camera and Brian said something like, "Thirty-six reporting in."

He looked at him and nodded as the monitor shut off and the elevator doors opened. We all got in and felt an immediate whoosh down the chute plummeting downward some two-hundred feet.

❧ Chapter Twenty ❦

Interesting Times

There is a Chinese proverb that says, "May you live in interesting times." Well, I'd have to say that these times are the most interesting times I have seen in my lifetime. It was unprecedented and we were to embark on something that we could only dream about some short decades ago. By this time, Peter Harper and the boys briefed Marcus as to the development of my crucial assistance with the missing robotic chip.

The doors opened and we were greeted by Marcus and a team of scientists eager to inspect what we had found hoping it was the missing link to robotic networking.

"Hello Dave, thank you for helping us with this. Your work is now even more important than you can imagine," Marcus said.

"Thank you sir, coming from you that is a real compliment," I responded.

"Follow me," he said.

Brian and the two others dispersed to areas where they could gather their thoughts, chatting with members they were clearly friends with. The one that had been struck by the bullet went to the medical room as the doctor looked to make sure he wasn't seriously injured. We had no doubt that he was okay, but precautions are always critical. As they separated, before I could thank them for their escort services I followed Marcus to the lab room. When we got there, there were two robotic models just waiting to be worked on, immobile it seemed. As I gazed in their eyes I noticed their trance like stares which gave me the creeps and made me wonder if we were doing the right thing. The robots were just beyond the examining table and as we got closer Marcus looked at the box I was holding as he helped me place it on the table for the examination. The scientists all hovered around the object as if it were magical.

I started to wonder if it was Pandora's Box we were opening. As he opened the top, a giant plume of cold air arose out from it as their eyes opened wider. *What in the world is going on here?* I wondered.

Marcus pulled the test tube from its holding case and carefully held it up to examine it as they all stared at it. "This is it," he said. "It's what we need to complete the project." He turned to me and eagerly said, "You did it, son—you found the missing link to what we were trying to achieve. We must start working on this at once."

I left them to do their work as I went to my work station, but first wondered if I would be able to speak with my family from a computer video screen. So I asked one of the workers nearby if this was at all possible and how I could speak with them. I knew that I didn't have to be present here in order to do this work of monitoring codes and working on those patents. I thought it might be interesting if I could contact Tom Pratt to see what he knew about all that he had uncovered from his Leakydocs operation. I asked if there was a private room from where I could speak to my wife. They directed me one that wasn't in use as they turned on the device for me to communicate with my family. They left the room and I waited as someone at headquarters peered through the screen.

"Hi, it's Dave. Can I speak with my wife, please?"

The individual at the other end said, "The new visitors?"

"Yes, her name is Laura," I said.

He responded by saying, "One second, please."

A few minutes went by and I wondered whether he had forgotten about me. Just then, I saw Laura's pretty face brighten up the screen.

"Hi honey, I miss you so much," I told her.

"Me too, when are you coming here?"

"That's a very good question. I'm going to see if I can leave right away because I'd like to be with you guys. I can do this work anywhere, especially since I know what they are working on," I responded.

"Okay, come as quickly as you can, it's boring here," she said.

"I will. How are the boys doing?" I asked.

"Good. I don't know what you told them, but they are studying their butts off in regards to that project."

"Okay, good. What's Pam doing?" I asked.

"She's just sitting in her room listening to her iPod and playing with Jigs most of the time. She keeps asking me how long we'll be here. I don't know what to tell her."

"Just try to keep her occupied and content and I'll make my way back there," I promised.

"Okay, I love you," she said amorously with sincere eyes. I responded the same and we went offline.

I went over to Brian to see if I could get an escort back to headquarters. He obliged and we were to leave in about a half hour. I went back to my work station and calculated where I had left off with watching if any new codes needed deciphering. I then read up on the technology patents that were bought up by the conglomerate companies. It was tedious work, but gratifying when problems were solved with good results.

As I logged onto my address, I noticed there was a private message waiting for me. The message was from a friend.

It started:

"Hey dude…sorry I couldn't tell you what I was working on. I'm sure it was a surprise to you that I was on your team. I tried watching your back without you knowing it. A few times you came close to being arrested by the government for interrogation, but I nipped that in the bud as I was made aware of it from our own intel. The guy that followed you at the bar was CIA and I stopped him from making the encounter. We have him in custody at another bunker on the west side. I'm sure you'll find out about this later. I can't tell you where I am, but I'm with another one of your friends. Stay cool and I'll meet up with you soon."

The memo wasn't signed and the computer address was scrambled as not to divulge his whereabouts. Computer addresses could be misdirected by use of satellites that were all around us. The address he transmitted from was located in a private home somewhere in Alaska, but I highly doubted that this was his location. Hackers had the capability of doing almost anything and I assumed this was Tom Pratt from the information he hinted, as he was the only one that knew about that near confrontation. I wondered who the other friend was, but even though I pondered the thought of his whereabouts I was more concerned with getting back to my family.

As I studied the patents, I was dumbfounded with the technology that had become available; many things that common people did not even know about, things that would blow our minds. For instance, we had the opportunity to make car tires that would last a lifetime without repurchase. We had the knowledge of automobiles that didn't need a tune up or oil changes—ever. These were minor patents that would have saved the consumers thousands of dollars over their lifetime. The things they hid from us were sickening, especially the medical cures for cancer that could have prolonged life. Murderers.

The guys asked if I was ready to leave and I told them that I was. I signed off as I got up and we made sure we had our gear for the ten-mile walk back through the underground tunnel. I dreaded the walk, but was happy that I would see my loved ones again, so it made it that much easier to start the trek. I was surprised that my ankle wasn't getting inflamed from all of the walking. I then looked around and knew it wouldn't be the last time that I saw this place. We then headed toward the elevator exit and got in. This time I was escorted by guys I hadn't seen before. We shot up the elevator chute in no time and the door opened. They introduced themselves to me and we briefly shook hands. Their names were Tim, Josh, and Kyle, three loyal members of the project.

As I was waiting to exit through the portal leading to the tunnel they opened another secret compartment with some odd-shaped gadgets with handles. There were two odd-shaped, sled-like boards with a rod on each connected to handlebars. They were connected to a power source.

They unplugged the sleds and looked at some gauge. Tim looked at me and said "Are you ready?"

I replied with a "Yes!" thinking we were walking.

Tim then ordered, "Get behind me!"

So I climbed on with my hands on his waist behind him. This was the freakiest thing. This gadget started to rise about two feet off the ground and I'm positive I didn't see any wheels under it.

I heard a whhhrrrrrr sound like a quiet motor. It was a Hovercraft. I'd only read about them in books and thought they didn't exist. We were flying, or gliding, or…whatever.

I shouted, "Wow! This is so cool!"

"Yea that's about the reaction we get with new users," Tim said.

They had just been constructed and were to be dispersed at all the underground locations for quicker transport. They ran on Hydro electrical power (HHO). The other two rode on our side as well, and we both headed down the tunnel toward the other bunker.

At this rate we'll get there in no time, I thought.

We rode like this without speaking for about fifteen minutes as I wondered how long it would take us. They were well-equipped with semi-automatic weapons. I dreaded the fact that everywhere we went involved the possibility of confrontation.

The craft had headlights so we could see where we were going and we saw much of the same. The walls looked the same mostly all the way through; so in that respect it was boring to see the same thing over and over again. The ride was so smooth and there was no wind to contend with down there. I could sense that we were almost there and noted where the opening was for future reference. We traveled for another seven minutes and the vehicles came to a halt.

Tim turned to me and asked, "How was the ride?"

"Extraordinary! I answered excitedly. "I love these things."

He said, "Yea, we just finished making them and there are more on the way for every location."

"It's a real, sweet ride" I said.

I saw them feel around for the opening. There must have been some marking that they could see for them to know where the wall divider was. I couldn't see it. Everything looked the same—dark and wet.

They took the hovercrafts and placed them in a hidden room by the elevator entrance.

This time they saw me in the elevator and said, "You're okay now; someone will meet you at the bottom."

"Thanks for the ride," I told them.

"You're welcome."

Off I went down into the facility. As the doors opened, my family greeted me and we hugged for a bit as we all walked toward our living quarters. I was tired, but hadn't realized it until that very moment. I went to lie down for a while to catch some sleep.

I awoke eight hours later. It was morning now and I got something to eat. The food that was available was in cans, as this method proved to be the best for longest preservation. Coffee was available, too, but only with powdered milk.

We all worked in unison, each having our own area of expertise. We followed what was going on around us, or...above us, I should say. It was bad. Items like gas, milk, and bread was so expensive that money had become worthless. Minerals like gold and silver were the trading commodity of choice and had some buying clout. My family was fortunate to be able to exist in this environment until things got better, even if they never gotten better.

The members all worked in their respective areas and our work progressed. We didn't hear much from government officials, as we were well-hidden and secluded away from the mainstream. I honestly believed that they didn't think we were a sophisticated organization, but we were.

Months passed and we grew and developed in every area. We were almost ready to start building the water cities, but we needed control of the existing government.

I thought, *How on earth could this become a reality?*

Then, I had another meeting with Marcus. Change was coming and it was faster than I had originally thought.

✷ Chapter Twenty-One ✷

The Secluded

Work was being performed with amazing speed and progress. We were very determined to finish. Besides overthrowing the government, the main focus was to make sure that the Geneva Project was completed to fruition and successful. This would prove to be the only system which could not fail.

The main target besides overthrowing the government was getting rid of conglomerates that caused such havoc in our society, the banking, oil, and insurance industries. These corporations were evil with no regard for human life. Their breeding ground was Wall Street as they burrowed through Main Street like locusts. Bank fees, service charges, twenty-three percent interest, twenty-six percent interest, it didn't matter. The more greed, the better. Even if there was no way possible to ever spend the money in a lifetime, they accumulated it in exponential fashion while the peons suffered more and more.

The Geneva Project was a system which must work in order to sustain a decent way of life for the future for all and not just the one percent. Already I could tell how well we were working together. This venture was an indication that the project would be successful. It just couldn't fail if the determination was there with all of us—and it was. It was pleasant to see.

Paul came over to see how I was doing and asked, "Do you need anything?"

I responded with a smile and a nod. "No, I'll be fine. I have all that I need right now. I am just anticipating the fight and how quickly we could end this thing," I said.

"Well, you'll know soon enough," he commented, as if to indicate that a confrontation was near—but it didn't matter because I was ready. I didn't really care because I just wanted to get this over with. I was so tired of all of this and wanted the next phase of life to begin as it couldn't come soon enough.

Paul then looked at me and said, "There's a surprise for you."

I said, "Really? What?"

Just then, I felt a nudge on my shoulder and I turned to see who it was, but there was no one there. When I turned to the other side, lo and behold it was Tom Pratt.

I shouted, "Tom! What's up buddy? I was really worried about you. Are you okay??"

He responded, "Yea why?" He was being the wise ass that he normally was.

"Oh, I don't know, maybe because the entire country wants to see you behind bars for what they think you did to them," I said jokingly.

"Ha ha yea, that was a trip huh? You never suspected anything did you?" he asked. "I was watching your back, dude, and you came close to being captured a few times. I had your back, bud. There was some CIA guy that was following you back at that pub we were at, but I took care of that imp."

I was so glad to see my friend again. We continued speaking to one another about work-related gossip. It was like talking around the water cooler. It was great to reminisce and feel normal again, even though it felt a little odd.

We went on and on for about an hour when I noticed a tall man walking toward us with his hand held out as if he wanted to shake hands. He introduced himself to me, and I shook his hand while trying to listen to what he was saying at the same time. It was a warm greeting.

"Hi Dave, Paul told me you were here speaking with Tom. I'm Michael Schooner. We spoke on the phone," he said with a smile.

"Michael! It's good to finally meet you!"

Little had I known that when the crap hit the fan Tom was hiding out with Michael on the Islands until it was safe to come home. Veracity members from the international front had helped these guys get back home during the struggle. Both Tom and Michael had been monitoring when the next Bilderberg meeting was to take place and where it would happen so they could infiltrate the proceedings to get more intel on what stage their plan was. Tom had so many connections by now that it would be easy to plant some special video/audio devices in the area for recording purposes. The meeting, however, was never planned. The

Bilderbergs knew about the intended attacks on the two cities so there was no need for another meeting. It didn't matter at this point anyway; our master plan was in full swing.

The ultra-wealthy had been prepared for these times and they were invested heavily in precious metals and other means of survival. There were many underground luxury bunkers that they could actually purchase to reside in like condos. They hoarded cash by the truckloads and major corporations had held onto billions of dollars in cash, further choking an already crippled economy. When spending ceased to exist, it further catapulted the fragile state of affairs deeper into depression. The final blow would have been to devalue the dollar by diminishing it. It had now lost status as the world's currency reserve.

These guys knew about this and they were prepared for the bad times that the mere peasants, the poor, and the middle class were going to struggle through. What they didn't know was that we had prepared as well, and were about to embark in a world-saving mission that would benefit the many and not the select few.

On every front preparations were being made. Everyone helped as they aided and assisted each other to push the movement forward and ready for war. This time, it was a war that the people wanted, not a war that was purported for profitable gains. We the people had been pushed as far as we could be pushed and we weren't going to be manipulated any longer. We wouldn't stand for tax cuts for the wealthy while the middle class faltered with the ultra-rich's tax debt. With every ounce of our strength we were going to make that a reality and it was evident that no one would stop us, not the politicians, not the lobbyists, not the political party members, and not the CEOs with their golden umbrellas. Enough was enough.

Every day we'd see sketches and models appear on our video monitors that were used to build the actual sea structures.

And robot construction was in full swing as well.

The item that had been attained by us at Computech was to assist in the most historic, futuristic application of this day. It was humanity's savior; and in the wrong hands, could have been as destructive as the atomic bomb, and as dangerous as the growth of the Nazi Regime. The beauty of this invention was that once applied to our robots, it could not be altered and could not be re-used in other applications for devious purposes, even by the robots themselves.

Their initial applications ruled the way they would be used for the eternal life of the machine much like unwritten law. Robots could teach themselves to think and in this case the initial application was to eliminate greed and hostilities arising from that self-indulgence. In the future this would be a moot point since money would not be needed for survival. I could only imagine the beauty of our new culture and I pictured those green pastures we used to run in when we were younger and times were simpler. These were the times we were returning to and it couldn't come fast enough.

⋆ Chapter Twenty-Two ⋆

The Robot Age

We were gaining in strength and…in numbers. We heard very little from the president and of officials from Washington as they were probably inundated with an onslaught of problems. Everything was crashing. This was even worse than the crash of nineteen twenty-nine. I thought about how they were doing in Chicago and Raleigh, but could only imagine their plight.

Meanwhile, back at our facilities, robots were being constructed by the thousands. John Hughes was right in the midst of the design of those grand creations. Although many scientists had played around with theories, John was the one at the helm putting them to use. He designed what they looked like and what they did. The robots were indestructible. Even a nuclear explosion aimed at them would not render these works of genius useless.

The plausible deniability that occurred in Washington for the past six decades was sure to come to a screeching halt. No more would they pull the wool over the eyes of their citizens for selfish prosper. This past decade they were so blatant that they just did whatever they damn well pleased and made a mockery of the citizens who had elected them to office. This was all about to change. In the past five years I had wondered how these guys could sit around a table, during the holidays, while millions of people suffered from lack of health insurance, poverty, and hunger—you name it. I just see them sitting there enjoying their huge feast with their servants on their precious ranch.

Those are the top individuals of the top one percent, the wealthiest of the wealthiest filthy-rich individuals, ladies and gentlemen, that had hidden behind the words, "The American Dream."

When I was younger, I had reveled in the thoughts of achieving The American Dream; becoming wealthy and having all that I could ever want. As they say, the first million is the hardest to make. I came from a poor family of immigrants as most hardworking Americans did. I didn't go to Harvard, I didn't go to Yale, and my Daddy didn't make sure of my future by paying for it like some had the luxury of doing. As I grew older, I saw the imperfections of this system. Too few people had the riches that many hardworking individuals didn't They started coming out with terms like, "The trickledown effect," to hide the fact that they didn't want to be heavily taxed. Well, "trickle" was a great propaganda word that politicians used to get what they wanted or to prove their point. However, it didn't work like they said it would.

The scales were tipped in such a way that it affected the entire country. Throw the crumbs at the peasants and we'll keep forty percent of all the world's riches and let them jump for the rest. It was so unfair. The other argument they used was that we all expected handouts and that the rich were paying for it. Sometimes you tell lies that are so big that you start believing them yourself and there's no escaping that. Yes, we needed a change to un-tip those scales for everyone, not just the select few.

Marcus was to hold an international meeting that was to take place in one week. I hadn't realized just how big this operation was, but I was to find out and right quick, as all the ducks were almost in a row. We were to start a revolution that would put our master plan into effect that would mobilize those forces that had ruined our world for so long. Our country was about to become exposed for the wrongdoings to many countries for our own self profit. No one knew the blackmails that had occurred. No one knew the threats that had occurred to leaders abroad, simply to exploit their country's resources for our own nation's use, our "way of life." Leaders who didn't get strong-armed, mysteriously crashed in a plane or some other inexplicable accident.

In the last ten years our country was hated by eighty-six percent of the world, but that made no difference to many citizens, they just ignored it and concentrated on their own backyards, so to speak. Many just buried their heads in the sand and accepted anything the mainstream media threw at them. They were spoon fed the information and the "normalcy bias" was in full effect.

The announcement was made for the worldwide speech and we went about our business for the next week until it was time to listen for what was about to occur. It was both exciting and frightening at the same time. I was in a better place now. I used to be worried, but now was empowered by the strength in our numbers for a just cause. I wasn't aware that the technology we were using with our robots had been transported overseas and the construction of these robots had been closely monitored by trusted members of our organization all over the world. The same formulas were used for all these machines and I now use that term loosely because, in fact, they weren't just machines. They were able to think with the same capacity as humans except there were no human emotions to get in the way of true progress.

They were the world's protectors and they couldn't be bribed or blackmailed into doing what the crooked wanted. They couldn't be bought or swayed in any way. They were Utopia's magnificent protector. With humans, this frame-of-thinking couldn't be at all possible. The crux of the matter was that these machines were to stop all of the selfish greed that had started at the top and had become increasingly vile. These self-seeking influential beings and world leaders wouldn't be safe to co-exist in our new world. We were to eliminate the old way of thinking and all the brainwashing that came with it. Our past leaders used the word freedom as a sword for personal, egotistical, self-indulgence that had helped only themselves and their friends. This was the war we were fighting, but this was the last confrontation we'd ever have to face.

With this new technology, Veracity Robots would see to it that these injustices would never occur again. With all the water cities being constructed, there was also a prison being constructed to incarcerate leaders or anyone who had abused their power from the old world. That was the number one agenda on our list for success. We wouldn't stand for rulers or kings or emperors or presidents or dictators. It would be just a supreme rule that was governed by the many. Law would be law and we'd all work for one common goal. Money would not be an option.

The next morning I awoke fairly early and realized that I had needed a good night sleep. My mind was so preoccupied with all that was going on, that I didn't think I was as tired as I was. Feeling refreshed, I went over to the coffee station and made myself a cup. Laura was already up and sipping her coffee near a table that had a huge HDTV on the wall. Although there were hundreds of movies available to watch; the screen had a beautiful panoramic view of some mountains and picturesque images. They were all spectacular views that were looped over a six-hour period. The images were so clear, that they just jumped out appeared so real. The mind works in funny ways. It could be pretty depressing viewing cement walls all day and all night for months at a time. It would be enough to make someone go bonkers. The designers of these underground facilities knew that, and gave thought to that aspect of living since using these provisions may be for a prolonged period of time.

"Good Morning, Honey," I said as I inched over beside her on a seat.

"Good morning," she replied.

I leaned over as she gave me a good morning kiss.

"How are you holding up?" I asked.

"Okay, I guess, I mean—what choice do we have? I know we are better off than most people, but I just want to get back to some kind of normal living," she said concerned.

"Yes, me too. I know exactly what you mean, but we have to resolve ourselves into thinking that a better life is coming for us. Just think about the horror the people on the outside are facing right now as we sit here. Think of the people in Raleigh. We have to be content that our family is safe and that we are in a better position than most," I said reassuringly.

"I know, but it's still hard. I'll be okay. You just do what you have to do to get us through this. I am with you every step of the way," she said lovingly.

"Thank you, Honey. That means a lot to me and gets me through the day while I work," I told her.

"I'll tell you one thing. I'll never take anything for granted anymore. When we get out of here, I will smell the proverbial flowers. I will look at things around me in a different way. You can be assured of that!"

"I know you will. Believe me, so will I!" I said as I nodded my head in agreement.

Just then an announcement came over the loudspeakers stating that Marcus was about to speak to the world members of Veracity. I gave her a kiss and left to go into the main control room to observe and listen in on his speech.

As I entered the room I was headed off by John. "Hey man, this is it," he said with a smile on his face.

"Yea, I can't wait for the next stage which should be pretty damn interesting," I said.

"You got that right. I have a feeling this is going to be intense. Wait until you see what these Bots can do!" he said speaking of his masterful creation in an exhilarated way. "I can't wait to see what these Aqua cities are going to look like full scale!"

"I know, me too. It should look amazing. I just hope living in one is not as confined as it is in here," I said.

"It's all good," John said.

Even though we had lived there for over a year, this was the first time I had heard the water cities being called aqua cities. I thought it sounded kind of cool and I visualized what it would look like in real life from the models I had seen over at Eastern Bunker One. Marcus began his speech:

"All members of Veracity," he commenced.

As he spoke, his English was translated into many different languages across the globe depending upon what country you were in.

"As I sit here speaking to all of you today, I want you to know that today is history. For the first time in the world's history, we are banning together as one nation, not as many divided nations. We will ban together to battle those forces that have kept us in chains for centuries. No longer will we be oppressed by the confines of a corrupt greedy system. No longer will we be manipulated in doing what they want us to do for their personal monetary gains at the expense of our well-being. These figures whom we trusted as our leaders, whom we've voted for and trusted with those votes, have not abided by our wishes and shall now suffer the wrath of our deep rage. I am speaking of the wishes of all mankind and not just those few who have monopolized on the riches of our lands. These are our lands too! All inhabitants have

the right to benefit from the resources that are available to us without paying an enormous price for it. They talk about world peace, but cloud that goal by corrupt propaganda that benefits only them. They mask our mission with talk of Freedom when Freedom is what they take from us so they could prosper from it as well. No longer will one percent of the population control forty percent of the world's wealth. We will abolish the use of money for the things that are available for all to use. We will abolish the media which is a vessel of propaganda for their own purposes. Money has enslaved us for centuries. It has segregated us as the human race. It divides us as a people. There will be no more hidden secrets of technology so that a few thousand can prosper profusely from that betrayal. These criminals will be taken into custody and brought to justice. The billions upon billions of dollars that they've hoarded will be rendered worthless and all people shall benefit from the earth's resources. Today we stand as one against tyranny, against deceit, against the gluttonous habits that these demons possess. They will not be able to hide. We will seek them out wherever they might be. The world will be a true paradise, the way it was intended for all walks of life. Those dishonest beings who have forsaken us by treachery, trickery and deception will meet their destiny. They are the ones who are the evil doers and they are the ones who have fraudulently raped our world. Their Domination, Cruelty, and Gluttony will be treated as the enemy to our way of life and our true freedom. Our 'Patriot Act' will be to incarcerate all those who have fraudulently acted on our behalf and were hidden by a secret agenda of voraciousness for personal monetary prosper. Tomorrow, October twenty-first, at ten a.m., marks history. We will rise up as one world power and bring down all those who oppress us. We have designated areas for which these scandalous villains will be kept until further notice. We will keep them there until our mission of saving our world completes. Our efforts of building these cities will not be diverted. There will not be any more peace meetings except those that we assemble. There will not be any more summit meetings that appeased the masses without results time and time again. We will take down the fences that have bound us. We will be victorious and we will emerge into a better place. It will propel our world to heights never before possible! Our people have suffered immensely from their vice grips. We shall overcome the tyranny! Tomorrow is history!"

His voice was getting louder with each paragraph until he was practically screaming with such a powerful force that it gave me the chills. There was a roar that could be heard like surround sound on a home theatre system in a small room. It echoed and reverberated throughout headquarters. It was a very powerful speech and well accepted because everyone was so fed up with how our world had been taken over by these greed mongers. That night I could hardly sleep with the anticipation of what was to happen in the morning. His speech made me feel personally vindicated.

That night I snuggled close to Laura as her touch always pacifies my inner soul.

✦ Chapter Twenty-Three ✦

The Struggle of all Struggles

I was tossing and turning all night as I awoke around 8:00 a.m., two hours from the great revolution. I grabbed a quick cup of coffee as my family was still asleep. I headed to the control room where everyone was bustling about. They were rushing around getting all the last minute details ready for the coup d'etat of our "civilized" rule. I broke out in a sweat watching all the screens from around the world as they recorded history.

I felt revengeful as I thought about those politicians who apologized to oil companies for a two month oil spill of over five-million gallons in our waters, and their flagrant negligence toward our environment. As if a hefty fine did not substantiate the massive oil spilled into our oceans.

How shameful, I thought, *that these leaders have a blatant disregard for human life and wild life for mere profit.*

For a moment I thought about how it was that that explosion which caused this spill was initiated and whether it was of malicious nature. After all, it's been happening throughout this sixty-year span and these guys knew that no one could stop them.

What's one more catastrophic situation? I felt equally ashamed at the same leaders who had kept interjecting the same failed policies that catapulted out national debt into the tens-of-trillions so they could have those wealthy tax cuts at the cost of our children's future. This was our day and we weren't backing down to these charlatans. I thought about all those poor birds and fish the government had killed while they tested experimental biochemical agents that were to be used on the human masses for population control. I further thought how sinful it was of them to even think about killing innocent people while sustaining their own family's lives. I was so tired with the corporate media and corrupt government.

I was tired of all the lies that the public had accepted wholeheartedly while they, the public, just didn't give a damn about our world. Oh, yes, they would utter their particular grievance, their hateful Internet posts but did absolutely nothing about it. When the government lies had been uncovered, only a few thousand people responded to the computer videos. I wondered why five-hundred-million people didn't respond with angry outrage and why they hadn't yet stormed the streets, the capitol, or staged another protest at the Washington Monument in 1960's fashion.

It was inconceivable how ten-thousand robots could overtake the nation's ostentatious military forces. But our guys back at home base were confident. I was privy to the information of exactly what these metallic concoctions could really do. I wasn't aware of what they were made of, but then again, I thought about who their creator was. John had thought of every possible angle in making this invention. They were the supreme fighting machine. Of course, he had them equipped with the latest submachine guns and grenade launchers, but that wasn't the special part of these superb creations. The outer layers of metal were coated with a special coating that could withstand a nuclear attack.

The material was the same material found on insect's outer shells—like roaches, for instance. They also had the capability of never running out of ammunition. They were like lizards that regenerated their limbs when severed. They had the capability to manufacture ammunition from their own bodies at a rapid rate. They even had the capability of firing heat seeking missiles at their enemies. There just wasn't any way to destroy these beings. They were truly indestructible. One robot could do the job of thousands of human troops.

I wondered if these robots could teach themselves to think, what would stop them from ruling humans? The answer was simple. The initial program was gospel and there was no deviating from it. All the good things that our old world had to offer were written into the software that commenced the robot's existence into this new world. The initial program could not be altered in any way, shape, or form. The robots elaborated it into the perfect utopian existence for all of mankind. They were as loyal as puppies. They were also taught of the way things used to be and taught to fight that old evil existence with every ounce of energy they had.

When the robots had completed their research on the old world, they would absolutely loath those who were voracious and destroyed our earth. Gluttony was the enemy and nothing stopped our friends from attacking those who were ravenous while attaining their self-centered gains.

With these guys on our side, I felt content in knowing our new world had a chance of survival. As I looked around the room at the video screens, I noticed members from around the world scurrying about just as we were too. It felt good to see international substations aiding in one common goal. The unification was so gratifying that peace, finally, truly had a chance without getting sidestepped into someone's personal project. Where deals were made and compromises attained while nothing was accomplished. We would hear politicians utter the same monotonous wishes for peace. It was especially tiresome listening to the peace process in the last few years. I was so fed up and had tuned them out.

I've been hearing about the peace process all of my life; at what point do we say, "Hey, it's not working!"?

But I finally came to the realization that it was all intentional.

It was 9:30 a.m. and I could feel the sense of the anticipated confrontation. It was as scary as it was exciting. Deep down I really couldn't wait to start the healing process so we could start living again. We started to see our robots being prepared for departure ahead of the commanders of each bunker from around the world. It was like watching a reality television program but this was real, it wasn't staged. All one-hundred-fifty bunkers were deploying thousands of Veracity troops, as well as thousands of robots.

The war was about to begin and our enemy wasn't even aware of what was about to happen. Or were they?

The initial mission for each country was to overthrow the nation's capital. We were to forge forward until each country was taken down and the elected leaders who had failed us, taken prisoner, or killed, whichever came first. If there was resistance, then we'd have no alternative but to shoot first and ask questions later. I didn't feel sorry for them because they had it coming and it was long overdue. They had failed the human race after being given ample chances to help, but chose not to. The focus of the international powers was to find and bring in members of Bilderberg for crimes against humanity. Once these crooks were brought to justice we could continue our mission in bringing the world to a better place in history.

Paul had given me the option of staying behind or joining the operation. I told him that he couldn't pry me away from this conflict. I would help in any way possible to bring them down.

We had been given the most sophisticated communication devices so we would be on point when handling any particular assault. The operation was well-financed by people who knew that a desperate change was needed for the betterment of all.

After everyone got their suits on we were ready for deployment. I stood toe-to-toe with all my fellow comrades behind, of course, our metal-coated guardians. They were motionless until they got the command to proceed forward. I could feel my adrenaline rush as we stood there waiting for the word to advance.

It would take hours for us all to exit the bunkers so we were told to synchronize our timepieces so there would be no mistakes. Then, we were unified for the attack of our lives.

We knew it would take some time before we could fly our victory flag and claim our new land. We were patient this long; a few more hours wouldn't make any difference.

It was time for departure as elevator-by-elevator load, we made our ascent upward toward true freedom. After about half-an-hour of deployment, we could start hearing some thunderous noises from above. Deep below ground level it sounded like a dull impact, but I could only imagine how loud it was above us. It turned out that the military was alerted to the fact that there would be a conflict—and they were ready.

They had no idea what they were up against when the robots started firing back at their meager power, meager in comparison to the power our forces had attained. It proved nothing in comparison to the commanding force of our guardians. It was really something to watch and I couldn't wait to leave the facility to help in the revolution.

It was now my turn and I eagerly left and entered the elevator. The explosions kept getting louder and louder as I went higher and higher.

Then, the doors opened. I followed the pack as we made our way to street level where I saw devastation of gigantic proportions.

There were bodies everywhere. I, along with the others, shielded ourselves behind buildings and anything solid. We watched massive amounts of their soldiers approach and fire upon anything that moved. There were bullets flying everywhere and I was grateful for my custom-made suit that I had on for protection. We were very prepared for this and it was time.

The fighting went on for weeks, and those weeks turned into months. We were fighting a nation of boundless strength that had been built up over two centuries. But, they had grown weak and had exhausted all their powers in countless and useless past wars that had benefited their bottom-line profits.

It was time to make way for a new era and a better way of life. The true definition of freedom would soon find its home once again in our country. In the coming months, one-by-one, each country posted its victories and its captures. As the FBI had its most wanted list, mostly comprised of Muslim Terrorists, so did the New Unified Nations. Our list however, contained all top 133 world members of Bilderberg along with their inner circle of thieves from around the globe. Our robots were trained well from the start, and that foundation made it possible for them to efficiently wipe out the tyranny and autocracy from the past century. It was most certainly a new millennium.

Chapter Twenty-Four

The Fall of an Empire

One by one, around the world, prisoners were being taken captive. The frustration from decades of scandalous activity would soon find resolve in the culmination of our tainted history. I couldn't wait to get started on our project of actually building the buildings and creating a phenomenal way of living life to the fullest.

There was still quite a bit of work to accomplish and this wouldn't be easy, but nothing worthwhile is easy. As I continually heard the fighting all around, I pondered the thought of when we would have control of the situation. I marveled at the thought of those magnificent cities relieving the stress of our over-populated lands. I speculated about the images of a bright future, free of the voracity that bound us. What was insatiable though, was the need to succeed. The need to prosper in life's many natural gifts that we had lost along the way. How could we have let that happen? Why did we stand idle allowing the locusts to ravish our land at a gargantuan cost to the pursuit of our happiness? I just didn't understand why. I guess mainly because our citizens were too busy working two jobs trying to make ends meet. We were undoubtedly spinning our wheels. Cries of Socialism, Communism and Nazism could be heard throughout the country, yet no one did anything except whine about it. Well, we were doing something about it now and we were getting the job done. It wouldn't be too much longer.

From around the world we heard wondrous stories of the victories won for the start of the new faction. We were close and our victory was around the corner. We could see a light at the end of the tunnel. Most of the villains were taken to prison and only a handful remained scattered throughout the world. Many of those who weren't caught, same as in the days of Nazi Germany, went into seclusion, thus avoiding capture. We knew it would be an ongoing battle throughout the new order. Many of the players had been caught. Our only concern was in capturing the remaining few. We would now search for the remaining powerful few who had destroyed our world. There were twelve figures that had eluded capture.

I worried that the twelve lingering criminals dug themselves in so deep that they would be incredibly difficult to find. What else were they plotting? Maybe their scheme was still in effect and we didn't know it? They were so devious and so powerful that I wouldn't put it past them to totally destroy the world since they couldn't get their way. But, nonetheless, we did cripple their efforts. But was it enough?

Our concern was that they contemplated defeat and what would they would do if the people rose up to combat their master plan, which was exactly what was happening. All we were sure of was that they went into hiding in some bunker somewhere on the planet. We were in a better place now and the victory announcement would soon be made.

Another two weeks went by and word got out that we had won our revolt. The day was grand. The news hit like a subtle wave of euphoria that soon developed into a loud crescendo of joyous dancing and wonderment over what had just been accomplished. The robots were our ace-in-the-hole for accomplishing this and they stood there with empty emotion toward what they had consummated. The robots worked diligently at fixing our communities, our homes, our schools, and everything else damaged in the resistance. Their speed was inconceivable and at the same time, amusing to watch.

As everyone retreated to their bunkers, arrangements were being made for their new lives. The streets were now patrolled by robots who kept order amongst any illegal activities. The highest priority for the time being was keeping everyone safe from those who exhibited aggressive behavior toward others.

The first part of the new order was to get everyone back in their homes while providing staples on a daily basis. The communities all came together quickly to help each other through that obstacle.

Rioting and looting was not possible as the robots put a stop to that immediately. Swiftly, wheels were put in motion for this transition period. We needed to move fast as people slowly repaired their homes. Things sped up rapidly when they were aided by the cyber beings. We all started giving them pet names as they seemed so, so,…human.

Solar and Hydro plants, already finished by the previous conglomerate energy companies, were now being utilized to bring in necessary power. It was an easy, quick hookup for this energy source and the beauty was—it was all free. These conglomerates had used this "free power" to charge people huge sums of money. The whole idea of it all was so villainous.

Some would go on to live somewhat normal lives in their previous homes as others would take up a new residence in the aqua cities being built. But still the transition period would not be a short one as we waited for the aqua cities to be completed.

I couldn't wait to visit these cities as they were being constructed.

As I lingered back at headquarters my family had not yet left as they were waiting for my word that it was safe to head back home. They knew that I wanted to relocate to the aqua cities, but were hesitant in doing so because the life they knew was back home, at our house. Still, we were curious as to whether we could get on with our lives after what we had been through. After all, our trying time was very similar to the time after the end of World War II. But it was different. There had been a long period of recovery before times became golden again.

In our lifetime, there was first the great depression which happened in 1929. It had been a fifteen-year recovery that had been slow going because of the way the government handled the cure. Then, we plunged into World War II. That time period thrust us forward for the next fifteen years into a great time of industrialization, from about 1945 to about 1960. We all know about the '60s and '70s. Those were some great times, great music, and great prosperity for all and not just for the top one percent.

Yes, we were headed into another fifteen-year period of growth with all the technology to date. If you think about it, we were back in the wild, wild, west flying by the seat of our pants into a new time that we hardly knew anything about. It was very exciting to envision a future only once written about and dreamt about by our fallen hero's from our past—Kennedy, Lennon, and King. These were great men that many of us didn't deserve and many of us did.

I thought to myself, *I only wished that they were here to help guide us through these next twenty years, but I knew they were here, I knew they were here in spirit.*

We needed another hero to get us through these tough years. These heroes were few and far between, but I guess that is what makes them great. Their unselfish actions are what immortalized them and catapulted them into prominent leadership. Their outstanding visions were far ahead of the times.

"Ask not what your country can do for you, but what you can do for your country."

~ John F Kennedy

After I made my rounds, watching what was going on in the main room, I headed toward my sleeping quarters to see what my family was up to. As I panned the room I saw the tired looks on their faces. I knew that they'd had enough.

"Okay, family meeting," I said. They all gathered around eager to hear what was to transpire next. "I think we should all go back to our homes and get things in order and see what needs to be done." I continued, "We have a lot of work to do."

"Dad, are we going to go back to normal now, I mean living at our homes, going to work and so on?" Robert asked me.

I tried to find the correct words, as any father would have in an extraordinary situation like this.

"Well son, the truth is 'I'm really not so sure' is the honest answer. We'll just have to take one day at a time and tackle it as it comes," I responded. This was the best answer I could give, given the circumstances.

Laura then turned to me and asked, "Should I start packing our stuff?"

I quickly said, "Yes I think that would be wise as we all need to get back to our homes. You guys start, I have some unfinished business to take care of inside."

I headed out of the room and toward the main room to see who was lingering about. As I entered, I saw John standing there looking a bit melancholy. I asked what was wrong.

"I guess you didn't hear," he said.

I looked at him concerned, "Hear what??"

"Leslie was killed in the revolution a few days ago," he said slowly and sadly.

As he explained how she died he had kind of a dismal smile on as it was the only way to help through his sorrow when speaking of how heroically she died and how much he cared about her.

"She was always so proud and fearless, you know?" he said humbly. "I just don't know how to deal with this."

I thought of what I usually said during times like this at past funerals, "John, if you need anything man, I'm here for you."

He softly said, "Thanks," while walking away. He knew there was really nothing I could do to make him feel any better short of bringing her back to life. I felt so bad for him. It seems he was always getting the short end of the stick in this life.

I wondered why some people were lucky enough to be born with a silver spoon in their mouth while not realizing what they had. But who knows if they were really lucky. I mean, I considered myself lucky growing up with the family I had and in a beautiful town near water. Meanwhile, good, honest people were getting garbage thrown at them at every turn of their life. I know it builds character, but someone like John had character up to his eyeballs. He deserved much more.

As I started walking toward the monitors I overheard Paul speaking with Michael and Tom about the next phase.

"These guys think it's over and we've won, but we are still very much in a fight," Paul warned.

Michael responded by asking, "How do you mean?"

"Well Mike, there's still twelve of them out there and it's a very good possibility that they are hunkered down good; having all the latest gadgets. They could be planning to destroy the entire earth with a push of a button. We need to find and incarcerate them…yesterday!" he sternly ordered with his usual deep voice.

⟡ Chapter Twenty-Five ⟡

A New Foundation

At that point they turned and looked at me. I had overheard their conversation.

"Sorry to interrupt, but I'm going to leave now so that I can get my things in order. I wanted you all to know that I will be meeting Marcus at Cape Cod City in about a week to help build the New City," I said. It was interesting how these new water habitats acquired their distinctive names almost instantly, while being constructed.

Tom continued looking at me and said, "That's a great idea. Get some rest and I'll hook up with you for the ride. We're going there also and have some unfinished business to tend to. How 'bout we meet here...say a week from Tuesday?"

"Sounds fine, see you guys next week," I said.

I started walking away to go help Laura with the packing and couldn't help thinking how Tom always put a smile on my face because when I looked at him I thought of all the goofy things he had done in the past.

"How are we doing Laura?" I asked.

"Fine, we really didn't bring that much with us and everyone had packed their things, so we're good. We are ready when you are," she said.

"Okay, we'll start bringing all the bags to the front in a second, I just want to wash up first," I responded.

I grabbed some clothes to wear for the ride home and decided to take a shower before I left because I didn't know how long it would be before we could use our own facilities. I didn't have to worry about work to pay for things as everything was being provided for by the organization. We wouldn't be at our house for a long period of time since we were being stationed at Cape City. We basically had to survive for about a week before we would be leaving.

I needed that time to sort things out and to get ready for our long journey into the future. I got washed in no time flat and got dressed equally as fast. I started gathering items we had brought with us and met everyone out in the main area.

As I arrived in the main area, I noticed all of our items together in a neat pile. I wanted to make sure we weren't forgetting anything so I headed back to our room to look in drawers and under the beds and so on for anything that may have been forgotten. Laura and the boys were pretty thorough in packing up as I only found one sock that had been stuck to the inside sleeve of the bed ruffle. I grabbed it and headed back to where everyone was waiting. I walked up to Paul and told him we were ready to head back. He shook my hand and helped us to the elevator.

"There's a vehicle waiting for you upstairs. They'll take you to your homes and if you need anything at all, just radio us and we'll have it for you lickity split," he said.

"Thanks man," I said. We gave each other a half-hug hand shake. We got in and the elevator took us upward.

The doors opened. We got out and started toward the stairwell at the old diner that had gotten us here. Some of the Veracity guys saw us and drove up to give us a hand. We all got on the riding vehicles and they escorted us to the stairwell. We got there in no time at all and thanked them for their hospitality.

We started up the stairs and dreaded the walk through the dilapidated facility, but to our surprise the diner had been worked on by the robot teams. They had cleared the wood and put it back to normal. They were still working on it, but it was a work in progress as to what it needed in order for it to look perfect again.

We watched as we passed carefully to avoid being hurt by the wood that was being thrown and the rapid pace at which they worked. Their perception was far more sophisticated than ours and they could perceive what they were doing before they even did it. In other words, they were very careful in making sure we wouldn't get hurt.

We walked outside to find our ride as Paul had mentioned, but to our astonishment our driver was a robot. I thought to myself that this was going to be very interesting. He said hello and helped us with our luggage, but we were so surprised, we couldn't even think about responding. It didn't give a thought about us being rude by not acknowledging his hello.

We all got in and kept staring at our driver. It looked at us as well which made us a bit nervous. It's not every day that you have a robot stare back at you. After about thirty seconds of staring, it said "Aren't you going to put your seatbelts on?" We smiled and all immediately put them on for fear of what it would do if we didn't listen.

Jigsey sat on my lap and barked at it for about a minute. Then, the robot looked at him with a stern look, but said nothing. Jigsey murmured into silence most likely thinking he'd better shut up. It then turned to us and said, "Hang on." The vehicle lurched forward. I gazed at the speedometer to find that we were doing one hundred and ten. We were frozen in our seats. No one uttered a word. We got there in about ten minutes, but this trip would have normally taken me twenty on a good day.

It stopped the car, got out, and headed toward the back to get the baggage out while we all sat there. It then came back and looked into our car and asked, "Aren't you getting out?"

We instantaneously unbuckled, got out, and then followed him around to the back of the vehicle. He took our baggage out and said, "Leave them there," when he saw we were about to get them. We wondered what he was up to as he went to the side of my house and out of sight. Thirty seconds later he appeared with a hand truck that I had kept under a crawl space. I had forgotten all about it. It was like it had a perception that was far advanced than anything we had ever experienced and x-ray vision like we had seen on old shows like "Superman."

He piled all the bags onto the hand truck. The kids were sleeping when we left. They weren't ready to come home yet, which was perfectly fine with us. I'd rather not have them with me until we were semi-settled inside.

We didn't realize that this robot would be our friend for the rest of our lives. It was assigned to us. Each home had its own robot waiting on them hand and foot, sometimes two robots. The reality was that I liked him already. He had kind of a dry sense of, dare I say... humor.

I found it funny how he acted. I called him Andy as he reminded me of an old friend, Andy, whom I once knew back in my home town. Back in the day, Andy was a guy that could fix or build anything including the motorized go karts we constructed with lawnmower engines. Well, guess who actually got it done? That's right, my friend Andy. He was another recollection that I had tucked away in the back of my mind. I smiled every now and then thinking about him. These memories are what keep us going, or at least it's what keeps me going. Well, I am sure it wasn't all fun and games back then, but it's always the good times we think about and not the bad, when times were much simpler. When times are simpler, the problems don't seem that bad—or maybe they didn't and we just would rather not think about them now. Well, anyway, I'm glad I was lucky enough to have experienced those times.

Andy's energy packs were made from high-efficiency solar cells. We got the solar energy patents from the oil conglomerates where they had been hidden for at least a decade. The technology was always there, but never utilized due to these hidden purchased secrets.

It was such a shame that we were manipulated into thinking that we needed oil so badly; it was so sad to think of all the bloodshed it had caused.

As I worked around the house fixing all that had been damaged, there was Andy right beside me, watching and helping any way he could. He seemed so loyal. He was like man's best friend. I could tell that he was learning from us. Andy was around, watching and listening during our discussions of what the future might bring.

The days went by one-by-one and we were into a new routine of what our work now consisted of. Our work was mostly comprised of our daily needs: water and food, as well as entertainment to pass the time and sleep to replenish our energy. Veracity also helped us out with that. They had tons of food supplies stockpiled for this trying time period. Arrangements were made for more food production as supplies reduced. We had an old-fashioned radio with a crank on it to keep us updated on any news.

I often wondered what had happened to our president during the struggle. We hadn't heard anything from him since his last transmission on what we labeled to be the last days of corporate owned media. The president was a good man who had been saddled by all the greedy damage from the previous president. He worked vigorously to try and fix the damage, but there was too much and trying to fix all those problems came with criticism and came from criticism from those who really needed the help he was providing. But they were too brainwashed to understand what had happened and they weren't very educated and too prejudice to understand. Our new president was black. One could certainly see how much he had aged in a three year period similar to that of Mr. Lincoln in the four years that he dealt with civil war in our country. How does one battle a situation when there are forces trying to bring down the entire monetary system? The president knew what he was in for when he was elected to deal with the mess and he knew he would get criticized for all his efforts. On the one front, he had to fix all that damage that preceded his presidency—and on the other, he had to solve them in a way that was acceptable to the controlling billionaires. It was just too much for one man to solve. If it were me, I wouldn't want his job.

There were twelve world leaders still in hiding and the hunting continued to find those last fugitives. Preparations were being made by Veracity for the construction of the aqua cities, while simultaneously rebuilding Chicago and Raleigh.

The remaining culprits were the most dangerous and the most protected. They were dangerous in the sense that they could arrange pretty much anything through their vast power, as they too had all the latest technologies. Although their power had been diminished, they were still a viable entity. They had ancient plans to implement if something like this happened. They were prepared to elude capture. Their plan was designed so well, that they were living a comfortable lifestyle underground somewhere while watching over our every move. However, our guys knew this as well and were already keying in on clues from captured hidden technology and communications systems. The existing satellites were being used efficiently for all of our needs. They were using them too as we were able to track what they were doing. As of yet, though, their locations had not been revealed. They were very shrewd in making sure their location was well scrambled making it difficult for even the most intelligent persons with the most sophisticated equipment to decipher.

From headquarters we were scanning the earth for anything peculiar far underneath the earth's surface. We could easily capture images up to a mile underground if it warranted doing so. It wasn't enough though, as there was so much land to scan and not enough time to do it. It had been reported that their final plan if captured was to annihilate the entire earth. Basically, being captured helped their eventual master plan of over-population control and the forming of a new world order. This knowledge would make them ten times wealthier than they already were, leaving the peasants—us—with nothing but to plow the lands and do the medial work that they needed done for their avaricious existence. The power was endless and that's all it was about at this stage of the game; control and power over the entire planet.

⇒ Chapter Twenty-Six ⇐

Saving the World

The days kept getting more interesting. I was almost finished with helping to get the house back to normal. A few days earlier we were greeted by another friend who had allowed things to progress a bit faster.

With this robotic assistance, we were able to get things back in order a lot quicker. The fact was they needed me to get back so I could assist with the final operation. I was to be briefed on the finalization of the new world when I got back to headquarters. We had no perception of time as far as when we would actually be able to reside in these aqua cities, which was the reason for getting our homes in order. It could be a few months, five years, or maybe possibly longer. For instance, look at how long it took to find and kill Osama Bin Laden. But of course the thought dawned on me that we had possibly found Bin Laden a lot sooner, but he was allowed to escape due to being friends with the prior president. One thing for sure though, finding these fugitives was not an easy operation.

I was curious to see how things would pan out and at what speed. I started packing my clothes not knowing really what to bring when Laura came in. She always knew what to pack. She was actually a pro at packing. I never met anyone quite like that. When we went away on trips she knew exactly how to pack the trunk with our luggage. I would look at the bags and say to myself, *There is no way we can fit all these bags in the trunk.* I'd always start placing the bags in the trunk and when I got to the last bag, which never fit, Laura would take everything out and start all over. She matched the bags like it was a puzzle that she had to crack and figure out. It was really an art. It was fascinating, as well as it was frustrating to watch her struggle with it and then rise up victorious.

I would look at her Dad the same way when he was working on a plumbing project. I'd think to myself, "What the hell is he doing?" It all looked so confusing; pipes coming out in every which way. As he was working at it, he'd be telling me some story about how cheap a part was forty years ago. He would chuckle to himself at what I paid for the same part today. A cigarette would hang from the side of his mouth as smoke rose up in a squiggly, white, grayish line.

These guys who lived in the industrialization era were amazing. I'd watch him work with his head tilted upwards at the project he was working on. Simultaneously, I would stare at the long cinder that seemed to never break from his cigarette. I was always amazed at how long they would get before they fell. Before I was able to see the ash break off, I would be diverted to his finished project of pipes with perfectly plumbed lines. Whatever he worked on seemed as good as new. He was certainly a fascinating person and I had such a deep admiration for men and women from his era. I got the sense that it was a very proud time to be an American in those days. We were extremely lucky to experience the '60s and '70s as children. It was a great time for our country regardless of the turmoil. We didn't realize that it was the start of the end due to those really running our country.

I said goodbye to my family wondering when I would see them again. I was hopeful that it would be soon, but I really didn't know. I trusted our new robot friend to protect them. I had analyzed their efficiency and their odd concerns over the last week. It was strange, really, trusting a machine over a human being to watch and protect your family. I had a feeling that they were in good hands from any evil that may be lurking.

Robert and Harry knew they would be utilized sometime in the future when it warranted it. Teaching skills were valuable in any society. They were always so organized and meticulous in their ways and I had every faith that they too would watch over the family. I took the boys aside and made sure they knew where the weapons were and where all the emergency equipment was located.

"Dad, don't worry. We've got it covered. You do what has to be done to get the job done and we'll see you soon. We'll make sure all the girls are alright," they both said, sharing the sentiment.

I felt honored that they had my back and a feeling came over me of how proud I was of my boys.

"Take care of Mom," I said.

"We will Dad, don't you worry," Harry assured me.

Just then, from between their legs, came Jigsey gyrating into frenzy as he leaped into my arms because he saw that I had my jacket on to leave. I was worried about dropping him because he was so excited. He wanted me to take him, but I knew I couldn't. It wouldn't be safe. I kissed him, hugged my boys, their spouses, and Pamela. Then I worked my way toward Laura as I gave her a special kiss.

Andy was already in the Jeep waiting with his eyes forward. I got my luggage in. I had two bags with me as I thought this mission wouldn't be a quick overnight visit. I threw them in the back and climbed into the front seat where I was expecting Andy to take off.

Instead, after about fifteen seconds, he looked over at me and said, "Put your seatbelt on, knucklehead."

Even though my initial reaction was to knock him out, I looked at him baffled in amazement for calling me a name. I was embarrassed because he was right that I hadn't thought of my safety. I smirked at his comment and put my belt on and off we went.

My mindset was not focused on what lie ahead. I really wanted to visit the aqua city to see all of the accommodations this project would offer. It's not as if I had seen brochures on what it was equipped with, so I had to use my imagination from what Marcus had described and from viewing the model replica.

All I heard on the way was the sound of the tires rolling on the asphalt roads. There weren't any radio stations to listen to and robots don't make for great conversation. I now again felt like smacking him in the head for calling me a knucklehead, but that feeling had left as quickly as it had come into my thoughts. We were in the dark from what was to happen when we arrived. I forced myself to be patient until we reached our destination at headquarters. I could now see the diner. Frankly, I was sick and tired of seeing it, but I knew that it was the entrance to where we were headed.

I made the best of it as we got out of the Jeep and started for the stairwell that led to our bunker destination. Andy somehow figured out how to wheel the luggage using his ambidextrous ligaments.

We saw some workers in the back kitchen as they looked at us, but it became obvious that they didn't speak any English. They too had a robot friend assisting them. Everything was back in order surprisingly sanitary and with all new completed construction. I smiled at them and opened the trap door to go downstairs—first me, and then my metal friend as he made several trips with our luggage. I wondered what monetary value would be yielded from reopening the diner for business, but I had more important things to think about than that. In the new unselfish world it would all be worked out. I was sure of that.

We put the luggage down, walked a few feet and Andy began pulling out a few Hovercrafts from their hidden location. I smiled in delight of knowing we wouldn't have to walk the lengthy distance to the entrance while at the same time lugging the bags. There were two bags and we tied one bag on each of the hovercrafts behind us so we could stand comfortably.

We zoomed away and were at the destination in no time. Andy immediately found the secret wall entrance, put our vehicles away, and huddled inside the waiting area as we waited for the monitor to turn on. We waited for a face to talk to, but it took a bit longer than usual. We then saw Paul's face appear.

"Hey Dave, I'll let you down in a sec, hang on pal," he said.

The screen went dark and about thirty seconds later the elevator doors opened and we piled in with our luggage. Down we went where once again the doors opened and we got out. Andy got the luggage out and I told him to put them into the area where my family had stayed during the revolution. I took a quick look around and noticed everyone was working intensely. They were eager in trying to locate the missing criminals hidden away somewhere in the world. I was tiring so quickly lately because each day was action packed with mental stress. Combined with the physical stress, it was an unhealthy combination. I wanted to wash up before I got to work and everyone was working feverishly at their particular jobs. The place exuded enthusiasm over what they were attempting to accomplish.

I went to my quarters and washed up. While I listened to some music, Andy sat on my bed waiting for his next command. I looked at him as I would look at one of my own children when they were bored. His head followed mine, but not in a threatening way. It was more like a *What are you staring at?* look.

I went in the bathroom and started running the water to wash my face and hands. I felt the warm water touch my face and soothe it gently. I really needed some warmth. It felt good. I had brought my razors with me and Andy had already taken them out and placed them on the sink. Tired of not having any conversation with him for all this time, I turned my head over my right shoulder and thanked him.

"Hey, thanks for taking my shaving cream out of my bag and placing it in here," I said not expecting a reply.

"Don't mention it," he answered.

I was taken aback for a moment. I was actually talking to this, this, this inanimate object. I wiped my face and walked out of the room where I stopped and looked at him. I said point blank, "Are you screwing around with me?"

He looked at me and asked, "What is screwing?"

Most people, when learning a language for the first time, usually learn the curse words first then the rest of the language. He was learning now and before he had a chance to really think about it, I said, "Nevermind, let's go."

He got up and followed me while uttering, "Okey, Dokey." I just shook my head while wondering if a comedian friend of mine programmed this particular android.

We got to the main room and I was ready to work. As I walked in, I saw Tom Pratt discussing something with one of the operators. I was happy to see him once again, but I wasn't quite sure what I would be doing. As I was looking at him, he turned toward me, while raising his head to his left and pushing up from the desk he had been leaning over, and smiled. I was only a few feet away so he walked toward me and gave me a fist-pound greeting.

"Hey Bud, you okay?" he asked.

"Yea, I'm kind of tired from all this new stuff, but I'm taking it one step at a time," I responded.

"How's your wife taking all of this?" he asked.

"Okay, as best as can be expected given the circumstances," I told him.

"Yea, I hear ya," he answered. "Well, I got the word to brief you on what's going on before you leave."

"You will be leaving immediately, as there have been some developments. I need to stay here for a while to work out some unfinished details," he said.

I responded quickly by saying, "Not a problem at all. I will see you when you get there."

"It turns out that the remaining Bilderbergs knew this day was inevitable and they were ready. As it stands, from the intelligence we have received from international bunker stations, they were all set for the final phase of their sixty-year operation. They have stockpiles of chemical and biological agents somewhere in Europe that could be launched at any time. They could take out two-thirds of the world's population leaving the rest of the peasants to plow the fields and do restorative labor while the masterminds reap the fruits of the lands where they will eventually reside. These guys are so demented. They value buildings more than they value human life. We've learned the reason they don't want to use nuclear is because it would destroy buildings that would cost time and money to rebuild. Using alternate mass destruction would only kill people and save the land," Tom said. I just shook my head but wasn't surprised just disgusted. But I immediately wondered how they were going to deal with the loyal robots that had defeated their armies.

Nothing really fazed me anymore, but deep inside I knew this wasn't over. I asked when I would be leaving. I had assumed the answer would be "right away." Although communications were developed throughout the organization, communication devices, such as cell phones, were not yet readily available for use. Residential households as well as all the major cell phone providers had been destroyed in the rebellion. Preparations though were being made for walkie-talkie devices that could stretch across the continent by one push of the button. Since this technology had already been developed by the conglomerates prior to the revolt, it wouldn't be much longer before this mode of communication was enabled. I wanted to hear my wife's voice because I knew I wouldn't be seeing her or my kids any time soon.

I tried not to think about it as I got ready for my departure. Andy was still sitting motionless on my bed, waiting for his next job.

"Why are you just sitting there?" I asked.

"I was just contemplating when we would be spending some more quality time together," he snidely remarked.

Whoever programmed this guy was a real wise ass, I thought to myself.

"You are one funny android, I must say."

"Funny, what is funny?" he asked.

I was hesitant in answering him because I didn't know whether he was pulling my leg or not, so I quickly responded with another, "Nevermind."

He then looked at me and said, "You say that a lot."

I smiled as I reclined on the bed for a moment to rest my eyes, and I immediately fell asleep. I hadn't realized how tired I was.

I awoke three hours later. I didn't get up right away as the relaxation felt so rejuvenating. Although I could have rested there for several more hours, I decided to get up to satisfy my hunger.

There was a small refrigerator stocked with all kinds of nutritional items. I grabbed a quick bite to eat and headed out again for my long journey. I told the robot to prepare itself for departure. I passed by the community lounge area on my way to the main control room and saw John sitting by himself. It was evident that he was still quite distraught over losing his girlfriend in the fight.

I went over and struck up a conversation to pass the time before I had to leave. I kind of gave him a soft rub pat on his back as I let him know I cared about his sorrow.

"Hey brother," I started.

John raised his head to acknowledge my words and said a faint, "Hi."

I didn't want to dwell on the bad news, so I tried keeping the conversation light by telling him about my trip. "They got me rolling out to the Cape today," I said.

"Yea, I heard. Wait 'til you see the creation. It even impressed me when I first saw it," he said.

"Is it all completed yet?"

"No, not as of yet, I think they are at seventy-percent completion," he responded.

"I can't wait, it should be fascinating to see," I said.

"It will be—like going to Disneyworld for the first time, when I first saw it; it felt like the scene from Jurassic Park when you saw the dinosaurs appear in the movie for the first time."

"I'm worried about you, you take care of yourself," I said.

"I will. I'll be okay—it's just the initial shock of it all and not being able to see her ever again," he replied.

"I know man. I can just imagine," I said.

"I'm going to meet up with you later in the month as I have to finish up some things here before I leave. My new residence is in that aqua city, it's on tier four #2332. I'll see you when I get there," he said.

I looked at him straight in the eye and said, "Until we meet again my friend."

We gave each other our usual half-hug handshake and I was off. Andy was already in the control room with my bags.

⊹ Chapter Twenty-Seven ⊱

Mission Earth

We started for our transportation expecting to find a Jeep, but instead it was an oversized transport vehicle containing sixteen seats. Andy was designated to drive us from point A to point B. The coordinates were then entered into his brain's GPS. The ride was about five hours which was approximately three-hundred miles or so. We brought enough food and drink to supply us for the drive.

The members aboard were a motley crew of people ranging from technical assistants to biological scientists. I sat just behind Andy so I could give him a swift slap in the back of the head if he made an out-of-line comment to any of the passengers. We all sat back thinking about our mission when we got to the new facility. From the way everyone was acting, if someone had been sitting among us, they would have felt the aura that flourished in our presence.

It was a common feeling to succeed on a very important and humane project that would ultimately affect future generations of people. It was a good feeling, yet mysterious. Figuratively, we were going where no man had gone before. We were pioneers working toward a new generation of life. From John's words, I couldn't help thinking it would be like the first time we experienced the scene in Steven Spielberg's movie, "Jurassic Park," where we first saw the dinosaurs that we had only read about in our childhood history class. I'm not sure about the others, but that's what I imagined I would feel when we saw the aqua city for the first time. I was excited yet reserved in my emotions. I wasn't sure whether we could physically house a-million-plus people in one area without problems of encroachment as we have experienced with lands like Palestine and Israel. When land was scarce, it became an issue. I had to reserve my opinions until I saw what we were dealing with.

As I stopped thinking about that, the more frightening thought that entered my mind was the idea that at any moment there could be a tremendous blast or something to that effect that would wipe us all out in a minute. Well, who knows what it would be like, as I've never experienced biological or chemical warfare nor did I ever want to find out. I looked around as we drove past bridges and bodies of water and tried to take in the beauty of it all instead of just worrying about everything as I usually did. I also took this time to catch up on some sleep. I wasn't able to lie down, but I rested my head back as the warm sunlight entered our transport unit. I fell asleep rather quickly. Most of the passengers were doing the same as they anticipated intense workloads when we arrived at our location.

After about three hours of driving, the vehicle stopped and we all slowly got out to stretch our legs. There weren't rest stops where we could buy a burger or soft drink. These places were nonexistent after the struggle. We had to get used to this way of life even though we thought about how much money we had on us for the trip. After decades of always thinking about money and how much you had on you, it was difficult to adjust when the times had changed. Money was worthless, but kept as an artifact or a souvenir symbol of the way life used to be. Today when we look at a dollar it only reminded us of the bloodshed and heartache it brought to billions of people. Not having it anymore didn't bother me much. In fact, I was relieved that we didn't have to worry about debt any longer. But there were understandably other concerns.

After about ten or fifteen minutes of stretching our legs and going to the bathroom, we got back into our vehicle and left again to finish our trip. Andy sat in the car the entire time waiting for everyone to get back. While he waited I had noticed a light on his body slowly flashing on and off and wondered why it was doing that. I later realized that when he was at rest he replenishes his electrical supply from any available light in the area, whether it was the sun or artificial light.

I was getting more anxious as the time went by and I knew that it wouldn't be too much longer before I would see Marcus's creation. As we passed through Connecticut I revered the beauty of the scenery. It is such a beautiful state. It wouldn't be long until we entered the small state of Rhode Island.

As an adult, many of us lose the capacity to slow down and really look at things as a child does. I try and stop myself every now and then to see the beautiful things that are close by. From time to time, I remind myself how important it is to do that ever since I recovered from cancer, what could have been a terminal illness. I do this quite a bit when I am a passenger in a car since there really isn't much else to do. I smell the proverbial flowers. I look at the trees or a parent holding a child's hand. What I liked to do most is watch people do kind things when they didn't know anyone else was watching. This was the true human being that we all have the ability of being one-hundred percent of the time. Stresses like debt and greed got in the way of living a good and honest life. It's interesting; I thought how much certain smells are correlated with a memory. I remember getting up on a Sunday morning and my grandparents cooking the usual yearly harvest of tomatoes into sauce on huge kettles in their back yard. I've realized that comforting smell was only comforting to me and not anyone else since it reminded me of my grandparents. I'm sure there are similar memories that others experience that remind them of special times. For me it was the smell of that sauce. Music had that same effect as a certain song brings back a memorable time, and it's also different for everyone as well. One thing that always amazed me through these senses was the speed of thought.

I was hoping that all that Marcus had taught us was now ringing true and our new existence would be a euphoric one, free of all the bad things he had mentioned. I hoped it wouldn't be really, really difficult, but then again it couldn't be more difficult than the life we were living; worrying about all the things there was to worry about. The way I saw it, was that all there was to worry about now was to make sure that we all had food, water, and all the essentials that made living good while excluding the material things that eventually ruined our lives.

We were going past Rhode Island now and could tell that there was much more water around us as we could see some openings. The water was as serene as it always most certainly always is on beautiful days. Beach waters are always so calming and the feeling being around it is a stress reliever in itself. If we could just harness that scenery, which creates serenity, into some kind of technology, it would prove to be another useful tool for the betterment of humanity. We knew it wouldn't be much longer before we reached Cape City. We were about an hour away. It was so exciting.

Rome, Italy

In a desolate part of the old city of Rome, deep below the earth's surface, (even beneath where many of the Catacombs lie) was the location of the Bilderberg's hideout bunker.

They had chosen this location as a decoy determining that this would be a great camouflage for their hideaway. From this location they were able to see exactly what was going on anywhere above them without being detected. Their tracking and scanning devices covered every inch of the Earth. They too were still able to utilize the satellite's that were way up above the Earth's atmosphere.

They paid their guards heavily in gold and silver to protect their whereabouts from above. As predicted, they were planning their final attack that would take out most of the world's population, thus leaving them masters of a new world.

What was ironic is that these influential world leader's ancestors were once involved in bringing down Hitler's German Empire just sixty short years ago. Even though they were the ones who initially funded the Nazi's efforts through the Union Bank owned by a prominent Wall Street banker, they vehemently strived at defeating an empire that now had the same plans or worse, of ruling the world themselves. Here they were, plotting to do exactly what they had feared Hitler would do and had almost succeeded. Well, that was understandable as Hitler—if he had succeeded—would have taken riches away from them, which was ironic in and of itself.

This particular hideaway was well equipped to sustain life for many years. Generally, it was built to house all one-hundred and thirty-three leaders plus other workers, technicians, and servants while they waited out the effects of a combination chemical/ biological bomb that would devastate billions of people.

Thanks to the struggle, there were only twelve of these people and their assistants left to complete the final operation. Of all the surviving Bilderbergers, the most powerful of the members had been left; five American, two British, two Russian, two Chinese, and one Japanese. What was left to be done was making sure the new monetary system was set up in such a way that these monarchs could monopolize on the perceived wealth that would ensue going forward.

The first world bank would be needed and set up properly for this to occur. Vegetation and irrigation would be needed for food and water supply and of course workers would be needed to plow the fields. People who had survived the cataclysmic blast would be used to plow the fields for the ruling class. These survivors would be at the mercy of these tyrants wanting nothing more than to feed their families to survive.

They also picked this location strategically because of Italy's perfect soil for growing crops. It is known that Italy's soil is very rich in minerals and perfect for growing just about anything successfully. Computers would be linked across the globe so that the monetary system would be set up and inter-connected with all areas of the world. In the past, apocalypse developers had already created a central business control system called, "The Cloud."

The Cloud was a system that was to be used for all visual entertainment including, but not limited to, video, games, theatre, and the Internet. The capabilities of this new system were endless. Its initial intent when first developed to be released was to eliminate the existing cable television companies from around the world while combining all of the world's communications into one system. But decisions were made to stifle its release until post revolution. The world's future control of humans would be monitored through this system together with the projected R.F.I.D.'s. It would be total and complete vindication toward Veracity's efforts to stop their mission. The world leaders were so snide in their thinking. It was as if they had already won and we weren't even aware of their sinister plan.

It was evident now that they were very close to completing the final chapter of this sixty-year movement to rule and control the world. The ducks were almost in a row. They were now calculating how much more time they would need to launch the final blow against humanity.

⇻ Chapter Twenty-Eight ⇺

To Rome with Love

A ll the groups that were talking amongst themselves had a different purpose for the final stages of devastation. There were translators present so communication wouldn't be an obstacle. They were situated in the conference room where each group was reporting what was left to do before they could launch the final attack. The meeting was slated for 2:00 and it was now nearly 1:45.

They had all finished a late lunch and were sitting back discussing the particulars while enjoying some fine cigars and the protocol type drinks for the wealthy scholars from prominent families—you know, single malt, double malt scotch on the rocks, etc. many who had no business going to an ivy league school if it weren't for Daddy's hand-me-down money.

"Well gentlemen, it's been a long road," one of the Americans said to another.

"Yes, indeed it has. Our father's would be proud of us if they could see the culmination of our long-awaited mission," one of the others responded.

"There is still quite a bit of work to be done, but I'd say we're about a week away from our final step," the first one responded.

They had become used to disguising what they really meant when they talked together very familiar tactics similar to those used in organized crime family syndicates. As far as I was concerned, these guys were a thousand times more corrupt. They shared pleasantries so they wouldn't feel so guilty about what they were doing. It was their guard or protection device built up from childhood while they watched and listened to their fathers talk. Picking a single malt scotch versus a blended scotch was the game they were taught. Regardless of the illegalities associated with Cuban Cigars since the Kennedy era, they had plenty Cohibas on hand. They didn't know any better. They had grown up in a world of entitlement and expected to receive anything they wanted. This was just another chore that had to get done so they could continue their glamorous lifestyles. At birth, each of these leaders was worth millions without having to lift a finger. Old money was the easiest; handed down through the generations that made up their way of life.

"Peter is finishing up with the central bank computer system. Once that is in place we'll be able to move the currency easily as well as making any future transfers. Energy systems are in place and we can use them almost without delay. It will only take a few months to make sure they are completely operational for the entire planet. How is David doing with the completion of the Cloud?" he asked.

"Fine, he's almost done. I believe he's just a few days away from the finishing phases," he responded.

David and Peter were technicians working hard at their particular tasks. They had been hired years ago and only now were they briefed about their assignment. The Cloud was something that was about to break into the mainstream before our country was devastated by revolution.

But as stated previously that all changed to post struggle, a way of controlling anything from currency to video surveillance of human activity. It wasn't necessary to understand the infrastructure of the programs or the software in order to use the information. The old way of doing things required users to receive technology-based services. This required individual use of a TV cable service, phone service, etc. With the Cloud, each of these services would have been supplied to a consumer at a particular rate within one system. In their new way of thinking the Cloud was still very usable and a natural progression in the world. The Internet would now be used for exchanging information and services monitored by these tyrants, an excellent means in fact for big brother to watch the "little people."

The meeting was about to start. Cigars were being extinguished and lunch was coming to an end. Papers were being shuffled and each department would report on their respective progress. It was a few minutes before 2:00, when a man stood up—one of the Americans—and he began to speak loudly and with authority:

"Gentlemen, this has been a long, long journey for most of us. What you are about to witness will be the

work of many decades of meticulous planning. Those who had the initial idea to unify the world's economy have since passed on. It will be an honor and privilege for you to see the final works. The purpose of this meeting is to make a determination on whether we are ready for the launch. We will be going around the room one by one to hear the progress reports of each individual."

There were about twenty people at this meeting including translators and assistants. One by one they stood up to report the findings of their progress. Achieving their goals was of the utmost importance to their overall mission. Everyone listened intently to the development that each had attained in their particular venture. What was surprising was that none of them mentioned anything about their enemy, Veracity. It was like it didn't exist. This was hard to understand as the only threat to their works would be this organization. But, in the main control room discussions of Veracity's progress was front and center.

Soon, the destruction that the launch would reward them with, would eliminate Veracity's advances and further threats. Surprisingly, they weren't overly concerned because fairly soon it would all be over and they would be victorious. They hadn't really viewed Veracity to be a major threat but only a hiccup in the master scheme of things. At the conclusion of the meeting, it was surmised that the launch would take place in eight days.

The control room was set up very similar to that of Veracity's bunkers; monitors and cameras having the latest of computer technology. They were everywhere. They were obviously well financed, and money or its now substitute was not an issue. This bunker had been around since the early seventys, so the developments of this particular facility far surpassed those of Veracity's. However, they used the same satellites.

These guys were very arrogant in their dealings with what they had planned because they were never deprived of anything they needed, wanted, or lusted for. This war was a rich-against-poor war in its purest form. The little people like us didn't stand a chance, so they thought. I couldn't blame them; this was how they were raised. They bought anything they wanted or craved. Most of us couldn't envision a world where anything we needed was at our fingertips or brought to us by asking without the worries of having our electricity shut off for non-payment and nowhere to turn if that occurred.

It was evident that a resource-based economy would be much better for all of the people than the current monetary economic system. The Bilderberg group fought a long fight to stop the spread of a resource-based economy. As Marcus had taught us, the difference between a resource-based economy and our current monetary system was that a resource-based economy was concerned with caring for all humans beings first and everything else was secondary; whereas in our current monetary based economic system, humans weren't necessarily the first concern and they became lost in the shuffle hidden by the idea of The American Dream.

I couldn't fathom how these people could live with themselves given the fact that they were just about ready to kill billions of people to control the overpopulation problem. How could a person go on living while knowing what they had done and the people that they had murdered?

Most of these people rationalized it as being a war, and this war had been going on since the beginning of time. This was all justified as they considered themselves "super-patriots." Ironically that was what the Nazis believed themselves to be in the Second World War as well, super patriots to the cause. A one world government would alleviate the problem of having any more wars, they reasoned. Yet, I couldn't understand this thinking as being rational. With our intelligence, with our new technology, surely there could be a better solution than killing billions of people while plotting to rule the world with their expected riches. I couldn't come to terms with that kind of thinking. That's the way I had always run my life though. Every decision I had ever made had resulted in the use of my heart. It had always been personal before business in my world. We had been eaten alive by that mode of thinking. The wolves were all around us and it was survival at any cost, even if it meant mass killings.

In the past, when the media spewed out facts about a dictator committing genocide, he was chastised then ceased from his violent and hateful killings. Yet, these people planning their current attack had thought nothing about their sinister plan.

I just didn't understand.

As they stood in the control room, they basked in the glory of their master plan. There they monitored the progress for the launch and thought of what the future held for them. They were so confident that they would be victorious, that the thought of them losing hadn't even crossed their minds. And why not? This is how it was throughout their lives born with the proverbial silver spoon in their mouth. They were so full of themselves that it made ordinary, good and decent people sick.

Some of them had gotten angry at having to stay secluded in those awful conditions, but they made the best of it as they knew they wouldn't be down there much longer. They were so far above the little people that even a mention of the middle class or the poor sent them into an outrage. Some thought that it was poetic justice for their final demise to have ended in this biblical destiny.

That was the sad part; most of these historic killers thought it was God's will, as if to say that God would have wanted to hate or kill in this way. It was so sad that they actually justified it in this fashion, but what history has shown in the past was that religion was the cause for many wars. That was ironic. I had thought of religion as being created and followed by peaceful people as a means to tranquility among the human race.

Humans, however, took the message and used it as a sword for their own particular conflict or differences. For instance, as if to say God hates homosexuals and they should be obliterated off the face of the earth. That never sat well with me and it doesn't get any more hypocritical than that. God is love...period. Anything hateful is not religion, it's just hate and that's all it is. Shame on them.

✦ Chapter Twenty-Nine ✦

Water Planet

It is a fact that the world is surrounded by seventy percent water and non-utilization of this particular fact for energy, for so long was just ludicrous. How could we have gone so long without the development of existence on water or use of water for free energy?

Marcus knew better as he was an intelligent being brought here to solve mankind's problems of co-existing together. When I first met Marcus I was so impressed with his vision that I couldn't get enough of the ideas he had for the human race. I couldn't wait to see them in action and I quickly adopted his vision as if it were my own. I wanted to help in any way that I could because his ideas just made so much sense and developing those ideas into reality was so invigorating. It was pleasing to know there was hope for a race that had been plagued by such negativity and manipulations. There was so much beauty to experience all around us. Yet, the selfish greedy criminals kept a wrench in the works while claiming to help their fellow man with the idea of promoting and attaining peace. These words were always thrown in the face of good, decent, hard-working people and fooled them into thinking that they could attain it. It made us sick when they took words like "peace", "freedom" and "The American Dream" and dangled it in front of our faces as if to say they were attainable, but at the cost of blood, sweat, and plenty of tears.

When we visited other lands we noticed that we weren't as free as we thought and we didn't live life to the fullest. We were shackled with the responsibility of making more and more while enjoying life less and less, six-to-seven days a week, both spouses working with sometimes not one, not two, but three jobs just to make ends meet. To add insult to injury we'd hear the sickening news reports of millionaires and billionaires making record breaking profits for the quarter while many others struggled.

We were about a half hour away from our first viewing of Cape City. We were close. Coincidently, at that moment, we heard Andy utter his first few words of the trip. "Thirty minutes from destination," he said in his automated voice.

"Well it's about time you gave us some information," I said jokingly to see how he would respond. I mean really, what could he possibly say in response; he wasn't human and had no emotions? I knew that his feelings couldn't be hurt by what we said to him.

He responded by saying, "There is no need for non-sensible repartee. I only deal in the facts and just the facts, sir. Everything else is just a waste of time and energy." He did have a point as joking can sometimes get you in trouble. I really hated that he was right, but I wouldn't admit it to him no matter how inanimate an object he was. I was starting to wonder about his demeanor, though, and whether at some point he would actually show emotion. I wasn't about to dismiss anything in this new, technological world. The others looked at me with maniacal smiles as they witnessed the robot getting the best of me.

As we got closer to our destination we noticed a lot more water around us. I couldn't help but notice how destitute and empty the land was and how it used to flourish with many people. It was evident, though, that most people stayed indoors because they didn't know what to expect from this shaky future. It was smart to stay indoors as the environment could be tainted with bad elements such as bio warfare. Little did they know how true that was. Then again, who knew if there would be protection against this threat staying indoors?

Everyone seemed scared of the unknown. They didn't know who to trust so they stayed to themselves and their families, making sure they had enough food and water to survive.

It was not a very pleasant way to live, but in these times it was the only way to live. By this time, many had built underground areas for evacuation in case of attack. The spaces were very similar to those that had been built in places like Kansas where hurricanes & tornadoes were prevalent and wind was commonplace.

I enjoyed the remainder of the ride as we got closer to the aqua city. Everything was so picturesque. I took everything in attempting to keep focused on what I was about to experience. I briefly thought about my family and how they were making out with the restoration of our home. I thought about Pamela and her partying days and how that was a thing of the past. Now, the clubs were nonexistent. I thought about

Robert and Harry and how they were so determined in teaching people the new ways of the future. They would teach everything from Marcus's teachings to environmental breakthroughs. I couldn't wait to be near them again and hoped it would be soon.

At that moment Andy spoke again. "Ten minutes to final destination," he said with that robotic-like voice of his.

As we were getting closer I noticed there were a lot more robots working on roads, homes, and all kinds of structures. There were even boats available as an excellent mode of transport to anywhere, and especially to and from the aqua city, parked a short distance from shore.

As we got closer there were literally hundreds of robots busily working. I easily noticed the magnitude of all these mechanical creatures working at rapid speeds. I looked around eagerly trying to see the aqua city, but couldn't see anything yet. I wondered how it was that we were so close and yet couldn't see something that was so colossal.

There were a lot of trees and shrubbery blocking my view of the coast and I started to see some shiny, metallic images through the trees until we came to a huge clearing that opened into a beautiful watery blue vision.

The image appeared right in front of my eyes. It was like twenty cruise ships had been strung together, probably more. I immediately got the chills from seeing something so massive and spectacular. The vision created an imaginary sound in my head and I could hear a crescendo of sounds of beautiful classical pinnacle composition while viewing this sighting for the first time. It was magnificent to say the least. However, the word magnificent didn't seem to do this sight justice. I was awestruck and could only imagine what everybody's faces looked like in the vehicle with me, but I didn't care to look at their reactions because I couldn't take my eyes off of Marcus's conception of utopia. It was outstandingly ostentatious.

Andy stopped the vehicle, looked at us and said, "Well, are you going to get out?"

We ignored him for a moment to compose ourselves. The structure was so high and so big and so shiny; constructed of metal and glass. We wondered how this huge construction could stay afloat. Boat transports flourished all around to and from the structure and from the seashore as well as many helicopters hovering above.

Now, there were literally thousands of robots working on the outside of this configuration. It was the first time I felt the impact of this new age. It was the first time that I was at a loss for words. The first time I had realized that what I had been briefed about was right there, right in front of me. It was very real. I felt goose bumps on my arms as I gawked at the operation and I was enveloped with emotion as a few tears rolled down my face.

Andy transported our luggage onto a beautiful yacht that was to take us aboard the enormous cruiser-like structure. It felt as though we were leaving on some cruise to an exotic island, yet this ship was stationary.

The trip in the boat was a brief one and as we got closer to the side of the building it kept getting bigger and bigger, like an optical illusion. We walked off the boat slowly and into the futuristic vessel.

All around us there were people working on something. They worked rapidly as if someone was holding a flame on their butts to work even faster. I was so stunned at the sight I was witnessing that it didn't dawn on me that they were racing against time. The villains needed to be stopped from launching a devastating attack against humanity. I had briefly lost sight of the mission. We were still very vulnerable and we needed to complete it to fruition. Although stationary, this vessel could depart at any time if it had to in any emergency.

I couldn't help taking in the enormity of the project that Marcus was epigrammatic about. It wasn't every day that one could witness such a production of great importance for the human race.

Robots were everywhere. I tried to grasp every inch of the project from inside now as I noticed hundreds of tinted windows that made up the entire circumference. I wondered why they were tinted but surmised that these were not ordinary windows, but solar panels incorporated into the actual look of the edifice.

Andy followed behind as it was apparent he did not know where we were headed and neither did we. We waited for some guidance. We were too occupied with looking all around us to wonder when someone would make their acquaintance and guide us in a direction where we could put our things away and get situated.

As I looked around there was machinery that I didn't recognize. I was curious to find out how they could use tidal wave power along with the other forms of energy to power this vessel at no cost. We were surrounded by water and that kind of power would be easy to use given our locality.

I can't mention it enough that there were literally thousands of people all around us. There were many boats docked at the edges of our vessel, and we could leave at any given time as these boats made runs almost continuously. They were powered by means other than gasoline, in fact gasoline and oil was now obsolete. These boats were also constructed from the new technology acquired from the patents, that at one time, were a big secret.

I wasn't sure what to call the vessel we were on, but used that word for lack of a better one. As I looked overboard I noticed there were hundreds of fishing and docking stations. I thought to myself that it would take months to cover every inch of this vessel. This was actually like a city and it needed its own zip code. Although I jokingly thought that to myself, it might actually have its own zip code given its huge dimension and capacity.

The deck I was on seemed to be used for living space as it looked like a big hotel on water much like a cruise ship, but vastly bigger. There were computer monitors all over that could be used. We approached one to input some of our information as we were instructed to do so before we left headquarters. When I input my name in the computer it brought back a response of where I was to reside for the time being, or possibly permanently. It was dependent on how large the room was and whether we could fit my entire family in that space. I would soon find out that my name was linked to Tier four #2328. It sounded familiar and I was almost positive that John was just a few doors down. I wrote down his room number, but I had it in my briefcase. I would wait until I was situated in my room before looking up his room number. I wouldn't be surprised if we were neighbors, since we had worked together in the past and our compadres were well aware of that fact.

After checking out where I was stationed, we all separated to make our own way to the living quarters. We were all so preoccupied with looking around that we didn't much care if we stayed together because we really didn't know each other. Because I was fixated at looking all around I must have tripped three times not watching where I was going. I was so interested and amazed at what I was experiencing.

So, it was Andy and I walking around and checking things out. Andy would follow behind me with my luggage wherever I happened to walk. I told Andy where we were going.

"Andy, we need to find room #2328 on Tier four," I said.

"Very well, we need to find the elevators, as we are on Tier one."

There were many levels as I stated earlier. My guess would be that there were about fifty floors from top to bottom. There were levels below us underwater as well, but I was guessing those floors were designated for work stations. I learned later on that the top two floors and the bottom two floors were designated for surveillance and the continued operations of this sector of the country.

The facility was equipped with many luxuries and protective devices such as alarms. There were also missiles to deflect or combat any defensive or offensive attacks. It was well known that our last strategy would be to locate and destroy the remaining players in the Bilderberg organization. That wouldn't be our last objective though, as The Geneva Project wasn't a perfect social system. We needed to work on perfecting it, but we were positive that this existence would be far better than the old money driven one.

Perfecting a resource-based economy would be far less exhausting than the money driven one we had in place for centuries. I was curious to find out what progress we had made in locating these criminals.

I unpacked my luggage, got situated, and noticed there were messages on the communication device in my room. The light on the unit was flashing much like it did in a hotel room. I had to figure out how to retrieve messages and thought that it wouldn't be that difficult to extract. I washed up, started fumbling through my briefcase and found the paper where I had written down John's address. I wanted to get this information so I could go see him when he arrived.

When I checked my message there was only one left from someone named Jack Singleton. He asked if I could meet him up on Tier

49 Control Room #1418 so he could brief me on what I needed to work on. That's really all the message said. It was direct and to the point.

I left Andy in the room so I could go wander about exploring the facility. When I was leaving, I noticed Andy was taking my clothes out and putting them in drawers for later use. He was very organized and I appreciated the assistance.

As I left the room I noticed how well lit everything was from the natural light. The use of glass made it easier for energy production. While I was still on shore, I had noticed energy windmills circulating for additional power as well. The combination of five energy sources proved to be sufficient enough to power the entire structure indefinitely. They utilized wind, geo-thermal, solar, hydro (HHO) and tidal wave to produce the essential energy to power all of the technology built within the edifice. It was such a thrill to know that all of this power was created from limitless resources. There was no utility company to pay and none to worry about cutting you off if you didn't pay the required, overinflated costs. That feeling was exhilarating in its quintessence. It made me feel so proficient and free from anyone controlling my existence. I felt rejuvenated and unbound knowing that what we were working toward, what was in fact, a present reality. We were on the right course where the many outweighed the will of the few. All that waste could have easily been used to feed hungry nations, yet it was all tied up in the accounts of the insatiable people. Prior to this world, the fact was that we had enough food available to feed the world twice over, yet because of covetousness many of our people starved and the ultra-wealthy could care less.

It wasn't our fault as we had been programmed with this system since birth. This new world didn't recognize divisions of nations, government, race, religion, creed or class. The only interest was survival of the human race as true equals, true sharing, and prosperity for all. We shouldn't have to pay for healthcare, education, energy, food, or water. It was our right as living beings to share what was all around us without someone putting an inflationary price tag on it.

I walked around examining all that I saw. I once saw a Woody Allen movie when I was very young that we had all laughed at. It was futuristic and I thought that I would never see this fictional world, but I couldn't help thinking that this place looked very much like the comedy, "Sleeper," that he produced.

The robots all looked so busy and so into what they were doing. With all this around me I forgot that the world could be over in an instant if the villains pushed the apocalyptic button. It was hard to think about that because I felt so empowered with all that I was observing. This was the closest thing to living in paradise every day. This was now my daily work to ensure that I helped everyone around me and they, in turn helped me. I couldn't help thinking about my loved ones, my elders, that had passed on. I wondered what they would think if they came back here for just a second and experienced something that was so innovative and revolutionary, so…ultra-modern. How would someone from their era even conceive of this being real? My dreams would never be the same.

I worked my way around the vessel like I belonged there and this craft was actually mine. I took the stairs because I wanted to experience everything first hand. I used my own mobility instead of riding in a tube upwards and it made all the difference as I saw ocean wildlife jumping and there were boats circulating and fishermen casting rods for a food source, thereby keeping the nitrogen cycle active.

It all worked and it was all so fabulous. I took in the entire wonderfully, surrounding, positive atmosphere I was now in. It was all so therapeutic for the body and soul. It took a while to walk up to Tier 49, but well worth the trip as the visual aspects was just breathtaking. But I needed a moment as I was out of breath, but didn't mind as I had also gotten some nice, well-deserved exercise.

Tier 49 was a lot different than the other floors as it had sort of a scientific feel to the area. Everyone wore white coats for instance and microscopes were everywhere, along of course with the usual computers and monitors. I realized that this floor was more exploratory, whereas Tier 50 was more defensive in case of an enemy attack. Our goal was still to rid the world of our own human enemies and secondly to rid the world of imperfections that would cause problems for our new society.

Marcus always said that The Geneva Project wasn't perfect and that it would need work as does any new project. Problems would be expected, but we were all ready to solve them as best and as efficiently as possible for our better existence.

Before I started bothering anyone with who Jack Singleton was, I watched what everyone was doing and tried to figure out what it was they were working on. It seemed to me that they were studying the atmosphere from fish, to air, to energy sources, to just about everything. What was interesting was that everyone had a purpose and I kind of figured what that purpose was. It wasn't about punching a clock or working overtime, it was a collective project for one common goal. We were competing for the goal of existence and being kind to our fellow man instead of competing against one another. We all competed together toward a better future and lifestyle and it was wonderful karma. Anytime the human spirit is lifted, it is magical. We didn't have to hope for a heaven for we had angels here on earth. And if there was a God, I know that he would be smiling upon us today for doing what we were always taught growing up to do and that was to, "Do unto others as you would want done to you."

I became aware of someone walking toward me which didn't surprise me as I probably looked like a sore thumb standing there in my regular clothes while everyone else wore their whites.

The man asked my name and what I was doing up here.

I responded by answering his questions, "My name is Dave Napoli and I was asked to come up here by Jack Singleton. Do you know where I can find him?"

He answered by saying, "Hi Dave, glad to meet your acquaintance, Jack Singleton." He reached out his hand to shake mine as we both smiled.

"You're probably wondering why I called for you. I've been told you've been with the movement for quite some time and your assistance has aided us in getting us to this point. You do realize the job is not yet finished to rid ourselves from the Bilderbergs, correct?" he asked.

I responded by saying, "Yes, I am well briefed and well aware of the confrontation."

He continued, "Any day now we expect the final saga of their mission to seize control of the world and minimize the population by billions of people. We don't know if it will happen in a day or in a month, but what we do know is that we must get to them before they detonate the final explosion causing the apocalyptic disaster. We know there are twelve of them left and know that they are somewhere in Europe. We have been getting some odd transmissions from Central Europe that only indicates that they are in that vicinity. Motion in any other area of the globe doesn't compare to the sounds we have intercepted from that region. We are about four days away from finding where they are within a one-thousand-mile radius. At that point it should take us another four or five days, maybe sooner, to pinpoint their exact location to within a few hundred feet. We speculate that the materials they have used in fortifying their chamber are far more advanced than anything we have ever seen before or we would have located them by now. This would explain our difficulty in knowing exactly where they are because it is not made from the usual, sedimentary ore. We suspect that it is something man made that was never released to the public. It could contain a mixture of up to ten different ores to make an impervious substance which protects them."

"How can I assist?" I asked.

"Is it possible that you can use your computer knowledge to try and find the substance they have developed? Scientifically we are trying to solve the problem, but it could take much longer as we are using trial and error. We were told that you were the best in your field at cracking codes. I wondered if you could apply the same theory you use to crack codes to decipher what these guys used and which substances were combined as our scientists are baffled. We thought you may be able to use your computer knowledge to solve it. Once we know, it will be easy to figure out exactly where they are hiding out to plan this attack. You must know that time is not on our side. We are racing against it," he warned.

"I will do my best to figure it out," I said.

"I'll show you to your area. Behind that wall is where your work coat is so you don't mess up your clothes should you rub up against anything we are working on. This place is filled with experimental liquids and substances. You also must wear protective glasses when you are in this area as we wouldn't want you to get hurt while helping us," he said kindly.

"Please could you give me all that's been figured out to this point?" I asked politely.

"Will do" he responded.

I said, "Thank you," as he walked away.

I communicated to Andy to come up and meet me as I would need his analytical help in solving the mystery of this material substance. Not only can these robots solve the problem at hand, but they use a different method to derive the answers needed. Together I am sure we would be able to figure it out but didn't know how long it would take.

When the robots were initially programmed to start their learning evolution, the scientists added the curious human element that enables them to think as a human. This was a very important quality to have since humans have to input the information into computers and if the right info is not inputted, then the answers can vary tremendously. Our robots see the solution and work backwards, which is an extremely useful trait to have in a machine. Our robots would prove to be quintessential to solving the complex problem we faced as well as futuristic problems. I wondered why they hadn't utilized them to figure it out and why they needed me to do it. I didn't want to waste anymore time asking them why so I just got ready to solve the problem at hand.

As I waited for Andy, I walked to the coat room and found a coat that wasn't too big or small for me. After I tried on two or three of them I found one that fit perfectly. I walked back to the area where I was speaking with Jack and waited until he guided me to the area of where I was to work.

As I waited, I wondered what the top floor looked like as well as the roof area. I didn't have time to go check it out as time was of the essence and we were running out of it. My gut feeling was that we didn't have too much time left and solving the problem sooner rather than later was important to the success of our operation. We didn't come this far to fail in the eleventh hour.

Just then Jack came back and asked that I follow him to my work station. This area contained many computers which were perfect for use with graphic design and ideal for the utilization of analytical formulas. I arranged items in my area that would make it easier for me to do my work while I waited for Andy to arrive. I needed the correct starting point which was usually one of the hardest parts in solving the problem.

Depending on which starting point you choose, allows us to solve the problem that much faster. A good place to start would be to use basic skills from when I was taught to solve my first problem.

Andy arrived and I greeted him with, "Hey, what's up pal?"

He answered promptly by saying, "Fine Mr. Dave, what would you like me to do?"

I proceeded to discuss the problem with Andy and felt as though I was in some Star Trek episode. I told him to input as many metals and possible combinations of metals that would make it difficult for radar or advanced satellites to penetrate. I already had a list of the possible metals on my screen which I linked up to him with a computer attachment directly to his side. After the installation of the information he rapidly computed the many different combinations and narrowed it down to within a few-hundred amalgamations of possible solutions. Within a matter of ten minutes I had all the mishmash back up on my screen and I started to play with them while Andy watched over my shoulder. I matched the grouping alongside our most advanced espionage equipment and all the blends were seen by the equipment. What was it that I was missing?

This went on for days. There could be hundreds of variations of all the different mineral deposits that had accumulated on the screen. My eyes were starting to bother me as I concentrated so intensely on the computer screen. I needed a break to rest my brain.

I was three days into it with no luck of finding the resolution. Andy and I literally worked day-in and day-out without a break until I couldn't take it any longer. I grabbed a biodegradable container of water from the fridge and started to walk toward the elevator as Andy followed me like a pet. I thought to myself that this would be a great excuse to go up on the roof and take a look around the perimeter. I had no interest at this time to see the 50th floor so we bypassed that floor and went up to the roof level.

The sun was shining brightly and the weather was about sixty-five degrees. It was a beautiful day with not a cloud in the sky. The ocean welcomed us like a breath of fresh air and like the smell of newly cut grass on a summer's day. It was exhilarating to view this marvelous sight. I tried to take everything in as it was all so stunning.

I didn't know where to walk first, so I walked to the edge of the periphery and viewed the vast water that stretched to a new continent on one side. There were boats from our enterprise all around, sailing to-and-from our vessel. Hovercrafts were being used everywhere and could be seen in the crescent of the structure we were on. There were flying things all around us, and as I looked around I saw that there were four heliports where helicopters could land in emergency situations or exploratory missions. It was so grand and my heart sang with delight and wished Laura could be here with me to witness this heavenly display of nature and technology.

I was tempted to sit on the lounge chairs that were provided for relaxation and tempted to take a swim in one of the eight Olympic-size swimming pools even though I had no swimming attire on. There were sixteen hot tubs and two running tracks with basketball courts, handball courts, rock walls; it was endless what they had up here for entertainment and recreational pleasures. It was a true manifestation of human contentment.

I didn't want to leave, but I knew I had to. I finally laid down on one of the lounge chairs without feeling too guilty that I should be working, as Andy stood by. I stayed about thirty minutes as I rested, closed my eyes, and took in the panoramic views as I now visualized them in my photogenic memory.

When I got back down to my working station Jack was standing there viewing my work. I immediately apologized for taking a break as he replied, "Don't even give it a second thought, I know how draining this could be."

I asked, "I notice all of these vehicles running on reserve power sources that never seem to run out of fuel. Can you show me the configuration and fuel source that powers these transport units?"

Without hesitating he brought me over to another computer and loaded up the diagrams and schematics outlining the operation of these advanced units.

"You see," he started, "The energy patents that were blocked from the general public put a stop to the distribution of these water (HHO) engines. The design allowed for the user to utilize these vehicles with only about four ounces of water at a time to sustain the engine for about one-hundred miles for instance. We never needed as much oil or any oil as the investors had us think. Our governments were in bed with these guys and the officials made billions upon billions of dollars by holding back this technology. Everything from the tires to the glass that is used in these vehicles can last hundreds of years."

He continued by saying, "The excuse they used for holding back this technology was that it would hurt the economy and spending which was beneficial to a successful capitalistic monetary system (as they laughed all the way to the bank with our money). Our vehicles are not solely powered by solar electric, you see, we also use hydrogen engines as well, in conjunction with solar. Our cities are powered by hydroelectric as well, since they are surrounded by water, the use of the technology is very simple. In all reality almost any kind of liquid would work."

He ended by saying, "It was just pathetic how the human race was manipulated by these greed mongers, but thanks to us, this will all soon be over. Our problem now is to find out what this material is made of."

I answered, "Well, I know I'm close. I just needed to stretch my legs a bit. I should have the answers by tomorrow or at least we'll be a lot closer than we are today. It's just a matter of dotting the i's and crossing the t's. I should have it for you quite soon, Jack," I said.

"Okay that sounds good. I'll check back with you tomorrow—but if you have a breakthrough today come and get me," he said.

I looked over at Andy as he was evaluating the information on the screen.

He turned to me and said, "Please input the seventy-three remaining combinations into my data banks."

I quickly obliged as I wondered what it was that he was looking at. We'd been through this a thousand times with little results.

"What is it Andy, what do you see?" I asked.

"One moment, sir," he replied.

I noticed his lights were flashing and blinking repeatedly, the same kind of flickering you'd notice on a computer hard drive when it was computing something vigorously. I left him alone and peered at the screen once more. As he did his thing, I did mine and tried looking at the problem in a new light and from a different angle. My grandfather always told me that if I couldn't solve a problem after hours of trying to, walk away and come back with a fresh head.

That's exactly what I did. Throughout life, whenever a problem presented itself, I realized that it worked every time. I took all seventy-three possibilities and placed it into an Excel spreadsheet and made up a macro that would mix up the combinations. I put the densest ore, Lead-Zinc Skarn, together with two kinds of shale, Marcellus and Utica. The result that spit back at me was an almost perfect barrier that would prevent anything from permeating it. Something was missing though. It could still be penetrated from espionage equipment that we had used to test for the composition.

I waited until Andy had his results and it looked like he was close to a solution. The information was uploading to my computer screen and to my surprise the three materials that I had found were the same in Andy's calculations except for one. Andy found the missing link I needed to complete the project, Epithermal Quartz-Gold-Silver.

I summoned Jack with a communication device on the desk at once. "Jack, I think we got it!" I said excitingly.

He made his way to my desk in thirty seconds flat and I proceeded to show him our results. I also proved it to him by using all the latest equipment we had to try and penetrate this newly formed barrier.

"Good work Dave!" he said with a gleam in his eye. "We just got the announcement that we are within a two-hundred-mile radius of finding their hideout position. We now must come up with equipment that can work through that barrier. This is our next endeavor as we close in on the spot. I assume this will take another four days before we are there!"

He patted me on the back and brought the result to another station that was working on barrier busters. He looked at me and told me to go get some rest and to meet him here in the morning. I obliged and took Andy with me back to my room.

✦ Chapter Thirty ✦

End of Days

When we got back to our room John had left a message on my phone that he had arrived and was in his room. I made myself comfortable and took a good look at where I was staying. It was a beautiful suite that could house my entire family, very spacious with a spectacular view of the ocean and the best part was that we had sliding glass doors that led to a balcony overlooking the ocean. I wondered why they had given me such a beautiful place to stay, but I guess it was because of all the hard work I was doing. This also got me wondering how the work would be split up with people in the new world. Although Marcus said that this new society wasn't a perfect system, I felt very secure in knowing that the fairest method would be derived for all. I couldn't think about that right now as we had an imperative assignment to take care of before we reached that point. I decided to cross that proverbial bridge and help solve that problem when the time came.

I listened to John's message saying that he got in a little while ago and that he was up top relaxing if I wanted to join him. I would have, but I was kind of exhausted so I decided to lie down for a while. My eyes were tired from staring at the monitor screen for a prolonged period of time. As I walked by, I saw Andy sitting there and he followed me with his eyes as I lay down on the bed. I looked at him and said, "Don't you ever get tired?"

He looked directly at me when he spoke and said, "I just need to recharge my battery as I don't know what tired feels like. I'm not human you know."

"I know you're not human, but maybe you should unplug yourself, you might feel more refreshed"

"As you wish," he said reluctantly. Then added, "Please plug me in when you wake up."

"Fine," I said.

The robot was disinclined in doing so because he knew that if he unplugged himself he wouldn't be able to protect the humans for which he served. That's how they were initially programmed, but one must wonder in some odd way whether they actually get emotionally attached to the ones they serve. I guess time will tell as we evolve into our new culture together.

I didn't see John that night because the next thing I knew it was the next day. The moment my head had hit the pillow I was out like a light. When I woke up I noticed Andy hunched over. I didn't plug him in right away because I wanted to wash and get ready without him sitting there staring at me like he usually does. When I was ready to walk out the door, I plugged Andy's power pack in and watched him turn on. Because of the android's sophistication, it took a few moments to get him activated once again. When he was completely energized I asked him how he felt.

"How do I feel?" he asked.

"Yes, how do you feel?" I asked again.

"I feel fine, how about you, how do you feel?" he asked.

Even though I thought he was being his usual wise-ass self, I said, "You know, I feel great! Better than I have felt in a while, thanks for asking."

He looked at me and said, "Don't mention it."

I looked at him and shook my head slightly and headed up to Tier 49 to see how my contemporaries were doing and offer my assistance as usual. Andy walked behind me with what I noticed was a rather interesting walk. He had long, lanky legs that bent at the knee, but the hydraulics made the bend rather smooth. I never heard any squeaking from the metal rubbing against each other. I've seen these guys run amazingly fast, which was another great feature that had been built into them.

Energized now, I rushed to help in the race against time. When I got there Marcus was leaning over, along with a group of people, studying the findings on my computer monitor. I instantly assumed that they had found a way to penetrate the protective barrier that was housing the culprits we were looking for. There were so many people standing around that I couldn't see what it was that they were looking at, but I could hear them discussing their progress.

Through a barrage of discussion from the group Marcus interrupted and said, "Okay, so this is it. Now we can proceed after we triangulate their precise locality."

As he turned around, I was only a few feet away, and we made eye contact.

"Dave, thank you for your expertise and dedication, because of your fine skills we are close to completing our goals."

I thanked him and added that I appreciated the compliment, but I was much more concerned with what they had found or worked on.

"Were the analysts able to break the barrier situation successfully and can they penetrate the protective shield our enemy has surrounding them?" I asked.

"Yes, once we found out what it was made of, thanks to your efforts, we backtracked and were able to create a special missile that could barrage the lion's den," he replied eagerly. He continued, "Making the missile was easy as we had missiles already constructed. We just switched out the warheads."

"Excellent, then we are all set? What is our next hurdle?" I asked curiously.

"Well, from here, we continue pinpointing as close as possible where they may be. When we get close enough that's when the challenge really starts as we will need our men on the ground speaking with locals to find any entrance possibilities to their lair. We have men from our organization that are milling about down there already, and we are in contact with them every hour to find out if there is any new intel," he explained.

At that point Jack joined us and whispered something in Marcus's ear then walked away. Apparently, the men spoke to some informants that had seen camouflaged trucks in a particular area in Rome. At the same time they were closing in through satellite transmissions. We were now within a one-hundred-mile radius. We were now about five days into the uncovering of an important target needed to save civilization or these monsters would take out a good portion of our population.

From reports gathered in our control room, our people stationed in Europe had reported to us that Europeans had already, with the help of robots, started forming solar highways and roadways, so that it could power the continent's energy thirst. I thought this was wonderful. Why was this hidden from our citizens for so long and why weren't these criminals who blocked these important patents interrogated and jailed for these crimes against our people? Well this was all history now and there was no turning back. We had to finish what we had set out to do to save the human race from this sinister plan.

Just then, John entered the control room and he approached me asking if I had gotten his voicemail.

"Yes, John. Sorry I got your message that you were here and I thought you'd be down anyway, so I didn't think it would be a big deal for me to meet you down here as I had work to do. Do you know what's going on?" I asked.

"Yea man, we're on the verge of a major attack," he answered. I was about to respond but I was taken back at how nonchalant his actions were. I was surprised at how shockingly cavalier he spoke about what was about to happen if we didn't stop the bad guys.

"Yea John, we could be weeks or even days away from them detonating the bomb and destroying more than half our population." I continued speaking firmly with concern in my voice.

With our men on the ground near the location and our computer technology combined with satellite help, we were closing in on them, but we didn't know if we would be in time to stop the attack. We were blind as to when this would occur. Still, we tried working as fast as we could. As I looked around, most of the computer operators were breaking into sweats trying to do their job. Everyone had a collective concern about the level of the state of affairs and I was glad that we were close to a solution yet apprehensive that danger lurked close by. I wanted this to be over, but it wasn't that easy. We still had to jump through hoops to make this happen and everyone from coast-to-coast was on high alert.

I remember the country having those silly color codes identifying the imminent danger the country was in from the terrorists. The system was used to appease the masses so they felt secure from danger. Little did we know that at the time we needed a terror system gauging the dangers, our officials were the ones causing havoc, instilling fear; all for profit, all for manipulation. But the intelligent people saw through all the catch phrases in the widely publicized presidential speeches.

The anxiety was getting insurmountable. I imagined what it might be like if the proverbial button were pushed and a massive explosion had ensued. On the other hand, I envisioned the capture of the final twelve. It would be gratifying to see them behind bars before they got away with their mass murder scheme. I wondered how they would like getting use to those accommodations after the lavish lifestyle they've experienced.

Just then, I noticed some odd blips on the screen coming from Europe. It looked like three—no, four—no, six images heading straight upward and then westerly bound. There was much talk back and forth in the room as to what these objects could be and where they were headed. I wondered if they were a diversion sent by the villains, like the snowball fight scheme I remembered from childhood. As we look upward at these attacking objects, the real threat may be heading straight at us while our attention was being diverted. Suddenly, there was a loud, collective round of chatter, but it didn't seem that it was coming from the newly formed series of flying images. I was to learn that we were within a one mile radius of the location. What this meant was that we could be right on target before nightfall. Our men on the ground were engaged in a firefight with security around the given area so we knew we were close to their hiding spot. What we were hoping for was the capture of one of them so we could gain intelligence quickly.

Once the bad guys were caught, there was no media to manipulate over their arrest and their crimes against humanity. As it stood now, there were only two areas for incarceration. The two currently being used in the west were Riker's Island and San Quentin. The other six continents had two each as well. Given our new system, we were confident that crime would not be nearly as high as it had been with the old monetary system. Mostly, because people didn't have to steal for what their family needed to survive. Not that that was acceptable but many grew up in ghettos and couldn't seem to escape the clutches of that environment. I couldn't even imagine being born in that environment and having to survive. I was lucky in that respect as my environment gave me chances to choose my own destiny. Well, not as lucky as those who were born into the ultra-wealthy environment with that silver spoon in their mouth.

By now we had determined that these images were actually missiles that were headed right for us. There was no cause for concern because our defense systems were set up to destroy these weapons in midair over the Atlantic Ocean. We were getting our counter-missiles ready for attack, and launching them would occur within the next fifteen minutes.

As we waited we continued searching for the culprits who fired these missiles. We had many of our people working on this so it wouldn't be long until our defense plan was successful, but it was a nail-biter. It looked as though it would get right down to the wire in finding these guys and stopping them before it was too late. I felt helpless even though I was doing as much as I could on my end. Triangulating their position was proving futile. *Too many cooks spoil the broth,* I thought.

I didn't usually remember all those old sayings, but I guess it's been rubbing off from Laura. As I said before, she had a ton of them. I basically stood in the background wondering where I would be the most help. Andy looked to me to see if there was anything for him to do. I was just too tense to notice what he was doing or how he was acting given the circumstances.

Things started moving faster and faster and voices got louder and louder. Everyone started panicking and sweating even more when our counter-missiles failed against the incoming arsenal. We had to think fast as the missiles would hit in approximately forty- five minutes.

It was evident that they were headed toward our newly constructed Aqua cities. The missiles were starting to separate and started veering away from where we were. We quickly deduced that they were headed toward other aqua cities on other continents like South America. We had to think quickly. We didn't have much time and all of our efforts had now turned toward stopping the attack.

While everyone panicked I tried thinking logically and calmly. I yelled out," It's the same material! It's the same material!"

They all stopped and looked at me, wondering what it was I was saying. "I bet it's the same material on those missiles as what they have supporting their bunker," I said.

"How soon can we place the material we are working on to penetrate the bunker, onto our defensive missiles?" one operator asked another.

Jack was looking on as they discussed this amongst themselves while everyone listened. Jack yelled out for them to start the process and for the rest of them to compute how long it would take.

209

It took two minutes to make that deduction and the operator yelled out, "It'll take thirty-three minutes to coat them properly and a few moments to launch. Impact will then take place in ten minutes."

Jack then yelled out, "Where will the impact take place?

Another quickly yelled back "Around the lighthouse at Montauk Point, Long Island."

We weren't even sure that the idea of putting the defense material onto our rockets would work. We all held our breath as the impact time neared. The time flew by and before we knew it, we had launched the new set of defensive missiles into the air.

Another computer operator signaled to the other aqua cities what we were attempting to do. It was now about six minutes to impact as we crossed our fingers for luck.

Simultaneously, reports were coming in on the progress of our ground war in Europe and the area surrounding our target. We weren't surprised that we were winning the fight, but the important information would be gained from interrogating the captives.

"Sixty seconds to impact!" someone yelled out. We all held our breath as an involuntary, nervous reaction. Then, just as quickly, we heard a countdown, "Ten, nine, eight, seven...three, two, one..."

We all looked at the monitor. After a few seconds passed by, a wave of euphoric applause erupted throughout the control room. Success.

Immediately, we radioed the other aqua cities and instructed them on how to take the bastard's missiles out. We aided in our own missile attack that was headed toward the western coast at the Malibu, Aqua City. We launched the counter artillery immediately and calculated impact as being somewhere over the Arizona desert. On the ground analyst deduced that there were no harmful materials when the missile exploded. They were a distraction to the real attack as I predicted.

We now refocused on what was going on in Rome and established communications with our people. An Italian translator had been brought in to assist with the prisoner interrogations as many who were bribed to protect the underground fortress spoke Italian and had no idea of the magnitude of the situation that would ultimately affect their lives as well.

After a day of interrogation, we were able to extract the information we believed to be credible. Three prisoners being held in separate quarters had recounted the same location of the fugitives.

The location was near a great monument called Piazza Venezia. The Piazza Venezia was located in the same plaza where Benito Mussolini, Fascist Dictator of Italy during the 1940s, used to conduct his speeches from his famous balcony. It was a grand monument erected in 1885 to 1905 to celebrate the unification of Italy. It was a historical place where many ancient structures could be found.

The Theatre of Pompeii stood nearby. History had revealed that this was where Julius Caesar was assassinated by his Senate and later avenged by Augustus Caesar. After the fall of the French Empire, in the western part of the Piazza, resided Napoleon Bonaparte's mother. Capitoline Hill where Piazza Venezia stood was also a very historic place where Roman Emperors had once ruled.

This was a fitting end to these horrible, present day criminals, but we had to be careful not to destroy the surrounding area and its many ancient structures. We were now about seven days into our pursuit. Capturing these cowards couldn't happen soon enough.

Our professionals were working on the exact location to penetrate the bunker. After much debate, we found an area behind the monument that we could start the procedure from and flank them from behind their lair. The timing was set for tomorrow. From where we were situated, and thanks to technological breakthroughs, cameras were set up quickly all around the monument. Those involved in the actual operation had now gone below the earth's surface to get their gear ready for the mission. They knew it would not be easy, nor did they know what they would encounter when they got there. These criminals were well financed and had all the latest inventions. These were inventions that we probably didn't even know about like the material used in shielding their position from us. I wondered what other technologies they had hidden that we had no idea about; ideas that could aid humanity for future generations.

Our operations team knew that they had to act fast making their way downward. Once the explosion was heard by the fugitives, they would counteract the procedure with a plan of their own.

We had been lucky in one sense. The material used to shield the bunker would protect anything above from destruction. The scientists were all in agreement that no harm would come to the monument from our doing. The plan was to immediately excavate downward until the target was reached. Then, blow a hole through the side of the bunker big enough for passage and take out as many of them and/or arrest them as quickly and efficiently as possible for those who did not perish. This worked well on paper, but in reality we knew it wouldn't work out quite that way. It never does in these situations.

It would be a one, two, three mission. Blow a hole long and deep until the blast is stopped by the bunker's hard material. Then, use our counter-material to blow a hole through the side wall. Then, enter and attack before they can detonate the world bomb. It was plain and simple but frightening.

Back at our location we tracked the progress of our enemy's missiles. Five of them had been previously intercepted and the last one was roaming toward a target somewhere over the Pacific Ocean. The missile would be destroyed in about an hour or so. We weren't overly concerned about the missile because we had effectively destroyed the others with little exertion. We could determine from its present course that the destination was most likely Hawaii, but regardless, it would be taken out shortly.

I retreated back to my room exhausted from all the mental strain. I went to sleep without hindrance.

When I awoke it was about 8:30 a.m. and I headed up to the roof to stretch my legs a bit. There were already a few people up there doing the same thing when I arrived. I concentrated on taking in the morning sun. I relaxed my mind and contemplated on the events of such an important day. I was anxious to get back to the control room and see what was brewing for our ultimate attack.

It was nearly 9:15 a.m. as I made my way down to the main room. Operators were milling about and people were already in full swing with their work. I thought for a brief moment that many of these workers had been here around the clock and were preparing for the culminating event.

I gazed over at Marcus. He was viewing some schematics and discussing last minute operations. Tom and Michael had arrived now and were checking to see how they may assist. I presumed John was still up in his room since I didn't see him anywhere, but on second thought I really didn't know where he was. John was very resourceful in a mysterious way. For all I knew he could have been working on one of his new innovations for the future. I started looking at the monitors that showed the place where Piazza Venezia was situated. It was the Palazzo di Venezia. I noticed similarities between Dealey Plaza in Texas where President Kennedy had been shot and this particular plaza. They both had roundabouts or an open area where cars can circulate in open view. There was much symbolism between the two places given the incidences of powerful leaders and images frozen in our minds from history. Sometimes, life was odd that way, two different places, yet both with powerful, historic similarities etched into our brains.

Forty-five minutes couldn't go by fast enough as our warriors were getting ready for the assault. This could go bad on so many different levels, but what we were concerned about mostly was the launch of the enemy's super weapon.

Unlike the dropping of the bomb on Hiroshima by the Enola Gay, we were certain that this would be a long-range type of detonation sequence. We got word from our Special Forces team that they had started to maneuver so they could align the coordinates with their bunker buster type missile. They only had one shot at getting this right. The wrong coordinates would alert our enemy and give them time to detonate their bomb and elude capture.

We wanted them alive so they could suffer for the transgressions they had committed against our nations for such a long time. We held our breath in silence for the next few minutes. We followed our combatants on the video screens and some prayed to keep them safe.

From behind the monument we watched as a long plume of smoke ejected diagonally upward. We watched as our fighters disappeared into the newly formed entrance path that led to the target. It's all that we could see as we waited for some sign of news report from our members. About twenty-five minutes had passed. It seemed the communication devices were having problems working at their present depths underground. We hadn't solved this technology yet, so we waited impatiently for a report.

Something odd happened then. We noticed on our screens a large flying object appear over the vineyards of Tuscany. It was traveling at a rather fast speed and was heading on a westerly course. We ignored that object for the moment as we waited for a report on the attack.

We then received a voice communication that we magnified on the surround system in the control room. It was Commander Anthony Longella who was in charge of the assault team. His voice was powerful and clear and the message was directed to Marcus.

"Sir, they are all dead, we lost two of ours, but I don't know how to say this. We couldn't stop the launch sequence. I'm not sure where the launch will start from, but I am certain that the sequence commenced."

Marcus thanked him for the semi-success in killing the scandalous criminals. Then, all of our eyes looked simultaneously at the radar screens that were tracking the flying object. It was heading directly for us.

We had established communications with our team members who had remained close to the area where the flying object had started its ascent. After receiving the coordinates, the team headed out on their new mission which appeared to be an open field. When they arrived, they were bewildered to find that there was a large gaping hole in the ground. The team reported back to command the dimensions of the opening and we quickly surmised that this had to be the massive weapon that was launched by the Bilderbergs.

Many of us broke into a sweat knowing that such a tremendous weapon could be upon us shortly. Some calculated impact times given the speed and trajectory of its path. Others were trying to figure out how to stop it from reaching the target—us. It certainly was a lot harder trying to think logically and clearly when there was a weapon of such magnitude heading toward you. We took into account that it had been traveling for a while before we were alerted to the apocalyptic weapon. We quickly calculated that it would touch down in five-hours and thirty-seven minutes. A few hours of time felt as though it might as well be a few minutes.

After heated discussions back and forth between the staff, a decision was made to try and destroy the object in midair with the same weapon we had used before. Our concern now was the fallout. What would the damage be, we wondered?

Our team was already calculating what the devastation might be if we were able to detonate it somewhere mid-point over the Atlantic Ocean. Mid-point was closing fast and the longer we waited, the closer it got to us, increasing the risk of fallout for years to come depending on what kind of bomb it was. It was evident that we didn't have much time. Five-hours and thirty-seven minutes seemed much shorter than it actually was.

Our people began calculating how fast we could get our missile coated and into the air for impact as we've exhausted the other coated missiles for the previous missile attack. We had exactly two-hours and seventeen-minutes to impact. Everyone was rushing around the control room bumping into each other, dropping glasses, spilling liquids—it was pandemonium.

Time passed by in the blink of an eye and after twenty-five minutes, we were ready to launch our preventative strike.

The command-to-launch sequence started, then the button was pushed, but there was no launch. We all panicked and scrambled to see why our weapon had failed. It wasn't the best time to think about when I was young. This kind of thing had happened to me at one time or another, usually when we would attempt to launch our model rockets. The thought instantly left my mind as swiftly as it entered because I was petrified of what might happen to us. I couldn't help but think about the horrific photos and films I had seen of the aftermath of Hiroshima and Nagasaki if this was in fact a nuclear bomb. But we weren't sure whether this was biochemical or nuclear.

Our staff ran out of the control room and down to where the missiles were launched from. There was no time to try and figure it out in the main room. They were down there quickly and looked all around the missile for anything peculiar. The worst kinds of problems were intermittent problems and we didn't have the luxury of trial and error. They tried testing everything as fast as possible. They were attempting to be as thorough as possible without missing anything obvious. If there's one thing I have learned about computers and equipment, is that ninety-eight percent of the time, the problem is a simple one.

Sure enough, they came upon a switch that starts the missile firing. The switch looked a bit burnt from all the sudden use after a long period of being dormant. They called up for someone to rush down a replacement part. While they waited, they took out the burnt piece. The new part had arrived and it was placed in the spot where the tainted one had been removed. They gave it a once-over and rushed back upstairs to the control room. One of them watched from another room to ensure a correct missile launch. Back in the control room, the launch was directed to commence. From the big windows that out stretched over the water we could see the launch and we followed the projectile as it rose in the sky. It was the faulty switch that caused the launch failure. We had liftoff. A straight, lengthy plume of white smoke trailed from the missile as it headed toward intercepting and destroying the target. We had lost quite a bit of time and the impact was now calculated as being much closer to our mainland then we would have liked.

So many questions entered my mind simultaneously. What if we miss the target? What kind of fallout would this produce and how would we recover from this? How long would recovery take? What if the plan failed? I just couldn't stand the tension any longer and I had about enough. My brain was fried and I wanted to be with my family. I wondered if I'd ever see them again.

The analysts figured out that impact would occur in about thirty-five minutes. There was much talking amongst the men and women in the control room. The unknown proved to be more than most of us could bear. I scanned the room and could see sweat on the backs of the operators as they worked on solving this gargantuan problem.

Some of them were working on what the expected aftermath would be given three different scenarios. Two were detrimental to our existence and one was bearable.

"Seventeen minutes and closing fast," one technician could be heard saying.

Now all the screens appeared in a panoramic view, connecting where the last screen left off. This created an entire view of the impact area over the ocean. As the time neared, one operator noticed weather conditions rising up from the south that were now close to the impact area. Strong winds had started to accumulate and gain velocity. We wondered if this could affect the flight path of both missiles.

"Twelve minutes and counting," the same operator called out.

As the collision time drew near, I could only think of speaking with my Laura. I tried not to think about whether I'd ever see her and my kids again. There wasn't much I could do. I thought about Jigsey, the gym that I frequented, my old job, the people that I had worked with, and the bar in my old neighborhood. They say that when you die you see your life flash before your eyes. I hoped this wasn't what was happening to me and I quickly changed my frame of mind. I tried concentrating on whether there was anything I could do.

"Eight minutes!" the tech called out.

If I were to use a word to describe what I was feeling it would be: overwrought. It all was coming to a head, all the worrying, all the preparations, all the tense feelings toward these horrible people that did this to us.

"Five minutes!"

We could see that our missile was traveling at a higher velocity than the target. We could see that from the two images on screen heading toward each other. Our missile was traveling at a speed one-and-a-half times faster than the target missile, probably due to the heavy load it was about to unload on us.

"Two minutes," he yelled. We were all sweating bullets as the time neared. Now, there was a silence as if you could hear a pin drop. We all were frozen in waiting for the anticipated collision.

"10, 9, 8, 7, 6, 5, 4, 3, 2, 1."

We held our breath, but the blips were still on the screen. We all gasped. What could have happened?

Then the operator called out, "The wind gusts affected the collision."

I couldn't take it any longer as I opened my mouth for the first time.

"What does this mean, are we done, is it over, should we brace ourselves?"

There was no answer as they studied the screens. Our missile veered off and we noticed something that we hadn't considered. We noticed the missile turning around at the same high velocity. Marcus called out to Mike Turner, who programmed the missiles for launch.

"What kind of missiles are these?" he asked.

"As a failsafe, I programmed these missiles as heat seeking," he said with half-a-smile on his face. "It's not over yet," he assured.

A few seconds later we could see that the missile had turned and was on a course chasing after the missed target. What propelled the enemy's missile must have given off enough heat for our missile to latch onto.

The operators were calculating some figures, "At this rate, impact should be in twenty minutes which puts the collision around." There was a pause. "There's 5,453 miles between our Eastern coast and London's coast, collision should be about two-thousand miles out from our position in aqua city."

Once again we waited for the impact and were now so drained from all this speculation, calculating, wondering, and worrying about what was going to happen.

"It's catching up and is on a steady course," I heard one of them say.

Many had hopes that our missile would reach the target in time, because the bomb was getting closer to our coast. The closer it got, the more damage would be sustained by our people. We frantically watched the monitors as the new countdown began. I for one felt like it was a déjà vu, in a dreamlike state. I watched in amazement at the surreal experience. I looked briefly at Andy.

He looked at me and said, "The impact will be in eight minutes, sir."

I nodded to him acknowledging him as his words were comforting, but we've been here before and I wasn't certain that the operation would be successful.

We struggled through the next five minutes, and in my trance-like state-of-mind, I could make out periodic shouts of time countdowns. I'm sure others were experiencing similar feelings as they gazed at the two little dots on our screens. And as the gap closed between the blips, hope and optimism increased. Would it be brief or continue on with success? Three minutes left and we'd know for sure. Those three minutes felt like an eternity. An image of my family once again entered my mind and I knew I was spiritually with them through the speed of thought.

Sixty seconds left and counting. My heart raced. I couldn't bear to see the reactions of others around me as I was glued to the screens and the thought of "*what if?*"

Thirty seconds left and counting. All the thoughts of what we had been through recently crossed my mind and I thought quickly that this was it. All or nothing…literally. I couldn't bear the thought of surviving the aftermath of all this and lingering through the suffering of disease.

10, 9, 8, 7……3,2,1.

There was a huge bright light that engulfed our monitors and it seemed to last infinitely. It couldn't have been any more climactic than this. For the moment, it seemed we had been successful, but we held our breath until we got confirmation that the target had been destroyed. After a long, thirty-seconds I noticed nothing on the screen.

One of our people yelled out to all listeners, "We did it, mission accomplished, the bomb has been destroyed!"

There was a roar that echoed throughout the facility and on all levels. We could hear the applause throughout aqua city, but it still wasn't over. Calculations were being performed to determine fallout patterns and casualty predictions, and the composition of the material detonated and released in our atmosphere. We still had unanswered questions and we were flying into new territory. We all fervently studied the atmosphere and wind velocities that were in the area. How would the wind affect what just happened? The windstorm was traveling in a northerly direction at this point, but we needed to determine if it would continue or stop before hitting our coast. If it stayed out to sea then the wind would continue in that northerly direction.

Most of us took long, deep breaths to soothe our anxiety and stress over the whole ordeal. For now, though, the danger seemed nonexistent, but again, only time would tell.

I didn't want to go outside because of the dangers that could exist from the fallout. Our best protection was to stay indoors. From the preliminary results of the explosion, the fallout was set to reach our coast within under a day or so. Time would tell how dependent we would be upon the prevailing winds, but after preliminary computations, it would seem as though the wind stream would push the fallout toward Greenland and the Arctic Circle. This was the best scenario. This was not a nuclear bomb as predicted from test sample reports now arriving from our crews. The cold would negate the caustic chemical gases and biological agents. Now though, we were still in a wait-and-see mode.

At that moment, as news of the victory spread, hoards of people began arriving for their final destination and resting place in this new world. I anticipated seeing my family appear, as well, from among the hundreds of people that were arriving. I thought about how much I missed them. They would be a sight for some very sore eyes.

I walked around downstairs and finally went outside. I wasn't worried about the fallout. We were sure that it wouldn't reach landfall for quite some time, if at all. As I walked out onto one of the balconies I got a clearer picture of just how many people were arriving. To my surprise, there were thousands who were given the word that it was safe now after the final conquest. I felt weary and my body was tired from the built up tension and from viewing the ordeal first hand. I didn't regret being here as my services were very much needed. We had a lot of work to do. At least I was doing something to help my destiny and my family's destiny.

As if in slow motion and in a fuzzy, dreamlike state, I saw a familiar girl pierce through the mass of people. Behind her was an entourage of familiar faces that looked fuzzy as well. As they got closer the fuzzy turned to clear and my heart filled with immediate joy when I noticed my family walking toward me. I thought for a moment that I had died and that I was in some paradise at that point. I froze in my tracks. I couldn't believe they were here, even though it was inevitable at some point to see them again whether it was here, or in another life.

I hugged them all, especially the love of my life and the power behind my success. I felt tears rolling down my face as my adorable pet lay in her arms licking my face with a thousand little kisses. All was good now with me and I could make it with them by my side. It was then that I realized that all would be fine and that we had made it.

After about five minutes of hugging and kissing everyone, I escorted them to our suite. I then looked at Harry and Robert and told them that a teaching facility was set aside for them and others on Tier 47.

As my family got situated in their new living arrangements and Robert and Harry went upstairs, I too took a ride with them to see for myself what was happening on Tier 49. I left them to do their set up for classes which would teach all about The Geneva Project and our new resource-based economy.

As I entered the control room people were working as usual. I noticed Mike Turner, the person who was responsible for planning the failsafe missile operation.

I walked up to him and said, "Mike, you don't know me, but I just want to thank you for your efforts in saving my life and the life of my family, as well as civilization." I stretched my hand out and we both smiled. We were content over the outcome, but a little nervous due to the fact that we had never met. It's not every day that you meet someone under these profound and unreal circumstances.

He acknowledged by saying "It was my duty. You're very welcome."

Instead of walking away, I made things a bit more comfortable by asking him if there were any new developments.

He said, "Yes, frankly, I don't believe we will have any problems in our area. The heavy wind gusts are pushing the bio-chemicals northward as predicted and the cold should minimize any harmful effects. We did it!"

At that moment I felt like hugging someone and almost hugged him, but thought that would be extremely weird so I stopped myself. As I looked over I noticed Marcus was looking at me and shared a mutual smile from afar. There are many kinds of smiles, some are short, some are half-smiles, some are nervous smiles, but this smile far surpassed any of those. We were literally smiling from ear-to-ear. We walked toward each other and hugged in ecstatic happiness.

It was then that I realized that our world would not end in dismay. It was at that moment that I knew that our lives had changed. It was in that moment that I was content with my soul and the joy of those summer days when I was little, and had a chance of returning once again. I thought about those blue laws that we once had in our history where no one was allowed to operate a business on Sunday except for emergency services like hospitals. I envisioned many more relaxing days spent enjoying our families each week on those days just like in days of old.

❧ Chapter Thirty-One ❧

It's a New Day

I had anticipated that in the following months we would start working on scientific breakthroughs, as they wouldn't be hampered by past political manipulations. No more would we have to deal with the smoke screens derived from the rich's political influence that kept the Democratic and Republican parties at each other's throats. The days of corporate-bought media—which enabled false propaganda to keep us at odds with each other—was over. Teaching facilities, agriculture, technology, science, mathematics would reach new heights. Diseases that were once thought to be incurable, due mainly to the health insurance industry's surreptitious management were very curable and life spans would be augmented dramatically. People would now live to be a hundred-and-fifty years old—and possibly even longer.

I couldn't wait to relax and do some fishing from one of the many fishing stations on the side of our building. I would get some entertainment and help feed the masses. I didn't care about any of that; that is, keeping the fish for my own use as this was irrelevant, but the joy and anticipation of wonderful things to come was elating.

I took a stroll up above and lay down on one of the many lounge chairs available. When lo and behold my good friend John Hodges was there. We gave each other a quick hug as we both knew how things worked out.

We chose some lounge chairs, laid down, and reflected on what we had just been through as well as some of the memories of our college days but, for the most part we said very little to each other. We just reclined there, basking in the warmth of the sun.

Kids were running around splashing each other with toy water pistols. Some of the spray hit our feet, but we didn't care. Others bathed in the pools. There was a different atmosphere brewing that included an amazing aura. We just laid there with our eyes closed and smiles on our faces. Later that evening at dusk, all around the world simultaneously, thousands of flying sky lanterns were released magically to signify our new independence. It was similar to our Fourth of July celebration. We all embraced in the newly founded world celebration.

Yes, things were starting to come into perspective now and with that, I realized that it had been quite awhile since I enjoyed a holiday or listened to a new song. I was excited about what we could expect in this new life given our new freedoms.

No more would we be subjected to propaganda-based rhetoric for monetary purposes. No more would we be subjected to personal views on religion which had been the cause of so many wars in the past. Yes, I could say with certainty that I would miss the Holiday season and those loving times spent with family during that time at our homes. I loved how people acted during the joyous season and wondered why it was that we acted differently throughout the rest of the year; road rage, disagreements, ridiculous law suits and such had become commonplace. *Why can't it be the holiday season all of the time?* I wondered.

I realized my real mission was to make it through. We all felt euphoric with everything in this new world we were developing. It was filled with a warm, reassuring sensation by knowing we were doing the right thing. The gifts bestowed upon all of us were magical. There would be no more screwing each other over money and material things. Now, all those things were readily available for all of us to enjoy, whenever it was needed. I still had memories of my youth when we had experienced those great and wonderful times. Maybe those days were back again?

I reminisced about receiving presents at Christmas time when we were surrounded by the joy of giving. I realized now that it wasn't about receiving gifts that had given us such an incredible feeling, it was about the giving and watching the expressions on loved one's faces, especially watching the children's excitement. I reminisced about how we had more fun with the big box that the special toy had come in, than the actual toy itself. I remember laughing with neighborhood and childhood friends until our sides had ached. Playing hide-and-seek in the dark and visiting the corner candy store; skipping and doing handstands and roly-poly and hula hoops. I closed my eyes and I could sense the smell of that hot sun on my face and work wasn't even a fleeting thought in my mind. I reflected on the wonderful smell of newly cut grass. When summers were sunnier and grasses seemed greener. I thought about when we chewed Bazooka bubble gum and watched the Road Runner cartoons on Saturday morning, stayed up late on those warm summer nights to watch the Honeymooners and Star Trek. I mean the real Star Trek with William Shatner as Captain Kirk. We would climb trees until we were out-of-breath and built igloos out of newly fallen snow.

My list was endless and I could sit for hours daydreaming about jumping on the bed and having pillow fights until our mother came in the room and yelled at us to stop.

I thought about PF Flyers and Keds sneakers that could make kids run faster and jump higher. I thought about the time and place where we knew everyone on our street and so did our parents. I thought about a time when it wasn't odd to have two or three best friends. I remembered not sleeping at all on Christmas Eve, anticipating the excitement that awaited us on Christmas morning. One time, in the middle of the-night, we were awakened by Santa Claus himself as he stopped by our house to give us the gifts we had asked for. Back then, things like taking drugs meant chomping on orange-flavored chewable vitamins.

Our brothers and sisters were our worst tormentors and...our fiercest protectors. Mistakes could be corrected by simply saying, "Do Over!" and it was yelled out as loud as we could. When we yelled out, "Car!" it meant that everyone needed to stop the game until it drove by. We would do this ever so patiently even though we were really irritated from the disruption. Hitting a tree with a ball was an automatic, "Interference!" which was also yelled out as loudly as possible. If we could have played for eleven hours continuously, we would and often did on many occasions.

One of my high school friends reminded me once how he used to wake up and wrap his baseball glove around his bicycle handlebars. He would then ride off as his mother yelled out, "Just make sure you're home for dinner." He'd ride off on his bike that had that comfortable banana seat. We would all gather up our brothers and friends to play in double headers of baseball like in the movie, The Sandlot.

Who could forget playing Jacks and Dodge ball or doing The Twist, and jumping down the steps while eating sunflower seeds or Jolly Ranchers, banana splits, wax lips or mustaches? We would swing on the park swings and went so high that we could almost touch the sky. Then, we would jump off as far as we could.

I remembered birthday parties where they made us wear those stupid hats and blowers and a million of our parent's friends would come over to help us celebrate while we ate cake and M&M's because that's what we got back then. Elaborate kid parties just didn't exist. Play dates? What the hell happened to us? Just open your front door and play with your neighbor's kids.

I thought about when it took two minutes for our television set to turn on and whenever milk would go up a penny, everyone talked about it for weeks.

I remember the times when girls didn't date or kiss until late into their high school years. When male teachers wore neckties and female teachers had their hair done perfectly every day.

I thought about how we felt when we went to the principal's office for doing something wrong. As I mentioned previously, we feared for our lives from what our parents and grandparents would do to us. They were a bigger threat to us and some of us are still afraid of them. I remembered when teachers threatened children to keep them back a grade if they failed. When it happened, the teachers kept their word and held them back. When we went to the gas station our windshield was cleaned and the oil was checked for free every time. We didn't pay for air in our tires. And who could ever forget when war was only a card game.

Yes, the choices we make affect us every day, every moment, every second. In the old world it required more from us to be a good person or a good citizen. In this new world though, being a good citizen and person is all that is important. Maybe with a little luck the good ol' days can come back again. The only requirement for this new existence is that we love what the earth gives us, are honest, sincere, and thoughtful of all human beings. We can do more than hope; we have the power to make it happen. It was inevitable that a new world constitution had to be written given the new age. We had a lot of work to do to make it all work.

We've lived this life, this past sixty years with the pain of knowing many spoken and unspoken facts and we still, as a people, live blindly, accepting the lies of what has happened in our history. Big business has killed one of our most trusted and honest presidents and his brother, killed simply because they were two of many individuals that strived for a better way of life for us all. They followed the constitution the way it was intended and cared about us enough to sign a peace treaty with our enemy, even when millions hated and feared the enemy and their concepts.

In the last sixty years the powerful big business oil tycoons (in tobacco-deception fashion) have bought technology patents that could benefit everyone. Then we allowed all the media brainwashing, the media manipulations, and the media propaganda that blocked these patents from ever hitting mainstream. Free energy is a right for all people. I must repeat, free energy is the right for all people. Even the people who are involved with energy production still do not believe that there are possibilities for new inventions, new possibilities, and free energy. As if we didn't learn our lesson from history when many believed the world was flat and couldn't be otherwise.

Today, big business has the audacity to build solar plants. They harvest the free energy from the sun and sell it at a premium to the public. The next resource they are after is water. Today there are water plants that are now being cultivated for more profit. Keep an eye on water as this free resource will not be cheap any longer. We must unify and rise up against this gluttony.

Why is it that many find it so hard to believe it possible that the very powerful and extremely wealthy oil conglomerates have stifled the surfacing of other types of energy which is much cheaper and almost eliminates partially or fully the use of petroleum especially given the fact of how deceptive human beings can be when it comes to greed? It's embarrassing to see how manipulative people can be and how people can trust wholeheartedly without aggressive questioning and research. Of the close to seven billion people, isn't it odd that not one person has come close enough for the masses to use that particular invention or combination of inventions to replace fossil fuels? I find it so sad.

John Lennon was feared by the government because of all the followers he had. Mr. Lennon imagined a world of peace for all humans and was very open on his views against the war. It is my belief that he was killed because of those beliefs and views. We live in a world where a life could be taken at the drop of a hat and getting whacked is as easy as one, two, three. J. Edgar Hoover, a man among many leaders of his time, who disgraced our country, once said that John Lennon was a threat to the "American Way." There were three hundred FBI pages on Mr. Lennon. Today, Harry Reid said it best, "J. Edgar Hoover is a stain on the FBI building."

Many have said that the world changed when the towers were hit. I say the world was changed a long time ago without our knowledge. It happened on November 22nd, 1963, the day big business took control of our country, our wealth, and our privacies. This was the day Mr. Kennedy was gunned down. Even today, the polls show that seventy-to-eighty percent of the public suspect that there was a plot in the Kennedy murders, dare I use that word, "conspiracy." It is the only time I mentioned this word and for good reason. Whenever this word is used at any time, an immediate trigger occurs in the mind of brainwashed Americans as if the word "conspiracy" is synonymous with the word fake theories or not true.

In Russ Baker's book, "Family of secrets," he points out that, "In America there is a tendancy to consider those who explore alternate stories and alternate accounts of the 'official story' as conspiracy nuts." So, might we use some replacement words as not to cloud the subject at hand with the same tired word that has been used negatively, whichever may suit you better, plot, scheme, plan. Be that as it may, there has been no investigation of the top officials involved in the killing of our president. I mean a real investigation without the manipulations of their murderers.

Officials, who were head of the CIA at that time, are still around today and are still free from prosecution. Maybe we should use the same illegal waterboarding methods against them to find out the truth. It's true that many of the guilty parties have died, but we must bring the guilty ones who are still alive to justice. We must release those Kennedy documents ordered hidden from the public. Then, and only then, can our country move forward and gain the respect of all people. There are no indictments of those who truly killed two Kennedys, John Lennon, Martin Luther King, Lee Harvey Oswald, and Jack Ruby. At every turn there was a scapegoat being framed. Oswald claimed he was a patsy. Be that as it may, criminal or no criminal, that phrase was widely ignored.

At every turn, the media was fabricated for the manipulator's objectives. We stood by and did nothing. Either because we are too afraid, or we were too damn lazy and trusting to do anything about it. But in reality we were powerless.

At the time of her husband's murder, Jacqueline Kennedy regarded her husband's presidency as an American Camelot, a period of hope and optimism in U. S. history. This is what they stole from us, hope and optimism. As a tribute, everyone should read the words that Mrs. Kennedy expressed in that hospital. They used to be readily available, there for anyone to read but those words are now difficult to locate. We should all live it and never forget what they did to us all. She refused to take off her memorable pink Channel suit that was covered in the president's blood. Mrs. Kennedy said, "I want them to see what they have done!" We should never forget what they have done. I loved President Kennedy and how he unselfishly protected this country. We owe it to those who were killed and, at the very least, we owe it to ourselves, to bring those responsible to justice before they are all dead. We must as, "We the People" demand to have the sealed JFK documents released to the public so our country can move forward.

"Imagine all the people living life in peace."

~ John Lennon

"I have a dream that all people are created equal."

~ Martin Luther King

"Don't let it be forgotten, that once, there was a spot, for one brief and shining moment known as Camelot. There'll never be another Camelot again."

~ Jacqueline Kennedy

These quotes contain profound words that have deep meaningful relevance. I am hopeful that this new world will serve mankind well. That those brave heroes; our beloved President Kennedy and his brother, Martin Luther King were advocates of true peace. And John Lennon killed for wanting a better existence for the human race. What they were working toward may finally be upon us. We must vigorously protect it and embrace it, while nurturing it and recognizing who our true enemies are. Always!

But for now, I think I'll just go catch some lightning bugs.

"Together we must learn how to compose differences, not with arms, but with intellect and decent purpose. Every gun that is made, every warship launched, every rocket fired, signifies in the final sense a theft from those who hunger and are not fed, those who are cold and are not clothed."

~ Dwight D. Eisenhower

⇒ Epilogue ⇐

At first, when you hear news reports of something profound that has happened, the very first emotion you feel is the terrible senseless loss of that person. Even though I was very young and have lived my whole life with the image of that awful motorcade it revels in my mind that we didn't just lose a person, it was all about what was taken away from us. How much better would this world have been hadn't they taken John Fitzgerald Kennedy's life away from us? I felt the same way with those three-thousand-plus people who were killed senselessly when the towers burned. Although each and every one of those lives was important, the chance of those lives affecting our world someway or another is what the killers took away from us all.

And as I heard the news stories report the killing of John Lennon, the initial shock is that the person is gone but what the killers took away from us is much more than just the person. John Lennon was the voice of harmony within our world and our world was a much better place to be in because of the lyrics he sang, the message he was trying give. Our world was a much better place to be in because of Martin Luther King Jr's words. How much more could Mr. King given our world than "I Have a Dream?" And I remember thinking when Mr. Lennon died how many more beautiful inspirational songs did we not hear for the next twenty or thirty years? But the emotion that stays with me that inspired me to write my thoughts down is the profound anger that I feel to this day of what these criminals have taken away from us all.

As Americans we should all be ashamed of ourselves. We cannot be ashamed of ourselves for allowing the JFK assassinations to happen as what happened has happened and we cannot change that fact. What we should be ashamed about is allowing these criminals to manipulate us, to control us, to allow three wars we should not have been in while thousands upon thousands of our people shed blood while these same criminals prosper from the deaths and their family's misery. Instead of storming the capitol in droves demanding justice, we have been complacent for five decades. How disgraceful that we allowed these murderers to get away with this. We go about barbequing in our backyards, watching publicized hyped-up television shows, going about our business, only debating amongst ourselves what we think happened while the guilty parties enjoy lavish lifestyles at the cost of our country's demise.

The question is, "Are we defenseless against the very powerful hidden government that Russ Baker proves through investigative witness accounts and documentation illustrated in his book?"

It is extremely evident who killed our president. The answer is very simply answered with a few questions:

"Who was the head of the CIA?"

"Who was the head of the FBI at the time?"

"Who was JFK's predecessor?"

"Why were these people not vigorously interrogated by the honest American public?"

"Are the highest levels of power exempt from interrogation and prosecution except for presidents?"

The JFK Files are sealed until 2029:

"Who signed the paperwork to seal these records or allowed for this to happen?"

"Was October 26, 1992 relevant in extending the concealment of these important documents?"

I am sure that the same people who killed our president, and manipulated our country can very easily manipulate the reasons why the killing occurred. What would stop them from interjecting more propaganda such as a "Coup d'état" that was very much needed to oust a president that they believed was making wrong decisions for our country in those sealed documents? What's to stop them from manipulating and controlling us even more?

We live in a society where our people, the little people go to jail for a very long time for far, far less a crime, yet when the crime of the JFK murder occurred we enlisted the same men who were involved to conduct the investigation, how convenient. Wouldn't it be nice if we could do that ourselves? If we—or our family members—got into a legal predicament? Since this homicide is not solved and the criminals not incarcerated, they have been given free reign to manipulate us again and again. Their children are among us and have been taught the same misguided principals as their Fathers. What's to stop them from doing the same in the future or this very moment as our constitution is ignored? These questions must be answered. This crime must be solved and records unsealed before those who committed this crime are all deceased. What will happen to our country's future only to say that if we all drop the ball here our country is doomed? But, it's probably already doomed because of all this greed. My speculation is that what is contained in those files will also exonerate these criminals from prosecution, probably with a statement that they had to kill the president for the betterment of the country; a creation of more manipulations and more questions to deflect prosecution of those guilty. Same as we are rationalizing today that we had to go to war to protect our country. But that brings a whole realm of debate. Of course it does. That's what these criminals count on. These criminal's biggest asset is the overwhelming trust that the American people have in their elected officials.

It is in fact irrelevant who pulled the trigger in the Kennedy assassination. From extensive research and from visiting Dealey Plaza personally, it is my belief that these were hired thugs from a very elaborate operation which was orchestrated by heads of the CIA, FBI, and the subsequent president along with the banking elite and big Texas oil tycoons. I believe they all had prior knowledge because they were directly involved. It is no surprise to me that this is what will be released eventually; long after the main players and everyone involved has died, but their children live on to follow in their footsteps. And we will brunt the new damage that will be incurred from their upbringing.

Who knows? Maybe we are getting too close to uncovering the truth and bring those who are left to justice. Maybe they actually do have a plan already in place and take advantage of the "end of the world possibilities" to deflect their guilt and incarceration as in the fictional plot of this book. If massive amounts of the public are struggling to stay alive from financial dismay, do you think anyone will be interested in incarcerating these individuals? Before Kennedy's death he had a speech where he spoke about how he was aware about secret organizations and would not let these secret groups prevail while he was president. He spoke about dismantling them, the special clubs that discuss and act on foreign and domestic affairs while conducting illegal operations that affect our lives. This, in and of itself alone, is considered treason. These groups are still active today.

I am deeply saddened that we'll never know the value, the gifts, the extraordinary things that all of these exceptional people who were killed, perished with.

Though this plot was fictitious; however, the de-industrialization of our country is not. This was a major concern of mine and was a tribute to those incredible people who worked hard after WWII, a generation that must never be forgotten. I wrote this book so it would be a concern for others as well. I acknowledged the hardworking people from the past sixty years who were and still are part of the middle class that have been all grouped together by the ultra-rich propaganda lie that they are on welfare and stealing from the system. These divisions within our society were brought about by the corrupt corporate controlled media. So divided have we become that facts are rarely even relevant. The poor are made to feel inadequate as a result of these powerful manipulations. By these rich tax cuts, these powerful leaders are attempting to abolish the middle class by evading their own fair share of taxes. Many of them, in fact, are taking their money overseas as well to avoid taxes. As we stand by and do nothing.

My friends, I leave you with one last thought—and that is to know that those who looked out for us have no more voice. Know that we are the voice of a slain president, brother, peace activist, and profound songwriter. Never let them take your voice away from you as they did our heroes. I am convinced in my heart of hearts that that would have been their last words to us all. It is for these reasons that we must never, stop turning stones over to expose these creatures, these evildoers who live under these rocks and at the very least bring some sort of justice to what's left of our world and— it is *our* world, not theirs.

⟿ About Nolan J. Reynolds ⟿

Nolan was born in 1959 in a Harlem hospital and grew up on the then-safe streets of Astoria Queens. His family started spending numerous summers in a house bought by his grandfather in 1965 in a suburban North Shore fishing town on Long Island about an hour away. As the area grew increasingly dangerous, his parents moved him and his siblings to that town in 1971. There, he experienced what most children felt growing up on Long Island during the '70s; the smell of the newly cut lawns and bright morning sunshine were a few memories of many that stayed with him his entire life to present. He developed a love for fishing, and it was there—floating on the timeless sea—that his mind wandered for hours thinking about his current life.

He always had a love for writing but it was always short, simple writings and he always noticed the reaction of recipients to the words he wrote. His favorite short dedications were the writings of special occasion cards given to loved ones. His wife was his biggest inspiration and the driving force behind his success in anything he did. Upon his wife's request, Nolan started to write. *And write, he did.*

The first subject that came to mind was his love for his childhood upbringing in that quaint little town with a small population, and how things have drastically changed. His book delves into those issues, mostly work ethics and values, which have molded him into the person who he is today. His love for his country and how things were is always at the forefront of his writings.